"Rebecca McClanahan's multi-generational memoir artfully weaves together more than a century of family documents, oral history, and historical records. With poetic elegance, McClanahan transforms ordinary life events into meaningful life stories. *The Tribal Knot* is not only an engaging read, but a literary model for those who yearn to write their own family story."

—Sharon DeBartolo Carmack, *You Can Write Your Family History*

"Rebecca McClanahan has written a magnificent book. *The Tribal Knot* is a loving portrait of a family across its generations. More than a genealogical trail, this is the story of a distinctly Midwestern family who captured my heart. I fell in love with, quibbled with, and worried over these people as if they were my own. I celebrated their joys, grieved for their losses, and mourned their deaths. McClanahan does such a marvelous job of making her ancestors come alive in this loving reminder of the ties that bind."

—Lee Martin, *From Our House* and *Turning Bones*

"To enter Rebecca McClanahan's memoir is to truly enter her life—her history, her geography, her tribe. The blending of photographs, letters, and diary entries into McClanahan's intelligent, lyrical, and thoughtful prose makes this one of the fullest reading experiences I have had in a very long time."

—Ann Hood, *Comfort: A Journey through Grief* and *The Knitting Circle*

"Book like no other I've read, *The Tribal Knot* combines genres to become something entirely new. Memoir, novel, genealogy, biography, survivor's testimony, study of generations of women, love story, catalogue of precious quotidian details, and portrait of Twentieth-Century American life, this book takes us where we've all been wanting to go but haven't until now seen how to get there. In this brilliant revitalizing of the oldest narrative we know, Rebecca McClanahan demonstrates how our lives depend on the story of our human family and why we can never get enough of it."

—David Huddle, *Nothing Can Make Me Do This*
and *Blacksnake at the Family Reunion*

"This lovely, unsentimental memoir spins the multiple strands of McClanahan's family past into a living tapestry going back into the nineteenth-century Midwest. I have never seen the familial panorama captured as living knowledge in such a moving way. Tragedies lie alongside daily struggles with McClanahan's own formation becoming intuitively known to the reader as she conjures her knot. When her time rolls around we already know her well. This is an unsparing book that is pulled into true by enduring attachment."

—Suzannah Lessard, *The Architect of Desire:*
Beauty and Danger in the Stanford White Family

Other Books by Rebecca McClanahan

◆

Mother Tongue

Mrs. Houdini

One Word Deep: Lectures and Readings

The Intersection of X and Y

Word Painting: A Guide to Writing More Descriptively

Naked as Eve

Write Your Heart Out

The Riddle Song and Other Rememberings

Deep Light: New and Selected Poems

THE
Tribal
Knot

break away b🚲ks

THE
Tribal
Knot

A Memoir of Family,
Community,
and a Century of Change

———◆———

REBECCA
MCCLANAHAN

Indiana University Press

BLOOMINGTON & INDIANAPOLIS

This book is a publication of

Indiana University Press
601 North Morton Street
Bloomington, Indiana 47404-3797 USA

iupress.indiana.edu

Telephone orders   800-842-6796
Fax orders   812-855-7931

The epigraph reproduces portions of "The Family Is All There Is," and is reprinted from *Firekeeper: New and Selected Poems* (Minneapolis: Milkweed Editions). Copyright © 1994 by Pattiann Rogers. Reprinted with permission from Milkweed Editions.

MANUFACTURED IN THE UNITED STATES OF AMERICA

Cataloging information is available from the Library of Congress
ISBN 978-0-253-00859-6 (paper)
ISBN 978-0-253-00867-1 (ebook)

1 2 3 4 5   18 17 16 15 14 13

for our families,
wherever we may find them

ACKNOWLEDGMENTS

Where to begin? Begin at the center of the present-tense tribe, with my parents, Paul and Juanita McClanahan, who generously offered not only their store of letters, documents, photographs, and artifacts but also the stories beneath the store, including some of the darkest chapters in their lives and the lives of their forebears. Thanks, too, to my living siblings— Jenny Dicks, Tom McClanahan, Claudia Marcolese, Rick McClanahan, and Lana Rubright. They encouraged me every step of the way, even when their memories collided violently with mine and derailed my writerly intentions. I also acknowledge our infant sister, Sylvia Sue, whose life and death are inextricably woven into our shared history.

My gratitude extends to other members of the family tribe, including my sisters-in-law, Chris McClanahan and Mary McClanahan, and my brothers-in-law, Dennis Dicks, Bob Marcolese, and Jim Rubright, who have survived many hours of their in-laws' stories with patience and good humor. I also count with pride my fifteen nephews and nieces, my thirteen great-nephews and-nieces, and my stepson, Darren Erik Devet, whose openness to new experiences has inspired me for over three decades. My father-in-law, David Devet, and his daughter, Bonnie Devet, also deserve thanks for their support of my writing over many years.

For her willingness to share the ancestral stories, I thank my maternal aunt, Barbara Clymer. Gratitude, too, to Barbara's husband, the inestimable Kermit Clymer, and to her daughter, Juanita Anne Linn. My father's sister Mary Lou Cougill is another close connection; her research into the paternal side of my family played an important role in this book. I'd also like to thank other relatives whose interviews, phone conversations, and correspondence helped to fill in missing pieces of the ancestral puzzle: on the Mounts side, Shirley Van Meter, Lorraine Komro, Colleen Trickey, Valerine Mavis Trickey, and Vicki Moskiewicz; on the Mead side, Suzanne Rayls, who shared genealogical documents compiled by her mother, Dottie Nixon.

A writer's tribe includes the community of readers, writers, editors, and arts administrators who nurture her work. Several editors encouraged me in this project over the span of many years, especially David Lynn and Peter Stitt (editors, respectively, of *The Kenyon Review* and *The Gettysburg Review*), who published excerpts and adaptations from *The Tribal Knot* when it was in manuscript form. I am also indebted to the editors of the following publications, where portions of the book appeared, often in radically different form: *Arts & Letters; Best American Essays; Dirt: The Quirks, Habits, and Passions of Keeping House; Kiss Tomorrow Hello: Notes from the Midlife Underground; Ms. Magazine; The Southern Review;* and *Waccamaw Journal.* Generous fellowships from New York Foundation for the Arts and North Carolina Arts Council provided me with time, money, and artistic support. Michael Martone encouraged me to submit the manuscript, which Linda Oblack later sponsored, with support from her enthusiastic assistant, Sarah Jacobi.

My administrators, colleagues, and students in the MFA programs of Queens University (Charlotte) and Rainier Writing Workshop served as my literary salon, along with a chorus of friends in the literary community who cheered me on and provided fellowship: Gail Galloway Adams, Barbara Conrad, Jennifer Delahunty, Joyce Dyer, Geeta Kothari, Kim Dana Kupperman, Joe Mackall, Marsha McGregor, Dinty W. Moore, Diana Pinckney, Barbara Presnell, Anna Duke Reach, Mimi Schwartz, Dustin Beall Smith, Michael Steinberg, Terri Wolfe, and Nancy Zafris. An even larger debt is due those who read the entire manuscript, offered critique, and talked me down from the ledge of despair more than once: Martha Allen, Gail Peck, and Dede Wilson.

But my deepest gratitude is to—and for—Donald Devet, my husband and partner of thirty-seven years, whose love, patience, and humor sustain me.

THE
Tribal
Knot

◆

Think of those old, enduring connections
found in all flesh—the channeling
wires and threads, vacuoles, granules,
plasma and pods, purple veins, ascending
boles and coral sapwood (sugar-
and light-filled), those common ligaments,
filaments, fibers and canals.

—from "The Family Is All There Is"
by Pattiann Rogers

◆

No living member of our family has ever seen it, but sources claim that a framed "hair picture," woven from locks of our ancestors' hair, figured strongly in one of the darkest chapters of our family history. If their claim is true, the weaving must have been an exquisite model of the form, for practitioners of hair art report that straight, black hair creates the most striking designs. Hair like Great-aunt Bessie's and her siblings'. Hair from their grandparents and from their father, uncles, and aunts, the eleven children of Mother and Father Mounts. Braided strands of rich, black hair from thirteen members of the tribe, each bearing its individual streak—chestnut, sable, lampblack, coal—yet coiled into one continuous loop. Double helix, coded chain. Hair of my ancestors, the tribal knot.

Last night all the roses opened, their yellow petals filling the dream arbor and spilling onto the bed. I woke in our home three states away from Indiana, my arms spread wide and empty across the quilt. Donald was already up, brewing the coffee I love—does anything taste finer than the first sip of the day? "Good coffee," I say to my cup each morning, as if to commend it for a task well done. "Good life," I often think. Then why this present-tense loneliness, a palpable homesickness for lives I never lived, for places that bloomed and faded so long ago? It has been many years since Briarwood passed out of our family's hands, two decades since the Circle S farm was emptied and auctioned. Two decades since the first letters began arriving in the mail—a shoebox here, a padded envelope there, until after several years my desk was piled high with documents. Letters and postcards and telegrams and water-stained schoolbooks and photographs and diaries and newspaper clippings and calling cards and hospital bills and tax notices and grocery lists and affidavits and wills and marriage announcements and death notices and unused checks and farm ledgers and audio tapes and handmade valentines cut raggedly by a child's hand—a great-uncle's hand—more than a century ago.

"I thought you might want these things," my mother said. "For your writing." It's true, I'd always written about family in one way or another. Hard to avoid the subject when you're one of six living children, an aunt to fifteen and a great-aunt to (at last count) thirteen. For years I'd been nosy about other people's lives, begging details from uncles, aunts, grandparents, and cousins. There's one like me in every family, I suppose: the cemetery haunter, archive junkie, keeper of all things outdated and moldy, professional prober. "Tell me about the time," you begin, urging them on, grabbing up the juiciest morsels, the funniest lines, aiming your high beam into the dark places—what secret will be revealed?

Then one day you open a century-old letter and realize that you know nothing. The questions you've been asking aren't the ones that matter. To answer your own needs, complete your own stories, you've assembled a supporting cast and assigned them cameo roles: the busybody aunt, the silent father, the jovial, drunken uncle, the nurturing grandmother. The truth of their lives is wider, deeper than you'd ever imagined.

The story of every life could begin with *Twice upon a time.* The time lived and the time recalled. *Re:* again. Recall: to call back, to summon. Remember: to put the broken pieces back, the broken members. Return: to turn again to a road you've traveled before. And with each retraced step, you move not only backward in time but forward as well, into a present and future containing altered versions of that past. When we return, it's tempting to look through a soft-focus lens. "The good old days," we say. But what of the nights? To lock the door on the lonely, desperate rooms of our lives, and on the lives of our ancestors, is to lock the door on memory itself. As I write these words, pushing forward into memory, my mind keeps flashing on peripheral scenes: a lumpy feather bed with iron railings, a sloping linoleum floor, a cobwebbed window opening onto a thicket of bramble and wild strawberry. Recalling the Briarwood of my childhood, I summon not only the arbor of yellow roses and the hiss and pop of bacon in the skillet, but also the ragged squeal of cats outside the door, the sour smell of curdled milk, the hollow eyes and mottled skin of a great-aunt whose oldness both fascinated and repelled me, an oldness I could not imagine ever growing into.

Fifty years later, I can imagine it. At times I catch a glimpse of the old woman I am becoming, in the veined, age-spotted hand holding the pen as I labor to write my aunt—and grandparents and uncles and cousins and neighbors and friends and lovers, the living and the dead, those I never knew and those who have yet to be born—into my life. Once, many years ago, *twice upon a time,* I entered a place where I was so thoroughly lost I knew I would never find my way out and didn't care if I did. Literature played an important part in my return, poems and stories I read and fought desperately to write. And music, threading its bright strands into the darkness. Small, domestic gestures also played their part in coaxing me home. The wind-dried sheets I unclipped from the line and pressed close to my face. The banana bread I slathered with butter and placed on the blue china plate an extravagant friend had brought to me, determined to help any way she could.

But finally what led me back to myself, long after I'd given up, was the sudden, piercing knowledge: I am not *only* myself. My life did not begin with my birth and would not end with my death. Not that I'd asked for this knowledge or even welcomed it. Like many people entangled in the knots of need and obligation, I had dreamed of aloneness and freedom, of lifting above the demands of home, family, neighborhood, and community, an ethereal presence soaring high. Perfectly whole within myself. Sans body, sans history, sans umbilicus tying me to past or future lives.

"To write one's life is to live it twice," writes Patricia Hampl in her essay "Memory and Imagination." She's right, I think, lifting yet another letter from its fragile, ink-smeared envelope. And to write the lives of others, entangled with our own, how many lives does that add up to? Where do we leave off and others begin? To what degree are we responsible for, and to, those forces that have formed us? As I search the family documents that span more than a century, these questions deepen and complicate. Here, the knot tightens. There, a strand pulls loose from the braid. Step back, I tell myself, far enough to see the whole design, the interwoven histories. Slide out of your own shoes and into Sylvia's or Juanita's or Lucippa's, or into the shoes of Great-grandma Hattie whose feet *hurt so much I can't think above them.* Untie the ribbon around Bessie's 1897 diary and slip inside its pages.

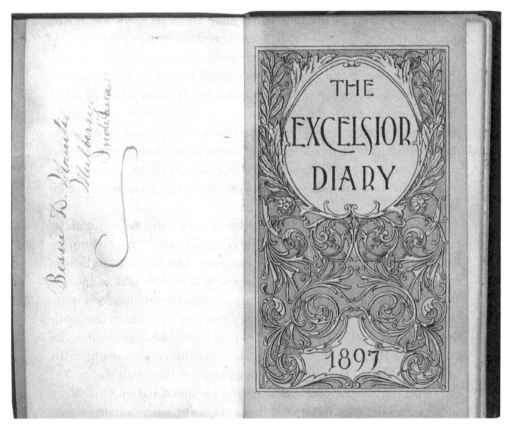

Great-aunt Bessie's 1897 diary, a gift from her teacher.

To read another's diary is to enter a private chamber. When the diarist is a sixteen-year-old girl, the trespass takes on another dimension. And when that sixteen-year-old girl is a long-dead aunt, the world flips on its axis. In the life we lived together, Bessie was seventy years my senior—always, and only, it seemed to me, old. My life stretched before me; hers, I supposed, was already gone. In the diary life we now share, she is nearly young enough to be my own great-niece. Even more disturbing is the time-warp quality of our encounter. Though her words toss me one hundred and ten years into the past, she abides in the pulsing, present-tense now. Sometimes, in the middle of an entry, she disappears for a few hours to attend to ironing or churning, or to answer her younger sister's call, returning to the page as if out of breath or flushed from the weedy garden's heat, or rapturous from a sleigh ride with cousins and friends.

Each page of a diary fills only with now. So, Bessie's diary of 1897 muscles along, day by calendar day, an inchworm making its blind progress with little care for what has gone before and no knowledge of what lies ahead, beyond a girl's vague landscape of hopes and dreams. I cannot reach through the pages and take her hand, warn her of what is to come. And if I could, would it change her course of action? The global things, of course, will be out of her control: the four wars she will live through, the bread lines, foreclosures and riots, the 1920s march of the Klan through Indiana towns, the assassination of a beloved president. But there are choices closer to home that she might make, roads diverging. If she knew in advance how the lives of those she loves would play out, would she choose not to grow so close to them? Not to visit the doomed family in Wisconsin or take in the smells of her mother's kitchen or toss the wedding rice over her cousin's shoulders as she leaps with her groom onto the train platform? Would foreknowledge of her brother's fate change her actions—her absence at the hard end, the regret she would carry to her death? And if she knew that one day a great-niece would sift through the diary and through stacks of letters and documents that open the closed doors of the family's past, would she have firmly closed that door? Locked up the evidence and thrown away the key? Or would she have given it all, gladly, into my hand?

◆

Half a century later, I'm still not sure why, on our family's summer visits to Tippecanoe County, Indiana, I chose to spend much of my time at Briarwood, the falling-down cabin stuffed with stray cats, dusty Mason jars, and stacks of outdated <u>National Geographic</u>. Maybe I wanted to be special, to be the only child of someone, even if that someone was Great-aunt Bessie. Not that I hadn't already had plenty of alone time with Bessie on and off throughout my earliest years. Childless, widowed, at times annoyingly eccentric, my grandmother's older sister had "traveling feet" as she used to say. Briarwood might have been "the old home place" and Bessie its last remaining resident, but she kept her suitcase packed at all times, joining our family wherever my Marine Corps father's orders happened to take us.

None of my siblings stayed at Briarwood longer than a few hours. They couldn't wait to get back to our grandparents' farm, to the creek and barn and chickens and horses, to Grandma Sylvia's cherry pies and rides in Grandpa Arthur's hand-built sulky cart. Plus, by then the Circle S farm had running water and a television that, if you positioned the rabbit ears just so, could get three stations. Briarwood was another story altogether. Arriving there was like climbing into the cartoon WABAC machine with Mr. Peabody and Sherman and going back, *way back*, in time. The only downstairs bedroom was so small that it barely contained the creaky iron bed and the dresser with its pitcher and wash basin. Bessie and I shared the bed, which was fitted with a feather mattress and several handmade quilts. On the floor beside the bed—careful where you stepped!—she'd stationed a white-enameled slop jar, though

Bessie preferred the term "chamber pot." On nights when I was too scared or lazy to make my way to the outhouse, I would crouch beside the bed and "do my business," another phrase Bessie preferred to the cruder expressions my Indiana cousins used.

The outhouse sat at the far end of what had once been, according to Aunt Bessie, my great-grandfather's raised garden beds. I hated outhouses, but over the years I'd learned to deal with them. Like the outhouse at my grandparents' farm, this was a two-seater, built for company on lizard nights. At Circle S I could usually convince Mother or one of my sisters to accompany me, to stand outside and guard the door (from what, I'm still not sure) or, if circumstances demanded, to share a seat beside me. I never actually sat. There was too much life crawling beneath the hole cut in the wooden bench, and I was not about to spread myself over such dangerous and unseen territory. I would squat on my haunches until my thighs trembled, but I would not sit.

Much of my time with Bessie was spent in the kitchen, an open room with an oak table, a high cabinet stacked with books and magazines, and a daybed that served as a sofa. Near the window, at the end of a long porcelain sink, a hand pump sprouted, attached to a cistern that had never worked and never would. First thing in the morning, the favorite time of day for both of us, Bessie would climb out of bed, button a sweater over her nightgown, lace up her low-heeled black shoes, and make her way out the kitchen door, across a covered porch, and down fifteen steep steps that led to the well house. This cold, dark space, located beneath a tiny outdoor kitchen, had been carved from the slope of a hill leading to a branch of Wildcat Creek. By the time Bessie made it back up the steps, bucket in hand, I was rummaging in the cabinets for Cheerios or Wheaties. Outside the screen door, a posse of wild barn cats had gathered, yowling for breakfast. But before she fed them, Bessie filled the percolator basket with coffee she'd ground the night before in a hand-cranked grinder. Within a few minutes, the cats were fed and the glass bubble on the top of the percolator had commenced its Maxwell House dance. Aunt Bessie drank her coffee black, in a chipped cup with a saucer to catch any spills should a cat startle her by leaping onto her lap or onto the table where I tried, usually without success, to guard my bowl of cereal.

Sometime in the early 1950s, power lines had been run to Briar-wood, but Bessie did not splurge. Yes for the icebox, and yes for the overhead light in the main room, and of course yes for the radio she kept on the kitchen counter. She switched it on each morning to check the weather report from the Purdue station, a habit from her farming days. Bessie still owned forty acres (several miles from Briarwood) that a neighbor, Eldon Zink, worked for her. He stopped by every few days to see if she needed anything from town. Short, with a pronounced hump on his back, Eldon resembled a fairy tale dwarf, but he had a soft, soothing voice and his face verged on handsome. He and his brother lived with their mother a few miles down the road. To my knowledge, neither son had ever married. Eldon was young in Bessie years, per-haps twenty years her junior. Still, he seemed old to me, too old to be living with his mother. Sometimes I imagined he might "fancy" Bessie. "Fancy?" Good grief, I'd been around her so long, I was starting to *imagine* in her language.

Where our days at Briarwood went, I'm not sure. They went, though, more quickly in memory than while I was living them. Aunt Bessie took her time: coffee, radio, outhouse, stove, sink, wash basin, bureau, closet. This is not to say that she was lazy. Every waking moment was filled with activity, each action purposeful and deliberate. Bessie Denton Mounts Cosby did not *lounge.* Unlike some women of her age who live alone, she did not pass her days in housecoat and slippers. She dressed for the day: white underwear, white brassiere, full slip with adjustable straps, cotton blouse, skirt and belt. Girdle and stockings, she saved for town or for visits to neighbors; on cabin days, she wore socks with her walking shoes.

After breakfast, we hiked to nearby woods, stopping to pick berries and wildflowers or, on occasion, apron loads of mushrooms that Bes-sie would later slice to cook in butter. The dandelion greens she craved grew along the roadside, and we'd carry baskets to collect them in. Once, we walked all the way along the creek road to Salem Cemetery, a small, well-kept graveyard surrounded by leafy trees that cast shadows across the grass. Bessie's parents were buried there. Her husband, too, and one of Bessie's brothers. I'd never known Uncle Dale, but Bessie talked about him a lot, much more than she talked about her other brothers—maybe, I imagined, because Dale was dead and my other great-uncles weren't. That made him more special, I guessed.

Afternoons, Bessie puttered in the garden, which by that time was mostly weeds. Mosquitoes and bees swarmed around her head, but she never got bit or stung. I stayed inside, swabbing mosquito and chigger bites with alcohol-dipped cotton balls and trying not to scratch the reddened welts. Some days I'd read a Nancy Drew book, or cut Betsy McCall paper dolls from magazines that Aunt Barbara had given me, or rummage in the bureau where Bessie kept old books inscribed with names of people I'd never known. One afternoon, after falling asleep over an unfinished crossword puzzle, I woke on the daybed with a strong urge to use the toilet. Hoping to make short work of this, I grabbed a roll of toilet paper from the cabinet near the screen door and headed out across the porch and down the weedy path to the outhouse. I lifted the latch and opened the door.

There sat Aunt Bessie, her skirt arranged around her like the pleats of an open fan, her black walking shoes dangling inches from the floor. She was holding a book close to her eyes and leaning toward a crack between two boards where a sliver of sunlight leaked through. She looked up from the book and smiled. "Welcome to my library," she said. I mumbled a hurried "excuse me" and turned to leave. It was one thing to share the two-seater with Mother, Jenny, Claudia, or, in emergencies, Grandma Sylvia. But Great-aunt Bessie?

"Have a seat. I won't bite," she said. "Did you finish the crossword?" I shook my head no. I was rocking back and forth, certain now that I would never make it to the bushes. Wishing I had a fan of skirts to cover myself with, I pulled down my shorts and fixed my gaze straight ahead. When I was finished I reached for the toilet paper, made a covert swipe, pulled up my shorts, and left, hurrying out the door without a word.

◆

Nights, after the thrill of lightning bugs subsided, after the last cat was fed and shooed out the screen door, after I'd soaked my chigger-bitten ankles in the washtub water sprinkled with baking soda, I'd climb up onto the daybed to read. Usually, Bessie was already there with a <u>National Geographic</u> open on her lap, lost in some Aztec ruin or snowy Himalayan peak. Sometimes she would put her magazine down, turn to me, and out of nowhere, start telling stories. Made-up stories, mostly, patched together from bits of the books she'd read when she was young, with plots that featured orphaned girls who pull themselves up "by their own bootstraps" as she liked to say, to become well-bred ladies who travel "hither and yon" among "the finest people."

On occasion, Aunt Bessie would talk about her family's early years here at Briarwood, when her youngest brothers were still schoolboys. Things were "altogether different than they are now," she'd say, going on to describe the swimming hole where neighbors gathered on Sundays, the summer kitchen, smokehouse, open-sided milking stable, the family's pet albino squirrel and cookie-grabbing raccoon. I'd glance around the dark, musty room, unable to conjure the lively home she recalled, with the tiny alcove housing Great-grandpa Mounts's reading chair and Great-grandma's sewing machine and flower boxes.

My favorite stories were about Sylvia, Bessie's younger sister. I'd seen photos of my grandmother when she was a young woman—holding a long stringer of fish, stretched out in a "bathing costume" on the banks of Ottawa Beach, perched up high in the branch of a tree or on a woodpile—so I was able to imagine her when Bessie told the runaway pony story. I could see Sylvia's long, black hair, and her strong chin and pretty face with the slightly upturned nose.

"Back then, traffic wasn't like it is now," Bessie began. "You didn't see much out on our little road. We had a little dun pony then. I didn't ride him but Sylvia did, you know your grandmother always loved horses. But she was just a girl then, maybe ten or eleven. One day—it was a hot summer day—the front door was open so we could catch a breeze. We'd let the pony out of the stable and he was feeding in the pasture near the road. Brother was sitting in the living room." ("Brother," I knew, referred to Bessie's brother Dale). "Back from one of his trips I guess, and I'd come in to tell him something, when suddenly we heard a loud noise and Dale jumped up from his chair—'What in the dickens?'—and both of us hurried to the door just in time to see that pony galloping right past us, too close to the road, then making a turn like he was heading back to the stable and then he was gone. And the next thing we knew, here he came again, and there she was, Sylvia, on the back of that pony, and she hadn't a thing to hold on to but a bit of his mane. She was riding that pony! Not a thing to hold on to but his mane!

"Now, that's something I couldn't do," Bessie said, shaking her head side to side. "That's what I said later, after everything calmed down and Sylvia led the pony back to the stable. Something I could never do.

"Of course, we didn't always live here," she continued. "We lived in Clinton County for a while. And before that, we lived down in Switzerland County." Bessie took a deep breath and leaned forward on the daybed. Oh no, I thought, another history lesson: the Mounts ancestors, the Mead ancestors. Rising Sun, Indiana.

"You were *born* in Switzerland County," I offered, dredging up the one detail I was able to keep straight. "Near a river."

Bessie nodded. "The Ohio. Dale was born there too. And of course our parents were too, a long time ago."

To a child of ten or eleven, at least to the child I was, nothing was more boring than hearing about relatives you'd never met. Dead relatives. Dead for years, decades. Forever. But the stories seemed so important to Bessie, the least I could do was pretend to listen. Again. So, I learned that Bessie's mother—I had trouble remembering her name—had been born during the Civil War. She lived alone with her mother, and they were very poor. Sometimes they went hungry. Later, the little girl's mother got married again, so the little girl had a baby sister, and a baby brother too. But the mother died when the girl was eleven.

My age, I thought, my interest perking up.

After the mother died, the children had to live apart, with different families. Hattie didn't see her siblings for a long time. As Bessie spoke, I thought about my own brothers and sisters, how it would feel to live apart from them. I liked it when they went away to sleepovers or to camp—I got more of Mom's attention. But to never see them? Especially our baby sister Lana, who'd only recently arrived on the scene? As for a mother dying, I couldn't let myself think about that. Just a few days after Dad had brought Lana and Mom home, Mom was rushed back to the hospital at Fort Belvoir. "Complications" was the word we heard. She was gone for days, all of us pitching in to take care of the new baby while Dad drove back and forth between hospital and home. It was weeks before we learned how close we had come to losing our mother.

"Who lived there, again?" I asked, resurfacing from my daydream. "In the house by the river?"

"My mother, Hattie, after her mother died. Her grandfather took care of her."

"The Mississippi River, right?"

"The Ohio," Bessie answered, shaking her head. I was a hopeless case.

"Sorry," I said. "Tell me one more time."

Bessie would take a deep breath, pause, and begin again. The lesson went something like this: "We'll start at the beginning, one generation at a time. Starting with you. Your mother's name is . . ."

"Juanita," I answered.

"And Juanita's mother is . . ."

"My grandma."

"Her *name*," Bessie said patiently. "What is your grandmother's name?"

"Sylvia."

Bessie raised her eyebrows. Obviously, "Sylvia" would not suffice.

"Sylvia Sanders," I said.

"What was her name before she married your grandfather?"

"Sylvia Mounts?" This was starting to make sense now—I saw a pattern.

"That's right. Mounts was my name, too, before I got married. Because Sylvia and I are sisters."

"And you have two brothers."

"Three. Sylvia and I *had* three brothers," Bessie said, lowering her head. She was quiet for a few seconds. Too quiet. "And who was our mother? Do you know her name?"

This was getting easier, like a multiple-choice test. "Mounts?"

"Her married name was Mounts. But do you remember her *first* name?"

I shook my head no.

"Remember the little girl I told you about, whose mother died?"

"The girl with the pierced ears?" The pierced ears I remembered from the photograph. I'd never seen a little girl with pierced ears.

"Yes. The little girl who lived in the big house by the river."

"Hattie," I answered.

Bessie nodded. "So, now, do you have it all straight? How many generations is that, altogether? Count them."

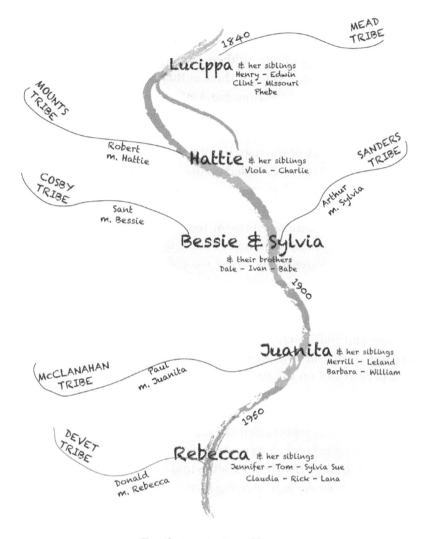

Family tree, maternal lineage

I tapped it out with my fingers. "Me, my mom, Grandma Sylvia, and Hattie. Four. Four generations."

"That will do for now," Bessie said, returning to her National Geographic. "It's almost bedtime. Lights out in fifteen minutes."

◆

In the hundreds of family letters I have inherited, letters spanning over a century, cousins write to cousins, uncles to nephews, aunts to nieces, teachers to students, soldiers to parents, lovers to lovers. But most of the letters are signed by three authors: Bessie, Sylvia, and Hattie. Two daughters and their mother. Letters written in good times on store-bought stationery or printed cards; in bad times on used envelopes, church bulletins, grocery receipts, wallpaper, wrapping paper, on unused bank checks or the margins of free calendars distributed from seed companies. Letters scribbled on the run, between tasks or smack in the middle of them: *I am rocking the baby to sleep with my foot and singing a little so if you get a few snitches of the song don't mind . . .*

Sometimes the intimate, present-tense quality of the writing catches me off guard, prompting homesickness for a life I never lived. *Baby is lying here doing something I'll bet you can't do, Putting his big toe in his mouth. Ha!* The women write while the cake is cooling, the lye for soap is boiling, the irons heating, the clothes soaking, the yeast about to spill over its bowl. The smear of molasses on Sylvia's elbow gums up the envelope, and Hattie scribbles while keeping a lookout for the freshly caged pig—*Well hear a racket now I expect hes getting out.*

In person and on the page, all three—Bessie, Sylvia, and Hattie—were skilled storytellers, but the liveliest descriptions were scratched from Hattie's pencil. In August, when it is *too hot to live anyway,* my great-grandmother reports that she has *melted and run all over myself* and *must fan myself to sleep.* In winter, she must *hump around and shiver to get warm.* Though her children often told their friends *you can never tell with Mother* or *she may be trying to run a bluff,* in her letters she appears to hide nothing. Reading Hattie's letters is like opening a window directly into her mind. Some letters begin breathlessly, in medias res, as if she's continuing a conversation with herself:

> *. . . And you ought to have seen the show last night about 1 o'clock Dale came running downstairs, something after the chickens, Turkeys flying Rooster cackling he grabbed the shotgun and I the lamp, him in shirttail & slippers and I just my nightgown and slippers it was a beautiful night to be out in such thin apparel when we got down there and peered in the shed here came two coons skulking out from under the wood house, so I captured them both and marched them back to*

their den and held the lamp for Dale to wire them in we came back
thawed out and went to bed again.

Hattie was never a religious person; her letters serve as confession booth, wailing wall and mourning bench, rosary beads she fingers one by one, stringing each item to the next in a chain of mostly bad news that often begins with her first few sentences:

> *Brands daughter came home for Christmas & went back, then*
> *on Thursday they got a telegram she was dead, wasn't that terrible to*
> *them. I moast dread the holidays anymore it brings so much sadness*
> *... The cement wall fell down over at Llecklitners and killed two sows*
> *and several pigs, some more of his good luck ... I feel rather blue this*
> *morning for out of 45 nice little chicks I have 4 left ... weasels, hawks*
> *and everything else ... but I suppose one ought to be glad it is no*
> *worse. Packards had a baby girl and it died ... Mr. Shalley is dead, so*
> *is Mr. Horlacher ... and on Sunday too.*

So it continues, the spilling out of troubles in one continuous stream until, gasping, Hattie must take a breath, rest a moment, and grab one more shallow breath before commencing, with much effort, the uphill climb of pulling herself out of the darkness:

> *... But it seems the good things are not for me ... I am moast too*
> *tired and out in heart to write ... the hens are still on a strike too. But*
> *what is the use to complain? Tell the news! Lilly is getting better. Ava*
> *has a new boy. The teachers sister & Walter Carr are to be married*
> *tonight. Jacksons will soon ... Dale dug out a skunk den last Sat. af-*
> *ternoon got 6 skunk and Pa got one in a trap you ought to have been*
> *here Sunday things quite highly perfumed around here.*

It is impossible not to admire Hattie's determination to talk herself out of herself—her efforts are so transparent, such poignant reminders of the courage and tenacity of ordinary lives. *But it is no use to cry although I felt very much like it this morning when I went and saw my nice Turkey that I had fed at dark lying stiff but then there are others are having worse luck so just try again.*

Years pass, decades, their words as immediate as on the day they were written. Here, huddling in the corner is a shivering Bessie with

they are like they havent
the least Idea how it
happend for they had eaten
a cold supper;
the Elevater burned at
ClarksHill and several
barnes, and Mr Bakers
over by Hayton had a
field of wheat burnt
up and the machine
was there ready to
thrash.
I suppose you had heard
that Ernest Carle was
struck by lightning and
killed;
Mr McCauley died two weeks
ago yesterday.
Clarance his youngest boy
fell and broke his collar
bone but is getting all
right

Page from one of Great-grandmother Hattie's letters, 1914.

her tiny, stocking feet stretched toward the stove. The frozen chicks are thawing beside her, and she is *writing while I warm.* For even the work-horse Bessie *must stop somewhere to write, so of course I would stop at the churn.* And the aging, exhausted Hattie must put her news to bed, *Well I will quit and maybe there will be some more to tell in the morning,* before picking it up, mid-sentence, with the rooster's crow, *and Good Morning I feel better don't you for the sun is shining even if the whole valley is a skating rink. Jolly is singing as loud as he can and the boys are skating I think they will get their fill. I will have to hurry for my scrub water is boiling and the yeast is ready to run over.*

The gift of a diary is a gift composed entirely of future: all those blank pages waiting to be filled. And with what sentiment shall he send Bessie forth? The small leather volume, <u>The Excelsior Diary 1897</u>, is inscribed in a careful hand, "Compliments of your teacher L. L. Kyger." Most likely, Kyger presented the gift on the occasion of Bessie's forthcoming graduation from the Clendenning grade school in Clinton County, Indiana. The teacher certainly hoped that Bessie would continue on to high school. But if she could not, for the facts pointed away from such hopes, she would at least have something into which to record her daily comings-and-goings, the books she was reading, her plans and schemes. She might even include lines from the poems she had recited before the other students. Bessie's was the most pleasant voice in the schoolroom, a singer's voice with deep, modulated tones that rose and fell, riding the waves of sound rather than thrashing against them as so many students did. Oh, how Kyger must have dreaded their weekly recitations. The brutality with which they assault Longfellow and Keats. Their reedy, nasal twangs. How had Bessie acquired such a voice? And what might she do with her gift?

Bessie liked to sit at the head of the class, so it is easy to imagine her, on a December day in 1896, perched on the front bench of the drafty one-room schoolhouse. A geography book is open on her lap, perhaps the very book found among her belongings after she died. With her index finger, she traces the snakelike route of the Mississippi then moves westward to the long chain of dotted lines marking the Rocky Mountains, eager to turn to her favorite page, which she has saved for last. "Map of the World," the heading proclaims, and below the heading, two circles barely touching: Western Hemisphere, Eastern Hemisphere. If you could stitch the two circles together, Bessie thinks, then fluff them out like the sleeves of a party dress, or better yet, if you could shape the whole earth in your hands like a ball of dough—no, that wouldn't work, it needs to be a real ball, a rubber ball that can spin swiftly above your head—then you could see the entire world in one glance. Bessie has never seen the great oceans, but she knows that America stretches between two of them, and one day she will travel the whole span of the nation and even farther, where, according to this book, all manner of peoples are living in all manner of climes. She will travel to every continent, even to Africa, "the hottest Grand Division of the Earth," where hyenas and leopards roam freely, and people ride atop elephants whose tusks are made of ivory. Ivory!

Bessie wonders if Africans look the same as the Negroes she sees on the train to Wisconsin or near the old family homes in Switzerland County. Bessie's mother is always telling stories about the Mead house on the Ohio River, how it was when Hattie was very young, before her mother died. How Hattie played with the Negro children and the mammy pierced Hattie's ears and taught her songs about chariots and robes and crowns. When Hattie tells the stories, her voice gets quiet and her heavy-lidded eyes look downward or away, like she is seeing something in the distance. Then she is sad for days. Sometimes she tells the biscuit story. Mostly, Hattie says, she remembers being hungry. So hungry that she feared the biscuit her mother placed in her dinner bucket might be her last. She might get even hungrier. So better not eat the biscuit. Better keep it in the bucket, just in case. So, the way Hattie tells it, she would carry that same biscuit back and forth from school to home and back to school until it was "no longer hardly fit to eat."

It's difficult for sixteen-year-old Bessie to imagine her mother as a child; she's seen only one picture of the young Hattie. Even harder to imagine her mother's mother: Lucippa was her name. Grandma Lucippa, Bessie would have called her, had she ever had a chance to know her. Bessie barely remembers Great-grandfather Mead, or Mother and Father Mounts for that matter. Sometimes she forgets they are dead. When you never see people, it's hard to remember if they are alive or dead. *Are you still among the living?* Hattie asks in her letters—to Aunt Phebe in Rising Sun, to Uncle Clint in Hammond, to Pa's brothers and sister up in Wisconsin. Mother is joking, of course, it's Mother's way, but Bessie sometimes wonders if Hattie isn't half-serious, considering the way things have gone in her life. Folks can be there one day and gone the next. Of all people, her mother should know that.

The December scene resumes, unspooling like a film before my eyes. Bessie isn't the only Mounts child in the schoolroom today. Her seven-year-old sister is here as well, surrounded by friends eager to share their bucket lunches and their pencils, to sit next to the girl with the smiling eyes, the open, pretty face, and the sense of humor she easily turns on herself. "Oh, go ahead, then," Sylvia says when she's done something clumsy or silly. "Just laugh and get it all over yourself." Then she joins in the laughter, endearing herself even more to those gathered around her.

Twelve-year-old Dale Mounts is present today, too, though his mind is hundreds of miles away, in the cold, leafless Wisconsin woods where he's sure his uncles and cousins are crouched with deer rifles, watching for a flash of white tail in the distance. Oh, he'd give anything to be there. To be anywhere but here, laboring over copying lessons, forming the lines a great-niece will one day discover in his 1896 composition book. Dale positions the pencil firmly between his short, broad fingers, noticing once again how much neater his teacher's letters are than his own. Then, following the model Mr. Kyger has provided, he begins to shape the words:

> Thought is deeper than all speech.
> Feelings are deeper than all thoughts.
> The mind has a thousand eyes
> And the heart has but one.

Dale's handwriting could use some improvement, but he's coming along nicely with his parsing, so well that Mr. Kyger has lately allowed him to supply his own thoughts within the patterns. Yesterday Dale had written:

> The roar of a lion is terrible.
> The love of a sister is precious.
> The president of the country is William McKinley.
> The hands of the lady are soft and white.

Strange, the thoughts that enter a child's mind, how they follow one after the other. Stranger still, the future hovering cloudlike around

Great-uncle Dale, age 12, and his 1896 composition book.

a child's head, taking years to settle. To a boy like Dale, to whom the softness of a lady's hand abides peaceably beside a lion's terrible roar, some thoughts are simply unthinkable. Should be unthinkable. Even decades later, when, I imagine, they arrive without his consent, a string of unthinkable thoughts linking each to each, and the thousand eyes of his mind are opened.

An eruption of laughter from the back of the room claims Kyger's attention, and he rises from the stool for a better look. Near the woodstove—which, Kyger notices, needs another log, and soon—Sylvia Mounts sits with the youngest students practicing for the weekly spelldown. Seeing Kyger, Sylvia claps her small hands across her mouth but cannot hide the smile in her eyes. Kyger lowers his head, attempting his sternest frown, but his heart is not in it. If a teacher is not mindful, he thinks, he could discipline the life right out of such a child, and everyone would be the poorer for it.

Dale Mounts sits alone at the back table, bent over his writing tablet with that worried look on his face again. Yesterday, Mr. Kyger assigned the middle-graders to write their first recollections. *My Early Life*, Dale has written, but has gotten no further. Dale is stymied. He seems to have no first recollections. How far back is he supposed to go? He scoots the chair closer to the table and scratches his head with the pencil he borrowed from Bessie this morning; he'd misplaced his again. Dale last saw it at the breakfast table, where he was rushing to finish his ciphering drills. He was certain that their pet raccoon had grabbed it up, but Mother said, "What would the raccoon want with a pencil when he could have a cookie?" So that settled that. Maybe the pencil fell from his satchel and he would find it on the path home, if the snow didn't start up again. Dale turns the page in his composition book, stares at the three words—*My Early Life*—and sighs his deepest sigh.

> I was born at GrandFather's house in Switzerland County Ind. The Year 1884. July 29. The first recollections of home was I would catch hold of a chair and Bessie would pull it around the room. One time when my Uncle Harve was plowing I went out in the field where he was. There was a large rock and he plowed it over and there was a large long black snake under it. I picked it up and showed the snake to him he was scaret very much and come and made me throw it down and he killed it. It was about four feet long. I am twelve years old now. I would like to be a Storekeeper.

First recollections. Brief. Imagistic. Floating to the child from who knows where. Why these memories and not others? A big sister pulling him around on a chair. An uncle plowing up a snake. In Dale's school report of his to-date brief existence, we glimpse a child's world from the inside out, a world of make-do play (a chair becomes a toy) where even dangerous encounters turn out to be not so dangerous after all. For someone is watching the boy. Someone is there to kill the snake that might bite the boy. Often, that someone is his mother or father, for this boy is fortunate enough to belong to both. But because the boy is part of a larger tribe, that someone is just as likely to be an aunt, a sibling, grandparent, cousin, neighbor, or friend. Or, in this case, an uncle. On the snake-plowing day the uncle happened to be Harve, but might have been any number of uncles—from the Mounts side, the Mead side. And perhaps to a boy so inundated with uncles, they might have seemed interchangeable.

Until Uncle Charlie came along.

Like a character who shows up late in a novel or a play, a character whose presence has been anticipated but as yet not revealed, Charlie gained the weight of importance chiefly through his absence during Dale's earliest years in Switzerland County. Dale knew that Uncle Charlie was his mother's brother. Hattie and Charlie had different fathers, but the same mother: her name was Lucippa. But Lucippa died when the children were small, so they had to live apart, with different families. Dale had heard of Uncle Charlie's wild years too, the knife fights he'd gotten into, and the scars that proved the stories. But in those early days in Switzerland County., Dale had yet to meet the man in the stories.

When Dale did meet his uncle, Charlie came attached to Aunt Mary, Pa's sister, an attachment that confused and delighted Dale once he was able to untangle the knot, the double family connection. Let's see, now, how did it go? Charlie is Mother's brother. Well, half brother. How could you have half a brother? And Aunt Mary is Pa's sister. Does that make Little Charlotte a double cousin? This was too much to figure. Dale's head was aching. And Mr. Kyger was looking at him again. He'd best finish his copying lesson.

> Every tree is known by its fruits.
> Each of the ladies was perfect in her part.
> No person should boast of himself.
> Let each of them be heard in his turn.

◆

Six decades past the diary year, as we sat propped up on pillows in the double bed we shared, Great-aunt Bessie would remind me once again that Byron was her favorite poet. "Always has been," she'd say, her loose dentures clacking. "Always will be." At eight or nine, I was too young to know of Byron's reputation as a poet, a soldier, a philandering lover. Had I known, I would have wondered at this wrinkled, scrawny woman so enamored of a young, wavy-haired poet that she kept a framed photograph of him on her side of the dresser we shared.

By that time, Bessie had read all of Byron's works, for in her later years, free of the toil and caretaking that had consumed her youth and middle age, she hungrily read everything she could get her hands on. But at the time her teacher presented the diary to her, Bessie had not yet read the poem from which Mr. Kyger's inscription was taken, stripped of context and irony. Certainly there was no copy of "Don Juan" at the log house where Bessie lived with her parents and younger siblings. Decades would pass before Bessie finally discovered the long poem considered to be Byron's greatest if unfinished masterpiece. Reading along—at the brisk clip with which she read everything, her round, dark eyes actively skimming the pages—did she pause at Canto XV, recognizing something familiar . . . "How little do we know" . . . and then, because Bessie was not one to linger on the past, move furiously on, eager to learn how things would turn out? Don Juan, fresh from a dalliance with the married Lady Adeline, has just met the adored Aurora, whom he loves from afar. If one can believe Don Juan ever loved anyone from afar.

In Byron's version, Aurora is sixteen, a year younger than Bessie's mother was when she married Bessie's father. Of course, that was a long time ago, or so it seemed to the young Bessie. Girls got married earlier then. It was hard enough for Bessie to imagine her mother being young, but married at seventeen? Why, who could conceive of such a thing! Though *most certainly,* some girls still married young. A few of Bessie's friends were engaged already, and she'd heard from her cousins, though they tended to exaggerate so she couldn't be sure, that Uncle Lafe's new bride in Wisconsin was only fifteen when they got married last New Year's Eve. Her name was Pearl, and she was about to have a baby. A baby, at sixteen! Bessie wondered what they would name the baby, and if she would ever get to see it. Pa went to Wisconsin more often now, in deer season, mostly, but he hardly ever took the rest of them along anymore except to help out with the threshing.

It was a puzzle to Bessie, how some folks got together. Who chose who. *Whom,* she corrected herself. Objective case: *whom.* Uncle Lafe and Pearl, for instance. "Lafayette," Hattie always corrected her daughter. "Your uncle's full name is Lafayette." But Bessie liked calling him Lafe, so as not to mix him up with the nearby Indiana town. Uncle Lafe was, let's see. Bessie stopped for a minute to calculate. Arithmetic was not her best subject, but certainly she could work this out. If Pa was born in 1856 and Lafe was a year older, that would make Lafe—well, it is 1897 now, minus 1855, let's see, yes, that would make Lafe forty-two years old. Older than Pa, and married to a girl my age! Bessie let the thought settle a minute, then put the thought away, deep down where she put other such thoughts, and focused on the line of uncles. Seven uncles was a lot to keep straight—and that didn't even count Uncle Charlie. Should she count him? He wasn't a Mounts, but he *was* Mother's brother. So certainly he should count.

Uncle Charlie and Aunt Mary, Bessie thought. Now there's another strange pair. A wife older than her husband. Bessie had never heard of such a thing. "Only eight years older," Mother had said. "But everyone is different so you mustn't judge, and besides, Aunt Mary is good for Charlie." Bessie figured Mother was referring to Uncle Charlie's dark moods and his temper. She didn't know if it was true, but she'd heard that one time Charlie got into a knife fight with a man—over what, it wasn't clear—and that he had a scar, a deep, long, diagonal scar across his belly. Well, people tell tales, Bessie thought, so who could know? She was curious to see the scar but she most certainly was not about to ask. Charlie was her uncle, after all.

◆

Seated on the tall wooden stool, Kyger looks out over the heads of the pupils clustered in small groups around the schoolroom. The diary is open to its inscription page, but he cannot seem to arrive at the proper quotation. Longfellow? Of course there is always Lowell or Riley. Riley, yes, that would be his pick—and Riley a Hoosier, too. But no, not for Bessie. For Bessie, something with substance and wit. Lord Byron?

Something instructive but not overtly so, for she would quickly sniff out such motives, this wiry, energetic young woman sitting before him, studying the geography text.

What is it that sets Bessie apart? Her determination? The curiosity that flashes from the dark eyes that rarely meet his gaze? The dogged will that will serve her well, Kyger predicts, if it does not take her into trouble? One thing is clear: Bessie Mounts will never be a beauty. Apart from her hair, straight and black and shiny—all three Mounts children have that same Indian-straight hair—she has little in the way of looks to recommend her. It isn't only the scar, cut deeply into the skin of her nose, from some type of burn, the teacher imagines. Even beyond the scar, there is something unfortunate about the way her face is arranged. Too small a canvas, perhaps, to contain the large features. Eyes planted too far apart, as if to make room for the rounded bulb of nose. A mouth that, were it mounted above the ledge of a firm, aristocratic chin, might seem generous, even sensuous, but placed as it is so close to the vague, indefinite jaw, seems comically wide.

Is Bessie aware of how she appears to others? Has she studied herself in her father's shaving mirror or in one of the full-length windows in the shops of Indianapolis or Hammond or one of those Wisconsin towns she describes in her compositions? At what moment did she decide, as she seems to have decided, to look not *into* the mirror but rather *through* it, to the larger world beyond? And if that world looks back too harshly, as if taking her measure and finding it wanting, Bessie knows how to avert those eyes, to look down onto the ciphering slate or deeply into the lesson book, or out, far out, past the window of the schoolhouse and into the distance and beyond. Is this merely her way to keep herself to herself? Or is there something only *she* sees out of the corners of those dark eyes?

A shame, to Kyger's mind. Of all his students, Bessie most deserves to continue to high school and even beyond. Oh, there are students who make better marks—Bessie struggles so with arithmetic—but no student is more curious. If Bessie lived in town, her story might be different. Or if her family were prominent, or at least landed. But the facts speak for themselves: Here is a poor girl living on a slab of land belonging to some farmer who hires her father to plow his fields, to plant and disc and harrow. Not that this labor is sufficient to pay for the extras that, to Kyger's mind, every child deserves. So the father also builds sheds, barns, poultry coops, and houses for other men. No matter how much he wants for his children—and by all accounts, Robert Mounts is a good father—a man in such circumstances can do only so much.

Bessie looks up from the geography book just as the first white flakes fly past the window behind Mr. Kyger's head. Bessie loves a plentiful snow, but Aunt Mary and Uncle Charlie are planning to come to supper tonight, and she's concerned that the weather might keep them away. Often, after Sunday dinners, Bessie goes home with Mary and Charlie, and whenever Charlie leaves to hunt or fish in Wisconsin, Bessie stays with Mary and Baby Charlotte. Sometimes Mary takes Bessie to town for a treat—a strand of ribbon, a pair of slippers—or to the dentist when Bessie's teeth act up or to the doctor when her face breaks out, as it has been doing lately. But Bessie hasn't seen Mary and Baby Charlotte for weeks now. The last time she saw her baby cousin, she was walking by herself, all the way across the room to Bessie's outstretched arms. Bessie loves Charlotte's hands. The pink, dimpled skin and the deep creases circling the chubby wrists. But if this snow doesn't let up, Bessie won't see her tonight. And who knows how much longer Baby Charlotte will be around? Mary and Uncle Charlie have been talking about Wisconsin, all the cheap farmland to be had in the Lucas valley, and Bessie figures they'll move there, too, like the others.

Oh, would she ever get to go anywhere? Lately, every chance she gets, Bessie has been studying the plans for the Tennessee Exposition in the illustrated magazines Aunt Mary passes on to her. Bessie is still upset that she missed the Chicago World's Fair. Her teacher at the time, a lady teacher with the blondest hair Bessie had ever seen, had told the class all about it. How long it took to build the White City, how many people were there from all over the world. Millions of people! And a zoo and balloon rides and electric boats and gondolas and a Moorish Palace and a Blarney Castle. And a giant lighted wheel with baskets on it, baskets that you climb into, that took you high into the air so that you could look down on all the lights and buildings and people. "'Tis a shame you couldn't go, Bessie," the teacher had said, tucking loose strands of blond hair into the bun at the nape of her slender neck.

Something in the teacher's voice closed a door inside Bessie. "No matter," Bessie had answered flatly, shrugging her shoulders casually then lowering her eyes. Just wait, she had thought. Someday . . .

Well, Someday is now. Come May, Bessie knows one young lady who will *most certainly* be aboard that train to Tennessee. She can see it clear as day—the great halls filled with steam-powered cotton presses, automatic brick makers, everything electric a mind could conceive. Electric-powered spinning wheels and dynamos. Electric sidewalks. Electric lights outside every building. Every single building. Miss Jane Addams will be lecturing at the Woman's Building, and Bessie definitely does not want to miss that. An avid reader, Bessie considers herself well informed on all the major issues of the day. She knows that McKinley was recently elected, which does not make her mother happy in the least, for Hattie is a Democrat through and through, though as she often complains to Bessie, what does it matter if she can't vote anyway? Bessie knows about Henry Ford's automobile being tested in Detroit and gold being discovered in the Yukon Territory and moving pictures being shown in New York City. Well, of course she knows about New York City. Great-grandfather Mead was born not far from there a long time ago.

The snow is not letting up. Well, that settles that, Bessie thinks. I will not see Little Charlotte tonight. Bessie closes the geography book and reaches for her satchel. Mr. Kyger allows her to read whatever she wants, once her lessons are done. Already this month she has reread Tales of a Wayside Inn and The Scottish Chiefs, a book that belonged to Great-grandfather Mead. Mother never gives up a book, no matter how long she's had it. The book in Bessie's satchel is An Old Fashioned Boy, which Mother gave Dale for Christmas. Mother always gives books for Christmas, and always inscribes them in pencil, even though she now has a fountain pen from Aunt Mary. Maybe, Bessie imagines, she does this so that the books can be given again, and again.

The copyright date on An Old Fashioned Boy is 1872. The year before Mother's mother died, Bessie remembers. Most all of Mother's books are about orphans; there must have been more orphans back then. An Old Fashioned Boy is a little different from the other books, though, for the boy Fred is only partly an orphan. But he is mightily angry at his mother for having remarried. Though Fred never says it outright, Bessie has the feeling that Fred wants his real father back. Of course he can't have him back, as his father is dead. Still, she sees Fred's point. If something happened to Pa, Bessie surely would not approve of some strange man marrying Mother and moving into their house.

Well, no matter, Bessie concludes as she opens to the bookmarked page. All will turn out well for Fred, as it does for all the orphans in Mother's books. Someone always finds the orphans and takes them in, someone richer and more educated and well placed than the dead parents. And the orphans grow up to be more famous than regular folks. Why, the author of <u>An Old Fashioned Boy</u> was an orphan herself, and a lady too. Some of Bessie's favorite books are written by ladies. And why not? A lady can write as well as a man and sometimes better, Mother says. Though of course they aren't the books people study in school, except maybe <u>Uncle Tom's Cabin</u>.

Bessie would like to write a book herself one day, about birds or about the ferns she studies in the woods. "The flora and the fauna," Mr. Kyger once said, "and Bessie, you are just the person to write it." But who has the time? Bessie can hardly read all the books she wants to read, much less write them. Besides, ladies who write books have a proper education. Some even have tutors. They can speak French and Spanish and German, and they travel everywhere, even to Europe. The architect who designed the Woman's Building for the Exposition is a lady. An architect! Seems ladies can be almost anything now. The architect is from Boston, so she must be well placed. Bessie pauses to study the flyleaf: New York. She should have known. Almost every book is published in New York, though a few come from Chicago. And of course some of the oldest books come from Edinburg, Scotland, where Bessie definitely plans to go someday. Definitely.

Kyger smooths his hands across the diary's leather cover. Keats's "Endymion"? But which lines would he choose? "A thing of beauty is a joy forever"? Or would Bessie see that as a cruel joke, a way to point up what she already knows too well? Though surely someone, someday, will have the right eyes, the right ears. A music lover, perhaps, a young man drawn to a lilting voice or the skip of a slippered foot, for at neighborhood gatherings, Bessie has proved herself a brilliant and inexhaustible dancer. Whenever Bessie is in motion—reciting verses, singing, dancing, strumming a guitar—her entire aspect alters. The furrowed brow relaxes, the tight lips soften, she forgets herself for a moment and, in that moment, comes as close to beautiful as Kyger imagines she will ever be.

But he fears he knows how Bessie's story will end: She will be put out to work like the other poor girls. Housecleaner. Baby nurse. A clerical job if she is lucky. Of course she will be welcome to return whenever she can get free. To be here among the books and charts. And perhaps the new teacher will know Latin and algebra and botany and be able to answer Bessie's unending questions better than Kyger can.

Questions: of course! He should have thought of it sooner. Kyger hesitates a moment, and from deep in the pocket of memory, he pulls Byron's words:

How little do we know that which we are,
Much less, what we may be;
The eternal surge of time rolls on
And bears afar our bubbles.

Great-aunt Bessie, age 17, with her teacher's inscription in Bessie's 1897 diary.

CHAPTER  3

"Through the young orchard, down a steep hill, over the footbridge and across the stream" is how Bessie recalled it decades later. Or "Across the young orchard, down the hill, across the spring," each recitation beginning and ending with the litany of the journey, as if the path itself were the main attraction. Bessie's voice on the cassette recording is surprisingly strong and resonant for a woman of ninety-seven, the click of her loose dentures serving as percussion in the pauses between phrases. A family friend made the recording in May 1978, less than a year before Bessie's death. I wasn't there in my grandparents' kitchen at the Circle S farm, where the friend had gathered Bessie, Sylvia, and Arthur as part of an oral history project. But as I listen to the tape, closing my eyes to bring the moment closer, I enter the kitchen, take a seat at the table, and lean my elbows on the oilcloth still damp from a last-minute swipe with Sylvia's dishrag as she brushed the pie crumbs into her hand. Voices, I believe, bring the dead closer to us than photographs can.

I close my eyes: clack, click, and an intake of breath as Bessie continues. "Down the young orchard, down a steep hill, to the valley to school." These were the years after Robert and Hattie had moved their young family from Switzerland County to Clinton County, where Robert found work on the estate of a prominent farmer claiming lineage to William Henry Harrison. Dale and Sylvia were still too young to attend school, so Bessie walked the path alone. She liked the feel of her feet, bare in summer and booted in winter, making their even progress. Walking got you from here to there, from there to here, and that is what Bessie liked best. The movement, the progress. Someday, she thought, I will have my own bicycle and my own buggy—let the others ride the skittish horses—and I will go wherever I want, whenever I want. And not just to Frankfort or Lafayette, either. I'll go on the train by myself. All the way to Chicago, to the Columbian Exposition. I will be twelve years old by then, nearly thirteen, so of course Mother will let me go.

Back home, her brother Dale was helping with chores—milking in the open-sided stable beside his mother, churning butter, sweeping the house, cleaning the yard, feeding the turkeys and pigs, and counting the days until he could accompany his father and uncles on hunting and trapping trips. Dale's little sister Sylvia stayed close to Hattie. Like most young children, my future grandmother would recall little of her earliest years, later borrowing the memories of elders to piece together a history. *Mother raised turkeys,* Sylvia wrote, *and they must have been pretty tame because one time she came and found me by the turkey who had some little turkeys and I had them in my lap and my feet under the old turkey hen.*

It is easy to imagine Sylvia holding Hattie's baby turkeys on her lap, her bare feet under the soft belly of the hen, and the hen blithely allowing it. Though all the Mountses were fond of animals (Bessie favored the lambs and barn cats), Sylvia, like her father, had a seemingly mystical connection to the creature world. Robert, it was said, could identify birds by their call or by a particular rush of feathers through the trees. And though he continued to hunt and trap throughout his lifetime, my great-grandfather often tamed wild animals, especially sick or wounded ones. Once, he nursed a crow back to health, intending to send it on its way. But the crow refused to leave, choosing to make its home in the top of a tree and occasionally swooping down to perch on Robert's shoulder. Inside the house, a pet albino squirrel was busy making mischief. Sometimes Hattie's ball of yarn would disappear and she would search for it, finding it unraveled behind the bureau or stove. Nearby, the pet raccoon, no doubt one that Robert had nursed from an injury, would place his paw deep into the cookie jar and grab so many cookies that he couldn't release his paw without assistance from Hattie or one of the children.

Once Sylvia reached school age, *I never kept up with my brother and sister,* she wrote. *I dident want to go and would go back with just the slightest excuse once I had the stomach ache and once I saw some dogs which I thought were after me and I went back home.* So there was Bessie, trudging to school on the road she had learned so well, her head filled with geography and arithmetic. There was Dale, following close behind. And there was the young Sylvia, hanging back, caught between home and the big world outside.

When Sylvia did make it to school, she was surrounded by girls and boys alike. Children, teachers, storekeepers, neighbors, aunts, uncles, and cousins—everyone loved Sylvia. The sweet child, the "light of our home," as her mother often said. If Bessie felt shadowed by Sylvia's sunny presence, she did not let on. Nine years separated the sisters, and Bessie had long laid claim to her portion of the sibling territory: books, music, history, birdwatching, greening and mushrooming in the woods, or hiking to local cemeteries where she studied the tombstone inscriptions. Bessie never felt afraid, she told me, and never alone, for there was much to see at the edge of the woods, and symphonies of birdcalls to trace in the highest branches: chickadees, titmice, flickers, sparrows, starlings, cedar waxwings. In later years, she would walk nearby roads alone even in the dark. In the 1897 diary year, she often hiked the three miles home from her clerking job, returning in the pitch black, one kerosene lamp burning in the small kitchen window.

"Aren't you afraid?" Sylvia would ask, glancing up from her needlework or spelling lessons as her big sister came into the house.

"Good heavens, of what?"

"The big dogs. And the hoboes by the railroad tracks. And the dead people in the cemetery."

Bessie shook her head. What was Sylvia talking about? The cemetery was the prettiest spot around. "They're *dead,* Sylvia. Dead people can't hurt you."

"The darkness. Aren't you afraid of the darkness?"

"There's nothing in the darkness that isn't there in the light."

Still, Bessie preferred the light, especially the pale, tender light of early spring. *Oh, I think I could live in the woods,* sixteen-year-old Bessie tells her diary. Soon, ferns would begin unfurling, and young greens would shoot up their first slender sprouts. Dandelions would be next, the "wish flowers" her little sister loved to shake into snow-like showers. Beginning in early March, Bessie started watching the trees at the edge of the forest, and when the dogwood leaves were barely the size of a mouse's ear, she started praying for rain. Not just any rain, but a warm, soft night rain to steam up the morning forest. *Earthstar, shaggy mane, bird's nest, morel.* Bessie went to sleep with the words on her tongue, and if she woke at first light with the damp earth smell rising outside the window, she crawled over the sleeping Sylvia and tiptoed up the loft stairs to shake Brother awake, his dark eyes still crusted with sleep, cowlicks sprouting. "Mushrooms," she would whisper, and Dale would nod sleepily, grabbing his trousers from the bedpost.

◆

Bessie's diary opens the way most diaries open, with dreams and hopes for the coming year, but also, as was often the case with Bessie, with a self-chiding resolution expressed in some unnamed poet's words:

> In the last year what have I done
> To make this great world brighter?
> Have I brought comfort unto one?
> Or made one sad heart lighter?

Anyone who has to talk herself into bringing comfort to others is generally in need of comfort herself, so perhaps Bessie was not the best candidate for the job of making this great world brighter. But she tried. She spends New Year's Day with her neighbors the Mitchells, a rollicking household of father, mother (Mrs. Mitchell won't die for another few months) and five stair-step brothers. The next day, Bessie is back home, sharing a celebratory oyster supper with the Monks, the Combses, and a few of the Mitchell brothers, along with Uncle Charlie and Aunt Mary and their baby girl, Charlotte. The young people are on holiday, but the new term will begin next week, and though Bessie is officially graduated from common school now, she is eager to begin her studies *with renewed interest,* for she plans to learn algebra and astronomy and who knows what else? But for now there is the snow, the glorious snow, and *a sled load of us went to Jefferson* and *how I wish I could express myself so one could understand how jolly it was. The bells jingled up to the door at seven and jingled away at one.*

The Mounts children were aware that friends and neighbors had more than their family had. Bigger houses and barns and corncribs. Fancier wagons. Some even had bobsleds and sleighs. The Mounts family had one wagon and one horse, employed mostly to plow other farm-ers' fields. Even their house, Bessie had recently learned to her surprise, did not belong to them! But it had a fireplace (*spacious, open-hearted, profuse of flame and of firewood,* she wrote, courtesy of Longfellow) and room for dancing.

> *Fri, Jan. 29: Had a little leap here in the evening. Those present were: Messers. Chas. Harry and Walter Mitchell, Elmer and Lawrence Clen, Orley Reichert, Maitie Combs, Sammy Lawson, Lec McDole, Ray and Chas. Fickle, Uncle Harrison, Dale and Walt Golden, Miss Julia Liebengutter, Lizzie Mitchell, Cora Allen, Winnie Allen, Ora Fickle, Lula McDole, Maggie Combs, Sylvia, Bessie, W. B Combs and wife. "Everybody dance!"*

Though some of the neighboring families are missing this night—the Yundts and Spitznagles and Zinks and Andersons, to name a few—the party list reads like a microcosm of the society in which Bessie and her family moved. Apart from a few immigrant families, nearly everyone in their rural township was native-born, and all were white. Many were of German descent, with a lively sampling of English, Swiss, Swedes, and Dutch thrown in for good measure:

> *Friday, January 15: Went to a party in the evening at Mr. Eli Rothenberger's. I'd have had a first-rate time if the lady of the house had not got angry because I closed a certain door. 0 well, the Dutch nature will crop out.*

> *Thurs., Feb. 18: Went to Mulberry in the evening. The Rev. Mr Satersbey lectured on "The Irish." I think I have heard discourses I ap-preciated more. The man of Boston showed his ability but I think he was a little "harrud on the Irish man begob."*

A few of Bessie's neighbors were from Ireland, and she concluded that the Reverend must have an ax to grind—who knew about people from Boston? She'd read that Irish immigrants were still swarming New York and Boston, taking all the jobs that no one wanted. Well, she thought, if no one wanted the jobs, who cared that the Irish took them?

To the modern reader, Bessie's community must seem claustropho-bically homogeneous. Still, Bessie was aware of differences among her neighbors, whether she observed such differences firsthand or simply absorbed the stereotypes that had been handed down to her: The Germans were frugal, the Poles strong and loud, the Irish hot-tempered and often intemperate, the English somewhat reserved—her mother came from English stock. And the Swedes? Well, the ones she knew were just plain old-fashioned. Over in Stockwell, just a few miles away, was a family of Swedes, the Cosbys, who raised horses and kept a livery stable. She didn't know the family, but she'd seen the sons working around Stockwell and to Bessie's mind *O my that family was as old-fashioned as the day is long!* Were they Lutherans? She'd heard as much. For whatever reason, they did not much believe in modern conveniences. The Cosby father had a thick, full beard and the mother always wore black. Black dress, black shoes, black bonnet. Some of the sons seemed old to Bessie, too old to still be living at home. Well, who knew about Swedes? Maybe they didn't even believe in marriage!

Like most Midwest communities of the time, the Mounts's community thrived on social, economic, and cultural unity. People knew their neighbors, and even if they didn't particularly like them, they either learned to accommodate or risked disconnection from the group. The community's shared and repeated rituals, centered on seasonal cycles of life transitions—planting, harvesting, threshing, barn-raising, butchering, births, weddings, illnesses, wakes, funerals—tightened the links of past, present, and future.

And if such bonds bound individuals too tightly? If a young woman like Bessie was seized with an early morning urge to hike the wooded miles between home and depot rather than bake seven pies for the threshers who would arrive at her uncle's farm within hours? Or a young man like Dale preferred to sit at the bedside of a sick friend rather than steer a plow horse through a neighbor's soybean field? Such is the cost of community. The individual losing himself to the group. Or finding himself. For what is an individual, finally, outside of the tribe? An island, a hermit crab, the lone hawk circling the lively scene below.

◆

To his cousins and friends, the short, stocky Dale was known as "Scrub" or "Bub." Bessie just called him "Brother," and she and Brother were practically inseparable. *At home* begins most of the diary entries, followed by an exhaustive and exhausting listing of that day's chores. But whenever they weren't at home or school, or helping a neighbor plant, husk, churn, or iron, Bessie and Dale were on the move together, hitching rides on friends' wagons, sleighs, or bobsleds to protracted meetings, Corn and Conundrum Socials, concerts, and neighborhood gatherings where they played duets on borrowed instruments, Dale on fiddle and Bessie on guitar.

Meanwhile, their father had a plan. There was an old barn on the Clendenning place that Robert could have for practically nothing. The logs were forty or fifty years old but still good, still whole. And Dale was big enough now to help out. Robert had been eyeing a plot of land, not quite three acres, on a low, sloping hill just south of Wildcat Creek. If they could purchase the land—and with the small inheritance Aunt Phebe had insisted on sharing with her niece Hattie, they should be able to accomplish this—they could start the dismantling right away. Robert envisioned a log cabin with saplings lining the front yard, raised vegetable beds, a rose arbor, and off the back of the cabin a smokehouse, springhouse, chicken house, and an open stable. Nothing as grand as the Ohio River place, of course, but something Hattie could call her own.

When Hattie sees the site, a steep thicket of bramble and burdock, she jokingly names it Briarwood, after a fine English estate in one of Grandfather Mead's books. But after months of clearing, then months of hauling salvaged logs by wagon across rutted country roads, Robert's three-room dream begins to take shape until, by the turn of the new century, Briarwood becomes a favorite gathering spot for masquerades, swimming parties, card games, and sing-alongs. Letters fill with Sunday dinners served to as many as twenty neighbors and family members, even if all that Hattie can offer is greens and possum stew. Or turtle, rabbit, frog, or squirrel in one of its many guises. *I don't know how to spell it,* Sylvia will write to her husband-to-be years later, referring to a squirrel her mother had served for dinner. *But we ate it anyway. But please don't tell anyone!*

The road to town was often crowded with folks heading to one meeting or another, waving to the Mountses as they passed in their wagons or four-wheeled buggies, and, years later, in their automobiles. Hattie and Robert never owned a "machine," so if they couldn't make it

(Top) Briarwood, the Mounts family homestead outside Lafayette, Indiana, circa 1900.
(Bottom) A gathering of family and friends at Briarwood, circa 1910.

to town, they would read in the local paper about what they'd missed. On one particularly busy Saturday, the Farmers' Institute in nearby Dayton offered talks on "Fencing for the Farm," "Small Fruits for Home Use," and "Our Daughters, and What to Teach Them," along with vocal solos, recitations, and music by the Mandolin Club and Chorus. The night the Rhineberger Quartet performed, the Methodist Church "was taxed to its capacity and the audience wept into ecstacies" over the singing, impersonations, and recitations, which included "The Message of the Violet" and "The Dead Cat." Turn another page and "Harry Freeman, the hustling young elevator man, is having his annual siege of hay fever," Aaron Yost's most valuable calf has been killed by lightning, Harry Goldsberry is "the possessor of a new Conn cornet," and Ed Dryer and wife are "the possessors of a baby girl."

Each week, the local paper fills with births, deaths, marriages, graduations, anniversaries, accounts of who is visiting whom, who has embarked on a trip, whose house is being renovated and at what cost, who is considering a move in or out of the community. Robert and Hattie's humble gatherings do not make the society pages as does the sewing circle hosted by Mrs. Moywers or the dinner Mrs. D. A. Dryer gave for her lady friends this past Tuesday. Great-grandfather Robert may have been among the builders employed by Professor Hooker, who, the newspaper reports, has just had the foundation of his house completed, thus "greatly improving its appearance." Dale might have been one of the workers laying the streetcar line or the track for the Interurban. But the Mounts name does not appear. My ancestors worked behind the scenes. They were hands, not voices. And, unlike most Hoosiers of their time, the Mountses were not joiners.

> Knights of Pythias Lodge conferred second rank on Messrs. James Madison and Charles House last Friday night. Their memorial services were well attended. The I.O.O.F., Grand Army of the Republic, and Modern Marthas joined in the march.
>
> On last Monday evening at Odd Fellows Lodge No. 765 Pat Slayback drew the lucky number which won for him Ed Keifer's slide trombone. Elmer Johnson drew Chas. Godfrey's tuba, having to pay 27 cents for the horn.
>
> The Rathbone Sisters (formerly known as the Pythian Sisterhood) will give a female negro minstrel and "white trash" entertainment on the evening of Nov. 14. The ladies are practicing regularly and the success of the event is assured. All are welcome.

All are welcome. To attend the festivities, perhaps. But not to join. The fraternal organizations to which many Hoosiers of the time belonged—Freemasons, Eastern Star, Knights of Pythias, Pythian Sisters, Patrons of Husbandry, Woodmen of the World, Rebekah Lodge, Odd

Improved Order of Red Men, Washakee Tribe #408, Oxford, Indiana, circa 1910. My great-grandfather G. E. Sanders is second from left in the middle row.

Fellows, Modern Marthas, Improved Order of Red Men, and, in later decades, the Horse Thief Detective Agency and the Ku Klux Klan—were not only ritualistic but exclusionary as well. If everyone could join, how would an organization define itself? Doesn't every like-minded community require exclusion?

The Improved Order of Red Men, for instance, a fraternity founded to revere the traditions of the "red man" but to which, until a few decades ago, only white men could belong. Enamored with the mythology of the American Indian and invited by his father, G. E. Sanders, to join the local order, my grandfather Arthur pledged in 1910 while he was courting Sylvia, who aspired to membership in the Red Men's auxiliary order for women. In Sylvia's letters, she tells Arthur that she is tired of being a Paleface and that she hopes if she is accepted into the tribe, her character will not be found lacking, that the others will find in her the qualities of a Pocahontas. According to the bylaws of the Degree of Pocahontas, these qualities include respect for the flag and the American way of life; reverence for the customs of the American Indian; charity to those in need, including Indians; and friendship and sisterhood among members. In both male and female lodges, mem-

bers who pass through the adoption ceremony are given access to secret signs and passwords so they can recognize one another outside
the tribal meetings. Within the Order of Pocahontas, a complicated
right hand gesture signifies "Who are you?" A left hand response signifies, "A friend."

For most of us, the need to belong is strong. My grandmother was
no exception, and as Sylvia grew into womanhood, she longed to be
worthy of the society of "better people." *My hope is that I will always
come up to your standards,* she writes to Arthur from Briarwood, a year
before their marriage. *I know you can put up with our poor quarters and
way of living for a week. We have to keep up pretty good spirits or we would
be too miserable to live.* Impatient with her lack of scholarly skills, she
sometimes censures herself: *If I live to be a hundred I will never be able to
write a decent letter. . . . If you can't make out whats on the lines why read
between the lines there's more there anyway. . . .* Reading between the lines
of anyone's life is a delicate, tenuous undertaking. So much remains un-
answered. For reasons unknown, my grandmother was not accepted
into the Order of Pocahontas. But other sisterhoods were waiting to be
born in small Indiana towns over the following decade, sisterhoods I
knew nothing about when I first began piecing together the crazy quilt
of letters and documents.

How little do we know that which we are, must less what we may be.
The years will fly by. Wildcat Creek will flood, droughts will decimate
fields, lightning will strike barns and horses and kill close friends,
fire will take the little springhouse, neighbors' farmhouses will burn
to the ground, boys will enlist in wars and not return, close friends
will die of diphtheria, influenza, cancer, freak accidents. Loved ones
will take their own lives. But for now, the Mounts children are safe
in the three-room dream home their parents have fashioned out of a
briarpatch. Each time I open a letter, the spirit of Briarwood pours in,
as if rushing through a hole in time. Bessie and Dale *have been prowling the woods after greens and gooseberries, got moast a gallon, and
hunting raspberries for dinner now and some beans too.* Open another
envelope and *Mamma is planting her roses, Babe is writing on his slate,
we have a daschund pup and the cutest batch of baby raccoons.* And
here comes Robert through the kitchen door *no luck fishing but my! a
shirt-tail full of mushrooms.*

Even in the darkest times, when Hattie is *boiling bones and sugar water for dinner* and the chickens have the gapes and die off by the dozens so that she must make regular trips to the sand bunk, she believes *though it may be dark right now the sun will shine again soon.* And so it does. And when it does, Hattie is resting on the back stoop, having *churned once and another about ready so Babe will have all the milk he can drink,* for the stubborn cow is finally fresh and *oh, we have been feasting on nice milk and cream—and you ought to see my nice gilt-edged butter. . . . The day is so fresh and livly—plants to set, a few pieces to wash, little turks and ducks hatching and several more things. Everything looks lovly this morning after the rain, yellow roses opening.*

CHAPTER 4

Monday Eve. Nov. 19, 1900
1152 Summer Street
Hammond, Indiana

My dear Mother.

I'm O so tired, I am afraid this night will not be long enough for me to get rested in. I worked hard today. I made eighty five cents. That is pretty good wages for me to make is it not?

There is no one home at the present. Jim has gone out somewhere, Chas. takes his third degree in the Knights of Pythias tonight, Ben has gone to the city to work at steam-fitting and just as I got home this evening word came that Aunt's sister is dead. Died at half-past five and we didn't even so much as know she was sick. She took sick some time last night, vomiting blood. Uncle Clint and Aunt have gone down there.

I had the toothache one whole week and made about fifty trips to the dentist but I have it filled now, but my, what a cavity there was after it had been drilled out.
(Wednesday evening.)

Will scratch a little more. Got home to supper at half past eight tonight with my feet almost killing me, made ninety three cents today. I'm going to make four dollars this week or "bust." I've made $2.24 already.

Say I dreamed about bed-bugs again last night, it worried me. If any of you get sick don't you fail to let me know immediately, if Pa should take another such spell such as he had last winter telegraph

*me as soon as possible. I must close for this eve. It must be late—ten
or after, Uncle was in bed when I got home from work. Good-night everyone. Your loving daughter, Bessie.*

Bessie folded the letter neatly, placed it in an envelope, and reached
for Uncle Clint's fountain pen. *Mrs. Hattie Mounts, Appolonia, Wisconsin,*
she wrote in her best hand. She was glad that Mother could get away
to Wisconsin for a few weeks, for Lord knows they needed the help up
there. But she worried about the others at home. Would Dale and Sylvia make it to school on time? What if Pa had another spell while they
were gone? Bessie sealed the envelope and placed a two-cent stamp on
it, wishing she had a calling card to enclose so that Mother could show
it to Mary and Uncle Charlie once she'd made it to Menomonie. A few
days ago, on her way to work, Bessie had stopped at the stationers to inquire about costs for the design she'd been sketching out for weeks now,
ever since she'd arrived in Hammond. She'd briefly considered "Bessie D.
Mounts, Book Binder," but had decided that the extra lettering would be
too expensive. More to the point, her job at the plant carried no official
designation, though W. B. Conkey was a bookbinding factory and Bessie did indeed work there, standing beside the large presses for hours at
a time, so if she wasn't a book binder, what in heaven's name was she?

Bessie had finally decided on a simple design for the cards, similar
to the one her mother had chosen for herself when she was a young
woman in Switzerland County. A card that could outlive any number
of changing circumstances. Her name—Bessie D. Mounts—in swirling
script, and above the name, a bird with a large feathery tail, resting on a
bed of violets and holding in its beak a banner: "Faithfully yours." But for
now, the calling cards would have to wait. What with her dentist bills
and daily dinner expenses and then sending whatever she can manage
back home, Bessie could barely make her weekly contribution to the
Hammond household, which from the day of her arrival at Uncle Clint's
she had insisted on doing. Bessie refused to take advantage of anyone's
hospitality, even—no, especially! she had concluded—the hospitality of
family. True, the Summer Street house was a bit crowded, what with
Uncle Clint, his three sons, and his wife and mother-in-law all together
under one roof. But even on evenings like this, when exhaustion seeped
into her bones and her feet ached and she feared the night would not

be long enough to get rested in, though certainly long enough for her to dream of bedbugs again, Bessie never forgot how lucky she was. Without her great-uncle's invitation, she would never have been able to come north and work at the W. B. Conkey Company, where, if all went well, she could earn more than three times what she had earned at Combs's dry goods store back home.

In the years since she'd left school to work as a housekeeper and mother's helper in towns close to Briarwood, Bessie had boarded in the homes of employers, often for months at a time. Unlike Sylvia, who'd always been a homebody, Bessie took pleasure in her away-from-home adventures; she rarely got homesick. But when waves of homesickness swept over her, usually at night, they broke suddenly and with great force, and nothing would do but that she make it home right now, right away, no matter the circumstances. Which had sometimes meant a three- or four-mile hike in the dark, all the way to Briarwood, where she'd step out of her shoes at the door, tiptoeing across the kitchen floor to the narrow daybed spread with Hattie's comforters. Early the next morning, as Robert crouched bleary-eyed beside the woodstove to start the fire for the biscuits, he'd look over at the daybed and shake his head in wonder. No mistaking his daughter's slight form, even buried as it was beneath the covers. Nor that shiny black hair, loosened from its pins and spread out across the pillow.

But Bessie was in Hammond now, and Hammond was much too far from Briarwood to allow for her accustomed escape plan. When seized with the urge to flee for home, she had to content herself with mementos she'd brought with her. Entries on the back pages of Bessie's diary suggest that the diary accompanied her wherever she boarded, so she probably took the diary to Hammond, along with several favorite photographs. One featured Bessie, Dale, and Sylvia at a springtime gathering outside a neighbor's barn. Seated cross-legged before the barn, an adolescent Dale holds a fiddle; Bessie, a small Spanish guitar.

Bessie liked this picture not only because she was holding a guitar but also because the photograph had been taken from a distance. Bessie was not fond of closeup portraits. She had long ago accepted that she was not nearly so pretty as Sylvia. What vexed her was that she was not even as good-looking as Dale. His nose, like Sylvia's, was straight. And though he had the Mounts's characteristic downward sloping eyes, which made him appear older than his years, Dale had inherited their father's strongly defined chin and, like Sylvia, their mother's full lips. Bessie had no chin to speak of, and though her mouth was wide, too wide for her small face, she'd decided, her lips were thin and tight as a knot. And with each tooth drilling or extraction—*O my,* she thought, how had I inherited such bad teeth?—her mouth seemed to cave in a little more. Finally, too, there was the scar across her nose. Well now, there I go again, I imagine her thinking, letting my mind get away from me, following the blue devils down the path that leads nowhere. For 'twas assuredly nothing to be done about the scar, so why waste valuable time dwelling on it? If all goes well, I will make four dollars this week. Four dollars!

◆

According to the postmark on the envelope found in Hattie's cache, Bessie mailed the Hammond letter the following evening, probably as she passed by the post office on her mile-long walk between the book factory on the outskirts of town and the Summer Street home of her great-uncle, Dewitt Clinton Mead Jr. November darkness would have already settled on the streets, though, characteristically, Bessie would not have been afraid. But *O my,* her feet in their high-laced boots were killing her, her back aching from standing twelve hours at the binding presses. To Bessie's mind, walking was decidedly easier than standing, though not nearly so agreeable as pedaling a bike. If only she could afford one of her own, a ladies' model, one without that troublesome bar beneath the seat. She'd jotted the address of the bicycle company on a blank "Cash Accounts" page of her diary, but goodness knows when she'd get a moment to inquire. For now, she was grateful to borrow her cousin's Rover. Bessie had never cycled before she came to Hammond, but Jim was a good teacher and Bessie had learned quickly, her small hands gripping the handlebar, the chassis wobbling slightly then straightening out and then *O my* the brush of wind against her face and the click of wheels beneath her. Much better than riding a horse, she had concluded. Sylvia would no doubt disagree, but Bessie had never been fond of horses as her younger sister was. Horses were too unpredictable, too likely to rear up without notice or to nip your hand

A page from Bessie's diary, 1902; Bessie with guitar; her calling card, circa 1900.

when you offered an apple. Besides, Bessie preferred being close to the ground, and when she pedaled with force, standing up on the pedals if necessary to crest a hill, the downhill coast was worth all the effort, and nearly as fast as a horse as well.

Although Hattie's reply to her daughter's letter was not found among Bessie's things, in all likelihood she responded promptly. Hattie was an inveterate correspondent who over the course of five decades

often posted three or four letters a week to her children and grandchildren, never mind the expense. In her reply to Bessie, Hattie probably
mentioned her dissatisfaction with the recent reelection of McKinley: Would Democrats ever have a say in this country again? And she
would definitely have reported all the news from Wisconsin, including the most recent sadness in the household of Lafayette Mounts and
his young wife. Bessie's clerking and housekeeping duties had kept her
from Wisconsin for more than two years now, so she'd never gotten to
hold Uncle Lafe's first child; Harry, named after Uncle Harrison, had
lasted less than two years. Five days after they buried little Harry, Pearl
had delivered a baby girl and named her Bessie, which of course pleased
Bessie Mounts beyond measure. Her own namesake! Why, Uncle Lafe
must think a lot of his niece, to name his own daughter after her.

Then, shortly after arriving in Hammond, Bessie learned the news,
and since then, try as she might, she could not get the image out of her
head: a small stone, set into the rocky Wisconsin dirt, and the dates—
September 12, 1899–October 6, 1900—carved into it. And, above the
dates, her own name. Fond as Bessie was of cemeteries, this was one
trip she would not hurry to make. She was not ready to see her own
name carved in stone.

Well, Bessie thought, at least it was still autumn. At least snow was
not falling on the grave with her name on it. Lines from James Russell
Lowell kept rolling through her mind, lines from the poem she had
recited before Mr. Kyger's class one snowy afternoon more than three
years before:

> I thought of a mound in sweet Auburn
> Where a little headstone stood;
> How the flakes were folding it gently,
> As did robins the babes in the wood.

According to Mr. Kyger, "The First Snow-Fall" was about the death of
Lowell's daughter, an event the poet called "our first great sorrow" and
which seems to Bessie to have hurt Lowell awfully bad. Pa often says
how lucky he and Mother are, not to have lost any of their children, and
if they ever did he didn't know what in the world he would do, he would
be so lost. Bessie wonders how you would recognize your first great
sorrow when it appeared. For several months this past year, she'd won-

dered if Harry Mitchell might be her own first great sorrow. She'd cried, she'd scribbled some lines from her favorite poets near the back of her diary, on the last few blank pages:

> *"We meet, one kiss, one sigh,*
> *And then we part forever."*
> *Scott*

> *"Dear heart let be the book awhile!*
> *I want your face—I want your smile."*
> *James Whitcomb Riley*

Then one day, Bessie decided enough was enough. She would not dwell one more day on such a losing proposition. Though Bessie would not be present at Harry Mitchell's wedding, she *most certainly* planned on sending a gift. A bowl, or some fine linen napkins from her favorite shop in Hammond, though such a gift would cost her mightily. If she herself ever got married, Bessie would like to receive beautiful linens and crystal bowls with which to set a proper table. And when she had her first baby, she would buy a tiny silver spoon. Bessie was certain that Pearl and Lafe's babies had never had silver spoons. Not that silver spoons, nor any luxury for that matter, would have softened the blows. Just think: Pearl is my own age and already she has known two great sorrows! For certainly, Bessie decided, the loss of a baby would count.

Is sorrow the same as sadness? Is it like the "blue devils" that Byron wrote about in his poems? Bessie got sad now and then, sometimes very sad. But she imagined that sorrow must be worse. It must be something you could never get over. Like, for Mother, when her own mother died. "A siege of sorrow," Hattie called those years. And, no matter what Lowell's poem says, Bessie was sure there were some things you would never get over.

At the time Bessie posted the letter to her mother, she seems not to have known Hattie's own surprising news. Perhaps Hattie was waiting for a more opportune moment, as this was the kind of news best delivered in person. Decades from now, my mother will overhear Bessie's comment to Sylvia, saying how embarrassed Bessie had been at the time, to learn that their mother, just shy of thirty-eight years old, was "in the family way." In 1900, in Bessie's small world circumscribed by neighbors, friends, and extended family, an unmarried woman of twenty remained, in many ways, a *girl* of twenty. Certain things were not discussed openly. True, young women like Bessie might have assisted their midwife-mothers with neighbors' pregnancies and deliveries, but such details were not aired in letters, at least not in the letters I have studied, and perhaps not even within sewing circles, around the neighborhood card table, or in private talks between daughters and mothers.

How much had Hattie told Bessie to prepare her for eventual marriage and motherhood? Probably not much. But like most young women of her time, Bessie would have pieced together bits of information to form a whole if uneven quilt of knowledge. More than twenty-five years had passed since the Comstock Laws had been enacted, and a young woman as curious as Bessie must have wondered just what kind of information was so dangerous as to have been banned by postal authorities. Also, Bessie must have noticed that though some of the Mounts's friends produced babies nearly every year without pause, some did not. Some, including her own mother, seemed to have spaced their children judiciously—well, until now, at least. How, precisely, did they manage that?

If Bessie's mother had pieced together any knowledge on contraception, in this particular year Hattie seems either to have disregarded such knowledge or to have been extremely unlucky. Or lucky, depending on one's views on the forces and purposes of conjugal love. Whatever the circumstances, one fact was certain: Hattie was four months pregnant when Bessie wrote to her from Hammond that November. (Hattie would give birth to her fourth child, Ivan Otto, the following April.)

Four years later, Hattie would again be "in the family way," the advanced state of her pregnancy preventing her from attending Bessie's wedding in La Porte, a northern Indiana town not far from Hammond. Knowing Bessie as I did, I imagine this turn of events was not only disappointing but also highly embarrassing for the private, decorous bride who, by the standards of the day, was no spring chicken herself. How to explain to the groom's family why her mother, age forty-two, could not attend the festivities? But for now, these events are unknown to the twenty-year-old bookbinder with the aching feet and sore gums, the young woman posting a letter on her way home from work, a letter fairly crowing with pride: *I made eighty-five cents. That is pretty good wages for me to make is it not?*

Yes, Bessie, never mind that your workday stretched far into the evening. One day's work for eighty-five cents was indeed good wages for a girl like you to make. Just months before you mailed this letter, the International Ladies' Garment Workers Union was established in New York. Factory workers fared the worst, but even those women working from their homes could expect, at most, thirty cents a day. Just look how far you have come in only three years, Bessie. Or have you forgotten how hard you fought Mr. Combs, the battles you waged to be paid what you were worth?

> *Mon., Feb 15, 1897, Dear Diary: Cold. Snow on this morning. Don't know whether Combs' are coming after me or not. Well they did not come after me.*

> *Tues., Feb. 16: I'll stay at home for those people today and if they do not come I will not daudle around anymore, if I am a poor girl and need the money I will not stay out of school and put myself out. I am decidedly independent.*

> *Mon., March 22: At the store. Gloomy, rained early in the morning. The question of my weekly wages came up. I set my price at $2.00. Mr. Combs refuses to pay it.*

> *Tues., March 23: Cold, windy and rainy. I do wish Mr. Combs would not be so obstinate. I think if my work is not worth $2.00 it is not worth anything. If he does not pay me more than $1.00 I shall not stay. So there!*

According to her payment record, Bessie's "So there!" yielded no result, and she continued to work for a dollar a week. But resentment was building against Mr. Combs and the power he wielded over her. Bessie consoled herself by using any leisure moments to read by the light of the store window—she finished <u>Knight-Errant</u> in two days—and in recording Combs's shortcomings:

> *A funny incident occurred today. Prof. Mortsolf was in the store, we were chatting and I said to Mr. C. "Have you read Hyperion?"*

(by Longfellow) He said:—"no I have no red Hyperion." He thought I meant calico or the like. We had a good laugh and Mr. Mortsolf went over & told the editor of the "Reporter." Mr. C. used to be a teacher.

◆

Hattie may have been right that Fate hardly ever manages things to our satisfaction. Still, Fate could have done worse than to place Bessie Mounts in Hammond, Indiana, at the turn of the new century. A sweet if small stroke of justice for a young woman who had long dreamed of being surrounded by books—as a teacher, librarian, or as an author herself. Just two years before, the W. B. Conkey Company had produced the first Sears Roebuck catalog. Since that time, the plant had produced textbooks, Bibles, biographies, and, most exciting to Bessie, special volumes of fiction and verse, most recently an ornate edition of a story-in-verse, Lucile. First published in England in 1860, the poem in its 1900 edition created by the Conkey factory was particularly beautiful, with its green and red linen cover and lithographed frontispiece portrait. Exactly the kind of book Bessie most coveted and could not afford. Still, I like to think that she at least got near the book, ran her hands over its fine cover and opened its pages to the story of our heroine, Lucile, the beloved object of affection of not one man but two—an English Lord and a French Duke! But what a sad story, Bessie would have thought. Do love stories ever turn out happily?

Had the twenty-year-old Bessie read the more notorious novels of the time, she would have concluded that love, whatever form it took, rarely guaranteed a happy ending. Theodore Dreiser's controversial Sister Carrie had been released a few weeks before Bessie posted the letter to her mother, so Bessie no doubt knew about the book's publication, perhaps from fellow workers at the factory. The plot of Dreiser's story would certainly have caught Bessie's attention, particularly the parallels between her life and Carrie's: a poor, independent girl traveling by train from her rural home to a large city to board with relatives and to work on an assembly line alongside other poor girls. Had she read further, Bessie would have been stunned at the sordid details emerging page by lurid

page: promiscuity, prostitution, alcoholism, embezzlement, marital infi-
delity, homelessness, and suicide. True, Carrie survived. Some might say
she triumphed. But, Bessie would have wondered, at what cost?

Kate Chopin's The Awakening, which had scandalized readers when
it was published the year before, would have made an even deeper impression on Bessie. After all, Chopin's main character is no hungry factory girl desperate for a way out of a bad situation. Edna Pontellier has
everything the young Bessie imagined a woman could want. She is a
mother to two young sons; her husband, a successful businessman,
provides her with a mansion, vacations, even a nanny to allow Edna
time for her own artistic pursuits. Yet Edna is not happy. How can this
be? What force could be so strong as to pull Edna away from family
and friends? To leave the mansion for the little "pigeon house"—and for
what? For a man? A young man who plays with her heart as he has with
others'? Or is there something else, something even stronger than love
pulling Edna away from the life she has known? From life itself?

Such questions would have troubled Bessie as she turned the pages
in Chopin's novel—if not as a young woman in Hammond then later,
when she was a young wife herself. Bessie, as my mother recalls, "had
longings. Strong longings. Longings that were never satisfied." Finally,
what were Edna Pontellier's choices? To live alone, lost in her art like the
embittered but passionate Madame Reisz on Chopin's pages? Or sacrifice her own needs for her husband and children like the long-suffering
Madame Ratignolle? Edna studied her two friends' lives. Was there no
way to satisfy her deepest longings, her true self, while remaining connected to those she loved? In Chopin's book, the broken-winged bird by
the shore supplies the answer, and Edna walks into the sea. The Book
of Bessie will not end so abruptly. It will continue for many more years,
moment by uncertain moment, road by diverging road.

◆

Scrawled sideways across two back pages of Bessie's diary, the unfinished poem is strikingly different from excerpts included elsewhere,
its hurriedly penciled lines riddled with dashes, asterisks, and em-
phatic underlining. No classroom-style flourishes, no famous poet's
name. This writer appears troubled, agitated, as if scrambling to get

the words down as quickly as they come, unbidden, through her, or trying frantically to recall words to a song or poem she memorized long ago:

> *Into the beat of love's bright measure,*
> *There has crept a curious jar and halt,*
> *It does not give us the same sweet pleasure*
> *But I have kept time,———it is not my fault*
> *When you struck false chords*
> *I winced and bore it*
>
> *You turned wrong pages*
> *And then blamed me*
> *You jumped whole bars when we tried*
> *To go o'er it*
> *And now we are hopelessly out of key.*
> *****************************
>
> *I played my part with power and passion,*
> *And now I am done with that duet,*
> *But you ran through it in idle fashion.*
>
> <u>*You'll play it better with someone yet.*</u>

Had Bessie met a man in Hammond—at the book factory, a community lecture, or at a dance she attended with one of her cousins? Had she reconnected with an acquaintance once she'd returned home to Briarwood, a fellow musician with whom she once sang duets? If the poem was original, did she ever complete it? I imagine her sealing the poem in an envelope along with one of the calling cards she had purchased by this time—"Bessie D. Mounts, Faithfully Yours"—so that the recipient would be forced to confront the name of the young woman with whom he had shared "the beat of love's bright measure."

In June 1902, when the entry was dated, Bessie was nearly twenty-two years old. Her first love, Harry Mitchell, had been married a year, and many of her contemporaries had already started families. Everywhere she looked, babies were sprouting up like mushrooms. More than Bessie could keep track of down in Switzerland County. Up in Wisconsin, Charlie and Mary's third child, Stanley, would celebrate his first birthday come November. Uncle Lafe and Pearl had a new daughter, too. I'm old enough to be her mother, Bessie thought. For that matter, I'm old enough to be my own brother's mother! Ivan Otto, for goodness sakes, is not yet two years old!

Sometimes it grows tiresome, this age business. Your friends tease you, your cousins tease you: "What are you waiting for, Bessie? Isn't it about time?" She brushes off their comments with a flick of her child-sized wrist, turning the conversation back to books, music, and current events. The newly independent Cuba. The Canal Act. The discovery of hookworm. But alone at night in whatever household she is employed, having washed her face in the basin on the highboy, hung her white blouse near the window to air, entered in her log book every penny of her latest expenditures, after turning back the quilt on the feather bed and climbing between the sheets smelling faintly of bleach and sunshine, the sheets she has boiled and stirred and wrung out and clipped to the line and ironed and folded and tucked carefully beneath the quilt, Bessie feels the aloneness sift down on her like a fine powder. This is the way it will always be, she thinks. Me, alone. In a single bed.

The thought in and of itself is not painful to Bessie; some nights it is almost welcome. Surely, aloneness is not the worst thing in the world. Why, some people choose to be alone. The heroine in Lucile, for one. And Mother's Aunt Phebe, who remained single all those years, only to marry at age forty-three. To her own cousin! A first cousin, a relative of the first degree. This thought no doubt ruffled Bessie's mind, stirring up unsettling questions that kept sleep away for several more minutes. Weren't there laws against such things? Well, maybe not down in Switzerland County. As for Bessie, she could not imagine marrying a relative. Not even a second cousin. And a first? A relative of the first degree? Under no circumstances.

What were Bessie's last thoughts before she finally sank into sleep those nights in Hammond, exhausted from her long days at the factory? Did she hear from the adjoining bedroom the snores of Uncle Clint, the quiet splash as his wife poured water from the pitcher into the ceramic washing bowl? Did she listen for the footsteps on the stairs, her three cousins returning late from the city? *First cousins, once removed,* she corrected herself. And Uncle Clint, though Bessie thought of him as her uncle, was actually Mother's uncle, one of Lucippa's brothers. Lucippa: such a beautiful name, Bessie thought, turning over on her side and plumping the feather pillow. Grandma Lucippa, she would have called her.

Sometimes when Uncle Clint isn't watching, Bessie studies his face, as she studies the face of Great-aunt Phebe when she visits from Switzerland County. Had Lucippa resembled them? After all, they were Lucippa's siblings, so there must have been a family likeness. If you could put their faces together somehow, Bessie thinks, side by side like the images in a stereoscope, you might see a bit of Lucippa slipping through. Grandma Lucippa, alive and well. Before all the sadness. Before the War of the Rebellion. Before everything began to fall apart.

CHAPTER 5

The Old Mead House, as Aunt Bessie called her great-grandfather's homestead, was an impressive place. That was how she remembered it. Not that she remembered much about the white farmhouse situated near the banks of the Ohio River. She'd been inside it only a few times, when she was very young. Bessie was just seven or eight when her family left Switzerland County, she and Dale and their parents; by the time they returned for a visit, Great-grandfather Mead was already dead. But Phebe was still there, taking care of things.

"I have a picture of the house somewhere," Bessie told me during one of my visits to Briarwood, "but I can't put my hands on it. Phebe lived there a long time. That's *Aunt* Phebe. She helped take care of my mother—that would be your great-grandmother Hattie—after mother's mother died. Mother's mother was Lucippa—that would be your great-great-grandmother . . ." Aunts, grandmothers, great-grandmothers, great-greats. Good grief, I'd think. Enough, already. I'd nod and pretend to listen as Bessie rummaged in one bureau drawer after another. Ancient history, to me. Dry as salt. Who cares about some old house in Switzerland County? Let's get going, now, to the creek or the woods. The morning is getting away from us.

Then Bessie would try once again to explain the connections: her mother Hattie, her mother's mother Lucippa, and on down the line. Just as, decades later, I would try to explain to my young nieces their relationships to their ancestors. Finally, when no explanation seemed to help, I resorted to metaphor: Russian nesting dolls. "Think of it this way," I'd tell the nieces. "Each generation is locked inside the next generation. You are the biggest doll. Inside of you is one generation before you: your mother, the next biggest doll."

"That's not right," one of the nieces interrupted. "Mommies are bigger than daughters. They can't be inside them."

I'd plow ahead: "Locked inside your mother is *her* mother, your grandmother. It goes on and on like that, for as long as you keep opening up the dolls. As far back as you want to go." Someday you'll understand, I thought. Our history is locked inside us—our mothers and fathers, our uncles and aunts. The further back we go, the more indistinct the features become, and the harder it is to recognize our image in theirs. But the likeness is there, all the same. You just have to look closely to see it.

"It was an imposing house," Bessie repeated, rubbing her glasses on the sleeve of her blouse. "White, with dark shutters. From the porch, you could see the Ohio River. Now where did I put that picture?"

◆

My great-grandmother Hattie was born in Switzerland County, Indiana, in 1861, less than nine months after her parents were married.

Within a year, her mother filed for divorce.

Who was at fault, if fault could answer the mystery, was never the issue with Hattie. Not then, not ever. The issue was her mother's deep and ongoing unhappiness, the "blue devils" that swarmed inside Lucippa's head. Things had not turned out as Lucippa Mead had hoped, though Leander had not been a mean man. And he *had* given her Hattie, her loved child. Should Lucippa have tried harder, lasted another year with him, and another? The War of Rebellion was on, and two of Lucippa's brothers had gone to fight with the Union, so maybe, Lucippa reasoned, *that* was why the months with Leander had felt like years, decades. Lucippa had thought, had hoped . . . but that was another story, another life. But oh, how she had missed her little brothers. Henry was twenty, Edwin barely nineteen. Still a boy. Nothing to his name but his horse.

And now, the horse too: gone.

Yes, Lucippa, I think as I retrieve yet another army pension document from the file box, eager to trace the connections. Yes, Edwin's horse is gone. And the boy who once rode the horse along the river road by the old home place: gone. Your mother is gone, too, Lucippa, but you know that already. She has been gone a long, long time. But you have a little girl, Harriet Zarader, named for the lost ones: Harriet, for your dead mother. Zarader, for a dead aunt. Hattie is a lovely little girl. But you know that already, don't you, Lucippa?

How much Lucippa's mind could hold is one of the mysteries of those years. The facts, though, are a matter of record. One year after he'd sold his horse for seventy dollars, leaving forty dollars with his father to pay the family's tax bill, Lucippa's little brother came home to the Ohio River house to die: *Diarrhoea chronica.* Not the most honorable way to die in the Civil War, perhaps, but definitely the most common. Edwin lasted a few days, and was buried "at my own expense," D. C. Mead would later write, as if it were notable for a father to pay for a son's burial. Assorted relatives would have attended the funeral, including Edwin's sisters Lucippa and Phebe; their brother Henry was still serving in Louisiana after surviving the siege of Vicksburg.

Most likely, Lucippa brought her two-year-old daughter with her to the burial, for there would have been no one else to care for Hattie. Lucippa's first divorce was final by then. Alone, she was waiting out the war, praying for the safe return of Brother Henry, trying to keep little Hattie fed and clothed, and battling the blue devils that swarmed her mind no matter how hard she tried to swat them away. Staying at her father's home would have eased Lucippa's money problems, but she couldn't bring Hattie into that mess of trouble, the battles between D. C. Mead and his new wife having escalated into violence. What Hattie will remember of these years is loneliness and fear and unrelenting hunger. Just the two of them, she and her mother. Sometimes it seemed to Hattie that the "darkies" living in the sharecroppers' cabin were the closest thing to family that she knew.

So when Lucippa met and married Augustus, Hattie must have thought she had gone to the heaven of family and home she'd read about in Grandfather Mead's books: father, mother, child. Enough to eat, and, wonder of wonders, in a few years a sister. Hattie was eight by then, the perfect age to be a big sister, and she could not get enough of little Viola. A year later, Charlie was born. The months swirled by so happily that Hattie hardly noticed the silences growing between her mother and the new father and then the darkness encircling her mother's eyes and then—what came next, what order of catastrophes left eleven-year-old Hattie alone once again with her mother, the new father and the babies nowhere in sight? Though who could blame him, Lucippa must have thought, with me as sick as I am and hardly able to care for Hattie, let alone two babies. Oh, Augustus would find someone to marry, Lucippa was certain of that. Little Charlie and Viola would be looked after. But Hattie was not his, she was Lucippa's only. And who would take care of Hattie?

> Know all men by these presents that I, Lucippa Frazier, being of sound mind but feeble in body and being desirous of making my sole property a gift to my child, Harriet Ray, do hereby, for and in consideration of maternal affection, give, grant & convey to Dewitt C. Mead, my father, in trust for the said Harriet Ray, all my property, and request that he will use the same for her good. I further request that he shall act as executor of this my last will and testament and shall act as the guardian of my child Harriet Ray.

> In witness whereof I have hereunto set
> my hand on this the 2 day of April 1873
> Lucippa Frazier

Only the signature is in Lucippa's own hand, and even that appears shaky and labored, as if accomplished with great difficulty on her actual deathbed. Lucippa died shortly thereafter, a thirty-three-year-old, twice-divorced mother of three. Hattie was eleven years old. Years later, Hattie would wonder why in the world she had not foreseen it. Silly girl, she should have known, she should have guessed, for it was common in those days for girls to lose their mothers—to diphtheria, cholera, influenza, tuberculosis, in childbirth, or from sheer, brittle exhaustion—before the girls reached puberty. Life was difficult, death swift and intractable, so why not prepare? Hundreds, thousands of girls losing their mothers every year, and the gravediggers barely stopping to look up from their shovels. A whole nation of girls losing their mothers. Common as dirt, these happenings.

But one girl, alone, is not a whole nation. An eleven-year-old girl with hooded eyes and long, wavy hair and bright gold bobs ornamenting each ear. A girl leaning out a large window, the dark shutters framing her face, a girl gazing out at the river, wishing back the days she can now hardly remember.

◆

Lucippa's will made no provision for her two younger children. Three-year-old Viola and her brother Charlie, who had not yet turned two, were living with Augustus and his new wife. When Lucippa entered her father's house for the last time, she brought only a few household possessions and her daughter Hattie. "I took care of Lusippi Frazier and child until she died, and buried her at my own expense," D. C. Mead would claim decades later as justification for bequeathing to Lucippa's three heirs a total of five dollars, to be divided equally among them.

Family legend has it that D. C. cared for his granddaughter Hattie in the years after her mother's death, with help from his youngest daughter, Phebe. What constitutes "cared for" is a complicated matter, however, especially with regards to my great-great-great-grandfather, Dewitt Clinton Mead. Apart from the national crises of the time—the Panic of 1873, the collapse of the stock market and railroad companies, bread lines and mass unemployment, a cholera epidemic that ravaged the nation—there were deep personal crises within the Mead household itself.

Marital discord had been an ongoing theme not only for Lucippa but for her father as well, ever since his first wife, the mother of Lucippa and her younger siblings, had died in 1854. Six years later, census records show two of D. C.'s sons still at home, but none of his daughters. There were, however, two females living in the Ohio River house: a thirty-two-year-old housekeeper and her teenaged daughter. In divorce proceedings begun two years later, the daughter claimed that at the time she came under "the undue influence" of Dewitt Clinton Mead and entered into a marriage contract with him, she was "of tender age, only fourteen years old." D. C. was forty-one. In the affidavit, the young woman avowed that she performed "the duties of a faithful wife" until D. C.'s "cruel treatment became intolerable," treatment that included acting in an "inhuman manner, frequently using violence upon her person."

D. C. countered by posting a notice in the local newspaper, stating that his wife, "having left my bed and board without just cause or provocation, all persons are hereby forbidden to trust or harbor her on my account." Apparently, a divorce was granted, for within months after the final affidavit was filed, D. C. married another woman, later fathering two sons with her; Daniel and Benjamin Mead are listed on the 1870 census. After that time, official records become more complicated, the details entangled. In 1871, D. C.'s wife petitioned the courts for alimony. Later affidavits claim that he had abandoned her and her children, compelling her "to find a home elsewhere" but "being destitute," she returned to him a few months later, at which time his "cruel and inhuman" behavior increased. Such behavior, she claimed, included not only calling her "insulting and degrading names" but also striking her in the face, driving her out of the house, and locking up her children in a room to keep her from them. On one occasion, so the affidavit states, the elderly Mead "did call for his daughter to get him his revolver," warning that if his estranged wife did not leave he would kill her.

If these allegations are true, the daughter D. C. called for was either his eldest, the ailing Lucippa, or his youngest, Phebe, who by this time had returned home to assist her father with a household that had grown to include not only D. C.'s two young sons but also Lucippa and her daughter Hattie. If the affidavits are factual, the young Hattie might well have witnessed this violent event, as well as other altercations between D. C. and his wives.

But "If," as my grandfather Arthur used to say, "is one heck of a word." People lie under oath. They exaggerate the truth to serve their needs. So, whose story do we believe? Disputes between D. C. and his wife continued for three years, finally ending in 1874, one year after Lucippa's death. Though we can never ascertain the whole story, one thing is certain: The Old Mead House on the Ohio River was anything but a serene shelter for a girl of eleven who had just lost her mother. Not to mention having lost her younger half sister and brother. Marriages start, stop. Start, stop. People die. And when it is all over, who is left to claim as your family? To Hattie, the answer was clear: whoever is left. That is your new family. Your new tribe.

◆

To an outsider's eye, the reconfigured family living in the Ohio River house might have resembled a conventional family: father, mother, chil-

Great-grandmother Hattie with calling card, circa 1873. Home of her grandfather, Dewitt Clinton Mead, outside Rising Sun, Indiana.

dren. In reality, the father figure was Hattie's grandfather, the mother was her aunt, and the siblings, though considerably younger than Hattie, were technically her half uncles. *Strange* (here I borrow Hattie's timeworn phrase) *how Fate arranges things.* Daniel and Benjamin were almost exactly the ages of the half sister and brother Hattie had lost. Did the presence of the two boys soften the absence of Viola and Charlie? For Hattie's sake, I hope so.

Over the next few years, Hattie tried hard to hold the memories, but details kept slipping away. The last time she'd seen her half siblings, months before their mother died, little Viola was, what, three? Yes, she must have been three. Why couldn't Hattie remember what Viola looked like? Baby Charlie was clearer in Hattie's mind, though she remembered mostly the feel of him, his bare plump feet and the silky place at the back of his neck, the little indentation Hattie liked to kiss when no one was looking.

Circumstances eventually improved for Hattie. When times were good, warm fires blazed in the Old Mead House, and Hattie would get full and sleepy from the fine dinner, and then warm and soft in the feather bed beside Aunt Phebe. Lying there, Hattie fixed her mind on what her Sunday School teacher called her "blessings," not wanting them to leave:

The big white house with all the windows and the dark shutters and the covered porch.

The Negro children she played with down by the river.

Here, Hattie hesitated. Does a horse count as a blessing? Even if it isn't really mine, even if Grandfather just lets me ride it? No, probably a horse doesn't count as a blessing.

But she was sure she should count Aunt Phebe. Phebe was there when Hattie woke in the morning and there when she went to bed. She would sit behind Hattie on the little stool in the upstairs room, brushing Hattie's thick hair with the soft brushes she kept on the dressing table. She made Hattie pretty clothes, too, high-necked dresses trimmed with lace and ruffles. Once, she had taken Hattie in the wagon to town to buy soft slippers and black lace-up shoes for Sunday School. She even let Hattie choose her own design for the calling cards that bore her name: Harriet Z. Ray. Hattie chose a fancy script printed in green ink and surrounded by swirling shapes that resembled leaves, above which a long-tailed bird with purple wings lifted its head, its beak open as if trying to catch the butterfly perched nearby. Hattie was very proud of the calling cards and liked to imagine who she would give them to. School had not yet started, but when it did she was certain she would meet many chums, and she would be "happy to make their acquaintance," as Aunt Phebe said.

After much deliberation, Hattie had decided not to put her whole name on the card, as it took up too much room; she wanted more room for the bird. But sometimes she liked to practice writing out her whole name. Harriet Zarader Ray. Harriet, for her mother's mother, who had died long before Hattie was born. Zarader, for an aunt who died the year Hattie was born. And Ray. Well, of course Ray. That was her real father's name, though she couldn't for the life of her remember his face. Her mother's face floated back to her now and then, mostly in dreams. Sometimes when Phebe brushed Hattie's hair, Hattie glanced at her aunt's image in the looking glass and pretended that Phebe was her mother. It wasn't hard to do, as Lucippa and Phebe had been sisters. Their mother had died when they were young, too. Lucippa had been fourteen, but

Phebe was only three. Well, then, see? There was another blessing I should count, Hattie thought. At least I had a mother for eleven years.

One day, Aunt Phebe sat her niece down in front of the mirror and told her that this was a special day. They were going to town to have Hattie's picture taken. Phebe took extra care with Hattie's hair that day, parting it expertly down the middle, brushing the long, thick hair until it fell in soft waves down Hattie's back, then lifting two thick strands from the sides of Hattie's face and securing the strands with a clamp at the crown of her head. At first Hattie protested. Lately she had been thinking that her ears were too big, that they stuck out too far. And the earrings just called more attention to them.

No, Aunt Phebe answered. You have beautiful hair, a beautiful face. Beautiful ears. And how many young women have earrings so lovely as yours?

Hattie turned her face to the mirror. Had Aunt Phebe just called her a woman? It was true, then, what she had been thinking. That the soft rags folded in Hattie's dresser drawer were indeed meant for her, that Aunt Phebe had noticed the changes in Hattie. She wondered if Grandfather Mead had noticed, too, and that was why he had been acting so strict towards her lately. He wanted to know the names of her school friends and he didn't like her riding out alone without telling him where she was going. But sometimes Hattie just wanted to ride, fast, not knowing where she was heading, just letting the horse go where he wanted, through the woods and down by the river, fast, until she was out of breath.

◆

In the photograph taken that day, a young woman stares straight out at the camera with an expression verging on defiance. Her hair falls over her shoulders; her heavy-lidded eyes are partially closed. She appears to be about twelve, perhaps thirteen, buds of breasts barely visible beneath the lace-trimmed dress.

In another photograph, taken at approximately the same time just up the river in Aurora, Indiana, a slender young man stands before the camera. His features are even, nearly aristocratic, the dark, deep-set eyes framing a regal, perfectly straight nose. He is dressed in a two-piece suit that has seen better days. Most likely the young man paid for the suit, and the photograph, with his own money. Even in the best of times, money was scarce in the Mounts household. But at the time of this photograph, the Panic of 1873 had grown into the nation's "Long Depression," which would not end for several more years. Robert Mounts was a middle son in a large family made up mostly of brothers. Three younger sisters rounded out the line, along with the youngest tagalong brother, Harrison, bringing the grand total of Mounts siblings to eleven.

These are the aunts and uncles Bessie is trying to keep straight in her diary, the names she will record decades later in the frontispiece of her dead husband's Bible. By that time, all of them will be dead, but Bessie will not record their death dates, choosing to keep them alive in her mind.

◆

My great-grandparents were married on an Easter Sunday afternoon at the Ohio River home of D. C. Mead. In the studio photograph, Harriet Zarader Ray and Robert E. Mounts make a striking couple, though Hattie's beauty resides almost entirely in her expression, the proud, direct gaze with which she meets the camera. She looks older than her seventeen years; it is difficult to believe this is the same motherless girl who had posed before the Rising Sun photographer just four or five years before. Yes, earrings still stud her large ears, and her hooded eyes still seem to hide some secret she will never reveal. But the long, thick hair is now parted straight down the middle, slicked severely back in the fashion of the day. And her breasts are no longer buds. A white ruffle frames Hattie's face, but if the ruffle is meant to draw the eye upward, it is not a successful ploy. For it is Hattie's voluptuousness that catches a viewer's gaze, the tightly laced bodice accentuating the hourglass shape that her younger daughter Sylvia would one day inherit: The full bosom and hips. The waist that, if not waspish, is, for this photograph moment, firmly corseted and defined.

Hattie stands beside a chair on which her new husband is seated. One of her long, graceful hands rests on his shoulder. Twenty-three-year-old Robert is slender and dark-eyed, his black hair sweeping like a wave across his forehead. The chin is pointed and strongly defined, and the thick, dark mustache—Robert's signature mustache, which he will shave only once in his long life, in a gesture of generosity and humor—nearly covers his top lip.

Some men grow mustaches to draw attention away from less than admirable features. But Robert Mounts is, to my eye, hauntingly handsome. (Recently, my mother told me that my husband, Donald, reminds her of her grandfather.) Had I been Hattie, I too would have fallen hard for this man, who by all accounts was as tender as he was attractive. Like most middle children, Robert had learned early on how to accommodate, to take his place in line, asking little, grateful for whatever came his way. Aside from his rare flare-ups of temper, Robert was more easygoing than his new wife. Accustomed to crowds, he seemed content to share what little there was because he'd always had to share, he and his seven brothers, and later the three Mounts sisters. Hattie, at the time of her wedding, had little recollection of her half siblings. And years later, even after she had reconnected with Charlie, she would continue to wear the loneliness many only children wear.

Both Hattie and Robert dreamed of making, out of their love, a home where all were welcome. But their dreams came from different sources and out of different needs. Robert's, perhaps, was not a need at all, but simply a natural continuation of the way he had always lived, in a sprawling, make-do home where children were as numerous and self-sustaining as the mushrooms he hunted with his brothers in the southern Indiana woods. Hattie would fashion her dream home not from childhood memory (her early life had been too sad) but rather from visions she carried in her head, visions nurtured by the books she'd read of vine-covered cottages and country inns and manor houses where fires blazed in the hearth, where the branches of Christmas trees bore the heavy weight of gifts, something for everyone—oranges and toys, satin slippers and leather-covered books—and where the long table was spread with bounty. No one who came to her home, to her table, would ever be turned away, she vowed. And no child in her care would ever be hungry or afraid or alone.

Bessie Denton Mounts was born on September 28, 1880, so small that Hattie placed her first in a bureau drawer and later in a doll-sized cradle

My maternal great-grandparents Robert and Hattie Mounts, circa 1879; their eldest child, Bessie, 1881.

Robert built for her. Bessie's diaper, Hattie would one day recall, was no bigger than a lady's handkerchief. In her first and only baby picture, Bessie takes up so little space on the photographer's velvet-draped chair that she might be a doll, except for the serious expression in her dark eyes. Someone has parted her black hair down the middle and combed it flat against her head. Her pose would be natural for a banker or a politician, but is oddly discordant for a child who, according to family legend, was already plotting schemes of mischief and escape. In this moment, though, Bessie appears confined, refined, one small hand resting casually on the sofa's arm, the other placed obediently at her side. Her doll-sized feet, strapped into high-button shoes, are crossed demurely.

How Bessie spent the first few years of her life is anyone's guess. There were few pictures or photographs in the extended Mounts household and even fewer books, just the handful that Hattie had brought from Grandfather Mead's house to the home of her new in-laws, Father and Mother Mounts, where the new couple shared space with several of Robert's unmarried brothers and sisters. The tribe that Hattie had married into was plain and simply poor. And the history of poor, uneducated families of the late nineteenth century was rarely recorded in images or written words, but rather was passed down through stories, quilts, comforters, and the occasional tintype and family Bible. The Tree of Paradise quilt still in our family's possession came from Mother Mounts, as did the mildewed, torn, and water-stained Bible containing the Scottish Psalter penned by an anonymous poet. Rhyming psalms were easier to memorize than free-verse translations, and when these rhymes were also set to music, a whole congregation could sing them together. Even the non-readers—and many of the Mountses were non-readers—could manage a rhyming psalm.

Though almost nothing is known of Bessie's paternal grandparents, stories abound of the eight Mounts sons. According to local legend, Robert and his seven brothers were "river rats" who made their modest living any way they could. If they ever attended school, there is no record of it. They fished, hunted, trapped, and sometimes farmed small patches of land. But most of their time was spent on or near the Ohio River. The brothers built rafts and flatboats, loaded them with logs or with corn, potatoes, and oats from nearby farms, and steered the boats down the Ohio. Sometimes they went as far as the juncture where the Ohio joins the Mississippi on its way down to New Orleans. At the end of their journey, wherever that journey happened to end, the Mounts brothers would sell the rafts and boats, then make their way back home to Switzerland County, Indiana, any way they could. Sometimes on their riverboat travels, the brothers came across their youngest sister, who had left home early on to work as a dancing girl on one of the gambling boats. Within a few years, the eldest sister, Mary, would leave home, too, to marry and divorce one Charlie and, soon after, court another, Hattie's half brother, who was eight years Mary's junior. Two of Mary's brothers had already headed north to Wisconsin, where land was plentiful and cheap.

The back pages of Mother Mounts's Bible contain what little we know of the larger community into which Bessie was born. Significant events are conspicuous by their absence. There was only one family Bible, after all, and only a few blank pages, so one could hardly commit to these pages anything that would not be permanent. Thus, in the

Mounts Bible, marriages are not recorded, for marriages invariably end—through divorce or death. Nor would one tempt Fate or Providence by listing the births of children or grandchildren; who knows how long *they* would last? Bessie's birth in 1880 is not recorded, nor is her brother Dale's, four years later. Death, being the only permanent condition, seemed the only event worthy of the labor it took for this writer—Mother Mounts, most likely—to sound out the difficult words, letter by letter, and to make the childlike, blocky marks of the alphabet that someone, long ago, had taught her.

> CARFEEL WAS SHOT THE SECON DAY OF JULY 1881
>
> JUNE THE TWENTY SECKEN 1884 PERRY KITTEL DROWNED TO DAY THIS IS SUN DAY
>
> MOS SURSEY DID THE THIRD OF OCTOBOR OLD 8T8 YEARS OLD 1884

Three deaths: One of public, national importance. (Though President Garfield would live almost three months past the July assassination attempt, Mother Mounts counted him dead as soon as the news was announced.) The second, of little importance except to Perry Kittel's family and to friends like the Mountses, who were as close as family, close enough to mourn this victim of the river's vengeance—and on Sun Day, too! The third, another friend and neighbor, Mose Searcy, dead at eighty-eight. And what better cause of death could one wish for, if death must come? To die at 8T8. To die of Old. Most probably, Mother Mounts and her daughters and daughter-in-law Hattie were called to the homes of the Kittels and Searcys to do what they could. To tend to the body, sit beside it during the visitation, wash and iron for the grieving families, bring food and fresh milk for the children. As they trusted that their neighbors would do for *their* family when it was time for their own names to be inscribed on the back page of a family Bible.

Another way for poor families of the nineteenth century to preserve the history of the tribe was through family "hair pictures." Civil War soldiers had carried locks of their sweethearts' hair into battle, and undertakers sometimes allowed grieving relatives extra time with the body of the deceased, to clip a bit of hair that would be saved, placed in a locket or brooch, or enclosed in a letter to be mailed to relatives far away. Victorians took the "lock of hair" practice a step further: Clipped locks were woven into intricate designs, knots and flowers and braids, then placed in brooches or incorporated into rings, bracelets, or earrings. Often, the hair for a single weaving was taken from several people, usually related by birth but sometimes merely by association; some weavings contained hair from the members of a school or church. Sometimes, entire memorial wreaths were woven from the hair of family members, the wreath growing larger and larger as the hair of each newly dead member of the tribe was added to it. Other weavers created designs from hair of the living members of the family, framing these works of art to hang on the walls of a family's home. If the infamous Mounts "hair picture" did exist, as sources would later report, most likely Bessie's grandmother created it a few years before Bessie's birth. Following the custom of the time, Mother Mounts would have clipped strands of her own hair along with the hair of her husband and their eleven children, and then hung the weaving in their home.

Imagine the scene: Switzerland County, Indiana. An autumn morning in 1880. Inside the house, the first threads of light through the muslin curtains illuminate the object suspended by a satin ribbon. In the main room, perhaps, above the long, hand-hewn table on which Mother Mounts's Bible rests. Or in one of the small bedrooms off the narrow hallway, where the three youngest of their eight sons sleep.

Or in the bedroom their middle son Robert now shares with his new wife and tiny, black-haired daughter, who lies tucked in the doll cradle her father has built, unaware of the strangely beautiful weaving hanging by a ribbon on the wall above her head.

Reading the hundreds of letters my ancestors exchanged is a journey through space and time. No, not *through*. Through, as Great-grandma Hattie would have said, "does not begin to answer the task." Rather, this is a journey into and across: *into* time and *across* space. The movement into time is a vertical excavation, each letter as focused and pointed as a diamond drill head boring into the buried layers of the past. The other movement, across space, is a horizontal journey my mind travels in one expansive sweep, peripheral elements vibrating at the edges of the central action. Sometimes the image grows so wide that to take in the whole picture I must rise above it, allowing each scenic panel its individual weight and portent. As I lift off, I try to forget how things will turn out. How lives will collide, old stars burn out and new ones appear. It is July 1903. Everywhere at once, 1903.

Sylvia Mounts
RR#5
Dayton, Indiana

My dear little sister:
You must write to me and tell me all about everything because I get lonesome here. I got you a little birthday present. Now if it doesn't suit you or if it is too small which I am afraid it is, I'll get you something else or a bracelet a little larger. There is the cutest little girl out in the hammock, her name is Helen and she says she was brought to her mama in a satchel and she says she is glad she came to her mama because if she had been taken to someone else she wouldn't have liked them.

Hoping that your present will fit you and that you will be pleased with it, I close,

Your affectionate Sister, Bessie.

I'll send you a <u>sniff</u> of my new perfume.

4 o'clock

Friday evening

Dear little "sis":

Am sorry the bracelet twas too little but will trot uptown in the morning and exchange it so you will get it tomorrow I suppose. I worked like "thunder" this morning and I was awfully tired this after-noon so I took a bath, washed my head, ate a piece of pie then went to bed and slept a couple of hours and I must say I feel tolerably well now. Got me a new tea jacket, lavender and white, trimming it in lace and inserting a lavender ribbon.

Haven't seen anyone I knew since I came down from Hammond, made a "mash" on a fellow I did not know, the day of the picnic. O no. I didn't mash him I just talked to him a little. Now don't forsake me but write again soon. Must close now, here's a hug and kiss for you

*_*_

Your loving sister, Bessie

Here's a scrap of ribbon to my tea jacket.

P.S. Isn't that too awfully bad about Mr. Lawson. What will that poor woman do with all those little children.

Everywhere at once, July 1903.

Here comes twenty-two-year-old Bessie, emerging from the front door of her employer's home at 513 North Fourth Street in Lafayette, Indiana, to "trot uptown" where she will exchange the birthday brace-let that fits Bessie's wrist but is too small for Sylvia, who at fourteen is already growing into womanly roundness the wiry Bessie will never know.

As Bessie disappears into the jewelry store, jangling its door-mounted bell, my mind lifts above the scene, sweeping fifteen miles southeast of Lafayette's central square to the outskirts of Stockwell, In-diana. Outside the Cosby family horse barn, the youngest Cosby son stands beside a plow horse, one hand steadying the right front hoof, the other dislodging packed rocks and mud with a hoof pick. Young-est son, yes; young, no. On this summer afternoon in 1903, Santford Marion Cosby is thirty-five years old. According to life expectancy standards of the time, more than half of his days on earth have already passed, though if such a thought ever occurred to Sant, he would have shooed it away as if it were a horsefly—troublesome, no doubt, but fi-nally harmless. Sant was not one to waste time worrying the details. Those things he could change, he changed. The rest, he didn't spend one extra minute on. Better to look forward, press on, take pleasure in the tasks set before him.

And Sant did take pleasure in tasks. His body, sturdier than the bod-ies of the older Cosby siblings, was well suited to the rugged, demanding pursuits of barnyard and field. In my favorite Sant photo, a straw hat is pushed back on his head, his signature forelock of dark hair curling out from the brim. Deep smile wrinkles crease his cheeks, which are promi-nent and ruddy as though polished by the sun. If, as the youngest Cosby child, Sant was indulged by his parents and siblings, the indulgence had served only to sweeten his disposition. Though his demeanor was for the most part serious, he could break into laughter at the slightest prov-ocation. Sant's laugh was deep-throated, contagious, irrepressible. The more he tried to stop himself, the harder he laughed, his eyes narrowing, his high cheekbones wet with tears as he leaned deep into the hilarity, taking everyone else with him until the room, as his future-mother-in-law, Hattie, would later remember, "fairly rocked with laughter."

In another photo, taken about the time he met Bessie, Sant sits cross-legged, flocked by a gaggle of young Cosby nephews and nieces. Though in his mid-thirties at the time, Sant seems more aligned with the children than with his thin, dark siblings positioned stern-faced around him. All three will die decades before him: his sister from con-sumption, one brother from spinal meningitis, the other from injuries sustained in a fall from a ladder while he was painting a house. Things like this happen all the time, Sant would come to believe. No why or wherefore about them. But how it did hurt. Burying your brothers, your sister, your parents. Well, at least we weren't orphans. At least all of us children (Sant would continue to think of himself and his siblings as children, even the dead ones) had our parents a long, long time. We were among the lucky ones.

◆

I open another letter. The scene widens. Below our eyes, Wildcat Creek snakes and turns, its waters eddying here and there into shallow pools where minnows dart between smooth, flat rocks. Close to its banks, beside a small garden of raised vegetable beds, a log house comes into view, tiny in comparison to neighboring farmhouses. The girl in the tree is harder to find than the house, camouflaged as she is in a leafy canopy of hardwoods. Yesterday, July 12, was her birthday, but since it fell on a Sunday this year and Sundays at the Mounts house always feel like holidays anyway, Mother had extended the birthday celebration one more day. "Your day, Sylvia," Hattie had promised. So, never mind that it is Monday, Sylvia has slept in late, eaten leftover sponge cake for breakfast, and borrowed Dale's trousers, which she cinched at the waist and rolled to the knee before making her barefoot climb up the tree whose branches extend over the narrowest part of the creek. Pa has promised to take her fishing, once he gets back from laying fence at the Packard's, so if luck nods in their direction, there will be fried sunfish for dinner. Her favorite.

Sylvia leans back onto the branch and looks up, watching flecks of noonday sun light the highest leaves. Fourteen: It feels strange to say it. Last month when her cousins were visiting from Rising Sun, they'd told her that once she turned fourteen, everything would change. Before long, she would get her monthlies, she would start noticing boys and they would start noticing her. Sylvia didn't tell them that boys were already noticing her and had been for some time. Not that she gave one flip about boys. You'll change your tune, her cousins kept saying. Just wait, you'll change your tune. Had one of them told her that within seven years of this moment, she would write to a young man named Arthur *I have always loved you Dear since before you were born,* Sylvia would have laughed. Laughed and got it all over herself. Impossible, she would think, slapping her hands against her trousers. You silly girls. Why, that's impossible. How can you love someone you've never met? Someone you've never even heard of?

◆

Twenty-five miles from where Sylvia leans against her favorite tree, another fourteen-year-old girl sweeps the porch of a small, seen-better-days hotel, moving gingerly between warped boards to avoid protruding nail heads. Situated in the center of the dusty township of Templeton, where the Big Four and the Nickel Plate railways intersect, the Sanders' Hotel attracts "all manner of men," as my grandfather Arthur will one day recall. City men passing through on their way to or from Cleveland, Chicago, Cincinnati, St. Louis. Men who stumble back late from the taverns, tote pistols, brawl in the alleys. Some stay at the Sanders Hotel only a night. Others board for months, filling the upstairs rooms.

The downstairs rooms belong to what is left of the grief-stricken family: G. E. Sanders and his two children. The girl sweeping the porch is Vena. Her father left early this morning to ready the grocery store for its first customers. The boarders have been fed, the dishes washed and put away, the oilcloth wiped clean of crumbs, and Vena turns her mind to her most difficult task: keeping a close watch on her little brother. Lord, what trouble would he get into today? A bantam rooster of a boy, twelve-year-old Arthur has always been scrappy, unable to let even the mildest insult ride, never mind the height and breadth of the insulter. And when words alone can't win the battle—quite often they can, for young Arthur has an impressive vocabulary—then fists must ensue. And if Arthur can't manage his opponent by himself, nothing will do but that Vena get into the scuffle, too.

Just yesterday, as Vena rounded the side of the hotel on her way to the clothesline, she'd seen some tall fellow punching Arthur, and out of nowhere, no, out of *somewhere,* somewhere deep, anger boiled up hot and fast inside her and before she could stop herself she was slapping the fellow's face with her open hand, hard, first with the right hand then with the left, then right, left, right until he cried out and ran, turning to point his finger and shout about what he would do to her. But he was crying. No doubt about it. Crying like the baby that he was.

Now, standing on the porch with the broom in her hand, Vena knew she should be feeling remorse. This was not in any measure what her mother had taught. Not in any measure how a Christian should behave. But Mother was dead now, dead six months and counting, and truth be told, Vena would do it again, slap that fellow until he ran like the baby he was. Truth be told, she could close her eyes and bring the moment back right now if she needed to. And she needed to. She closed her hand tight against the broom, released it, tightened it again. Her hands were hot, still stinging. And it felt good.

◆

Had Hattie known the Sanders family at this time, known the extent of their suffering, she would have done what she could. Even if it meant leaving two-year-old Ivan in the care of Sylvia for a few days, robbing her own egg money, walking the three miles from Briarwood to board the Interurban to Lafayette then the train to Templeton, and depositing herself on the steps of the Sanders' Hotel. Not that anyone could take the place of a child's mother. The motherless Hattie knew that. Aunt Phebe, a motherless child herself, had known that, too. Had never tried to make Hattie into her own daughter, much as she would have liked to. No, Phebe just did what she could. Made herself of use.

For Hattie and Phebe and their neighbors, there were plenty of opportunities to make themselves of use. Besides helping out at butchering time, at huskings, thresherees, or barn-raisings, there were the ongoing duties of birthing rooms and sickrooms. From mumps and measles to influenza, cholera, typhoid fever, diphtheria, tuberculosis, cancer, and dozens of undiagnosed but deadly maladies, sickness swept through their small communities, claiming the young as well as the old. Occasionally someone would be taken to the "detention hospital" for smallpox or other infectious diseases, but for the most part, people stayed put. They were born in their homes and they died there. Rarely did a physician appear at the bedside, though neighbors were often called in, especially midwives like Aunt Hattie, as she was known to her neighbors.

> *Company came and stayed all day I had hardly got the work done and had not ate yet till our new neighbor across the creek came after me so I was there all night they have a new little boy. I was too tired and sleepy yesterday my arms are sore yet this morning. We had callers last evening and then about 1 o'clock we all got up to see about the cow, have a fat little boy calf this morning. Marshal's were here their baby is so cute it looks like a doll. Haas baby allmoast died the*

next Sunday after they were here, had Pluro Phenmonia and Everts McDoles have twins. I certainly been busy this week. Tried to make soap too.

Hattie kept homemade toddies and tonics in the cupboard and often administered them, along with advice she included in letters: *Be careful what you feed Baby. If you could get some blackberry cordial and give him a little once in a while when his stomach and bowels bother him I think would be good for him.*

As a child, Hattie had known her share of trouble, but she had been lucky with her own children, managing to raise them thus far without severe mishap, though there was that time, not long after they'd built the little house on Wildcat Creek, when Sylvia got so sick. Yellow with jaundice and burning with fever that wouldn't break and of course it was the rainy season and the Wildcat out of its banks from flood, so the old road was useless for coming or going. Hattie was beside herself with worry but nothing compared to Robert—why, that man could not bear to see any child suffering, and his darling Sylvia, well, that was unthinkable! Sylvia's fever was raging and Robert was pacing the floor, cursing and praying all at once, and then suddenly he was out the door and Hattie following behind, down to the creek where he commenced to strip off his outergear and then he was in, diving under the water then rising up top of it, and then he was swimming, hand over hand, in that strong sure way he'd always had with water, and then he was out of Hattie's sight.

In an hour, maybe two, Robert appeared, his muddy boots tracking across the kitchen floor, a block of ice strapped to his back. So he'd made it downstream to the mill, Hattie thought, and this ice what he had to show for his labors. Ice that Hattie would shave off in slivers to slide between two metal cans, the smaller one filled with cream from her only fresh cow, and shake and shake those cans until the cream hardened and she could spoon the sweet coldness into her daughter's mouth, again and again, until the fever cooled.

Like their mothers and grandmothers before them, young women like Bessie were expected to go to the homes of the dying and the dead, to

Sanders' Hotel, Oxford, Indiana. Great-grandfather G. E. Sanders operated this hotel and lived here with his wife and children. The little boy is my grandfather Arthur; to his left is his sister Vena and their mother, about a year before Golda's death in 1903. The two men were probably boarders at the hotel (note the pistol in one man's hand).

sit with sick or grieving neighbors, and to help out any way they could. Someone had to wash and iron, to keep things "slicked over" as Hattie called it. Here, as recorded in Bessie's 1897 diary (by then she had, as her teacher feared, been forced to leave school to help with the family's livelihood) Bessie is called away from her clerking job to a neighbor's house:

> *Fri., April 23. Dear Diary, Mr. Combs brought me home from the store and Ma and I went up to Mitchell's in the afternoon. I staid. Sat up all night, helped the next day. O how I do pity them it is so sad.*

> *Sun., April 25: Raining this morning. O I do wish it would not rain, it is so bad to put anyone away in the rain. The Mitchell boys brought me home in the evening, they wanted me to stay so bad.*

Mon. April 26: I washed in the forenoon. Went up to Mr. Mitchell's in the afternoon, helped wash up there. Staid all night.

Tues., April 27: Washed and ironed at Mitchells all day. 0 how I do miss Mrs. Mitchell. I can't realize it hardly. She was so kind to me and made everything so jolly, it seems so lonesome here without her.

In the larger community, the sickroom was the women's domain, but in the Mounts household, gender divisions were less defined. Dale and his father often pitched in with cooking, cleaning, mending, and even nursing. So it isn't surprising to learn from Hattie's letters that *Dale set up 3 nights last week with little Robert Fickle* or that he was the one called to the Funks when the parents were grieving their daughter's untimely death. Had Dale been born in another time and place, he might have received training in the healing arts and lived happily within this profession. I imagine him sitting quietly beside the bed, relieved not to have to make small talk or hold up his part of the conversation. Conversation was hard for Dale. Half the time, he wasn't sure what to say, especially to girls. They made him nervous. Sure, he liked a good time as well as the next fellow, he liked clowning around and singing and dancing, as long as he wasn't the center of attention. Here by the bedside he wasn't the center of anything. He could just sit in the dark, listening to firewood snapping in the stove. He could rest his tight muscles—putting up fence was hard work—and rise now and then to tend the fire or pour a dipper of fresh water from the bucket, or empty the bedpan, a job that never really bothered Dale like it did some people. For years he'd watched Bessie, so he knew what to do. Bessie was a good nurse, if a touch fidgety. She was always up and about, fussing over something. The only thing that kept her still was reading, but even the quiet ruffle of pages turning was enough to bother some sick folks. Dale didn't need a book. He could just sit. For as long as it took. And if the silence grew too dark and heavy, as it did for some, Dale could soften the silence with a song, for Bessie had taught him hymns and folk tunes and even a few sad mammy songs she'd learned down in Switzerland County. Singing was easier than talking, anyway, and soothed better, or so people told him. Mostly, though, the sick ones just want someone to sit with them. Maybe hold their hand, but mostly just sit, breathe in and out with them and not be afraid of the silence that fills the room.

In the envelope containing the 1903 birthday letter to Sylvia, Bessie included a separate letter to her mother, detailing the new tea jacket, Uncle Clint's latest news from Hammond, and the Groceryman's picnic—but not the fellow she'd *made a mash on.* Bessie knew better than to mention such a thing to Mother. Never mind that Hattie had married at seventeen, she was fiercely protective of her children. Better safe than sorry, Hattie reasoned. Better single than divorced. To Hattie's mind, 'twas infernally tricky, this marriage business. Especially as regards her eldest child. It would take a special man, one possessed of godly patience, to abide Bessie's moods. Even as a child, Bessie had a mind that no one, not even Hattie, could wrestle from its intentions. Determined. Stubborn. "Recalcitrant," a neighbor once called Bessie, and had Hattie been near a dictionary, she would have looked the word up right then: *recalcitrant.* Could be the neighbor had a point, though Bessie wasn't exactly unruly. Had Hattie followed her finger down the dictionary page, she would have found *restless.* Yes, that's closer to the truth of Bessie, she would have thought, nodding.

More than a century later, looking up from my desk spread with countless family documents, I nod right along with Hattie. Bessie Denton Mounts seems to have been born restless. Restless, curious, and incurably independent. The eldest child of Robert and Hattie, Bessie had inherited the best and the worst of her parents' history. From her mother, a passion for books, music, and story, but also a streak of dark longing growing from the self-described "siege of sorrow" that had been Hattie's childhood. From her father, a connection to all things wild (birds and foxes, creeks and woods) and a stubborn tenderness toward the helpless and weak, but also a restlessness that would keep Bessie, whenever possible, on the move.

As early as 1883, three-year-old Bessie was already in motion. At the old Mounts home near Rising Sun, the rooms of the Mounts sisters had emptied, leaving Robert's bride, Hattie, along with her mother-in-law, to tend to the household and farmhouse chores—the cooking, gardening, canning, churning, milking, washing and ironing, cleaning and scrubbing, and supervision of livestock and chickens. No wonder Hattie couldn't watch the inquisitive Bessie every minute. One morning while no one was looking (*action, roll camera*) Bessie toddled off behind her father and uncles out the door and down the lane. When Hattie finally found her at the edge of the woods, Bessie was resting a moment from her adventure. Hattie leaned down to give her daughter a brisk swat and a warning, neither of which fazed Bessie, who looked up into her mother's face and announced with stubborn pride, "I runned away and I just plunked 'er down." Another morning, a soap-making morning while Hattie's back was turned, Bessie, curious to see what all the fuss was about, headed straight for the lye bucket. Fumes from the harsh chemicals burned her nose, creating the disfiguring scar that Bessie would carry the rest of her days.

◆

I retrieve another envelope from where I've stored it, remove the photograph, and step through time: 1903, the Sanders' Hotel. The screen door unhinges on its own. I walk inside. Across the vestibule, behind the closed door of the front bedroom that comprises half of the family's living quarters, a double bed is positioned near the window. The Wedding Ring quilt on the bed is rumpled on one side, as if its single occupant had fallen into an exhausted sleep. The other side of the bed is smooth, undisturbed.

Beside the bed is a mahogany highboy with an oval-framed mirror, a small cardboard plaque propped against it:

> IN LOVING REMEMBRANCE OF MRS. G. E. SANDERS
> BORN NOV. 15, 1871 DIED JAN. 22, 1903
> AGE 31 YRS., 2 MO., 7 DAYS
> GONE BUT NOT FORGOTTEN

If we were to open the top drawer of the highboy, we would find three copies of an obituary column, one copy neatly trimmed with pinking shears, and a stack of cards and letters whose envelopes have been carefully eased open—with a kitchen knife, it appears—so that their contents might be slid in and out and in again without defacing one single word. Some letters offer more comfort than others. No need to say much, G. E. has concluded. A simple "We are sorry" goes a long way. As do the flatly practical notes—"If there's anything we can do

. . . "Heres a little treat money for the children" . . . "Enclosed find easy recipe for cornbread. . . ." All are welcome to the grief-numbed widower. Even the meddling ones from his dead wife's sisters, who seem to think that Arthur and Vena would be better off living with them, now that their mother is gone. The most formal letter is from G. E.'s uncle in Illinois. Every time G. E. reads it, something seizes up inside him.

> *Dear Nephew,*
>
> *We deeply sympathize with you in your bereavement and hope you will find strength to bare it. You have the consolation of having done all you could for her, and your children are not as helpless as if they were younger. And yet bereft of a good Mother it will require great care on your part in forming their character that your son may grow to be a good man and your daughter a nice lady. You will no doubt feel greatly broken down for a while but time assuages all griefs and it will be yours to plan and to do the best you can for yourself and the children.*
>
> *With good wishes for your welfare I am*
> *Sincerely Your Uncle*

Time assuages all griefs. Six months now, G. E. thinks. Does six months count as Time? And this work my hands busy themselves with, the endless repetition of tasks. Is this *the best*? The best I can do for myself and the children? This rising from bed each morning, this stacking and counting and clerking, the customers staring past my eyes as if nothing has changed, does this count as Strength? The strength to bear it?

Bereft. The word looks strange to G. E, no matter how many times he's studied it. It looks incomplete, unfinished. And just try to say it: *Bereft.* It sucks the air right out of your lungs.

Feb. 8, 1906

Mrs. Sant Cosby
Cosby Ranch, Clarks Hill, Indiana
Hello! Sis.
Dale says please bring your guitar over with you when you come. This is Sun. Eve. We kids are all sitting around the fire.
Yours Lovingly Sis.
P.S. Saw Wiley, is very proud to be Uncle, he asked me if my sister had any babes and I said no he says then its not Aunt Sylvia is it? Ha. Ha.

Dec. 24, 1907
Red Cedar Dam,
Menomonie, Wis.

Mrs. S. M. Cosby, Clarks Hill
Hello Sis!
We are going over to Charlie and Mary's for Xmas this year. You and Sant can have a little Xmas tree all by yourselves.
Sylvia

As the eldest child, Bessie had always been the big sister to Dale and Sylvia, but once the other siblings began arriving, Bessie was now closer in age to her mother than to her younger brothers. Ivan was twenty years younger than Bessie; Babe, born a few weeks after Bessie's wedding, twenty-four years younger. *The boys,* Bessie called them in her letters. *Send over the boys.* And Hattie would ship Ivan or Babe off to Bessie and Sant's farm, or in later years to their house in the small town

Photo on left: The five Mounts siblings, circa 1910. Bessie (on left) was 20 years older than Ivan (in center) and 24 years older than "Babe" (little boy in bowtie). Dale and Sylvia Mounts were the middle children.

Photo on right: Bessie's husband, Sant Cosby, holding one of his nephews, circa 1914.

of Stockwell, Indiana. The fact that Sant was twelve years older than Bessie, nearly as old as Hattie, added to the atmosphere of aunt-ness and uncle-ness permeating the Cosby household. In a Washington's Birthday postcard to Bessie, a teenaged Sylvia writes *Can you remember when Washington was there? Ha! Ha! I expect Sant can anyway if you cannot.* And describing a Christmas visit to the Cosbys, Sylvia writes to her soon-to-be husband, *We kids broiled rabbit steaks over coals and baked apples on a string here in front of the fireplace, It's grand. . . .*

We kids. Bessie and Sant were the grownups. The rest of them— Sylvia, Ivan, Babe, and later Sylvia's children and grandchildren—were *the kids.* Kids whom Sant took great pleasure in spoiling, much to Bessie's consternation. When the kids were visiting, no matter how hard Sant had worked weeding, plowing, discing, harrowing, harvesting—"every inch I am worth" he often said—at the end of the day he would walk the children to town to buy taffy squares, caramels, small toys and trinkets. Bessie spent time with her younger charges as well, pointing out gravestones in nearby cemeteries or teaching the names of various birds or mushrooms, but she expected the young ones to comport themselves in a dignified matter at all times—in short, to "behave." Sant, on the other hand, delighted in their antics, letting loose his signature belly laugh.

Perhaps Sant had had enough of behaving. His parents were old-fashioned Swedes, churchgoing Methodists who rarely raised their voices and never uttered profanities. The Mountses enjoyed dances and card parties and were known to let fly a few curses "if the situation warranted," as my mother remembers. Apparently, the situation often warranted, and the Wisconsin Mounts uncles were particularly eloquent in this area, which may be how Bessie's little brother Ivan acquired his highly peppered language. One spring evening about a year after Bessie and Sant married, five-year-old Ivan was walking with Sant down the lane that led from the Cosby farmhouse to town, on their way to buy a treat. Imagine the scene: Sant having changed out of his "overhauls" (as my Hoosier uncles pronounced it) into white shirt and dark trousers, his straw hat pushed back on his head, and beside him the young Ivan, his thick black hair sprouting an aggressive forehead cowlick. Sant probably held Ivan's hand, which would have felt small and soft inside his own rough farmer's hands. Had a stranger been passing on that lane—an unlikely event, as few strangers passed on that lane—he would have thought *father and son.* Certainly a stranger would not have thought *brothers-in-law.* Technically, of course, that is what Sant and Ivan were, though more than thirty years separated them.

What happened next is the stuff of family legend, a story we will tell and retell for decades to come, complete with punchline. What I would give to have witnessed the moment: Ivan in the middle of some childlike tale then suddenly, without missing a step or taking a breath, he explodes with "Liars, thieves, sons-a-bitches!" shocking Sant into silence. As the moment settles and the tickle of hilarity begins to move through Sant, it requires all his willpower to force back the laughter trying to squirm its way out. But Sant does not flinch. He does not chide. Ivan has had his say, that is the end of it, and the two brothers-in-law continue on their walk as if nothing has happened.

◆

Though letters from the Mounts menfolk are rare, the men and boys make cameo appearances in the women's letters. Usually the men are out somewhere—hauling fodder, making fence, tending to crops and livestock, trapping, hunting, fishing, or in the case of Dale, sitting up nights at the bedside of a friend or neighbor, prompting his mother to report that *he looked like he had been through a mill.* More often than not, though, the eldest son of Hattie and Robert is gone to Uncle Charlie's in Wisconsin, only occasionally returning to the tiny log house where Hattie has sat herself down *in the midst of it all* to scribble a few lines. *Pa is filing his saw and Dale is sitting here sewing a patch on his pants he is having quite a time I guess he has sewed it clear through by the remarks I hear.* The young sons Ivan and Babe run in and out of her letters, too, and every now and then Hattie grabs them by the back of their patched-up britches and sets them down with pencil and paper: *All of the trees are out in leaf,* they write in their childish, blocky handwriting. *The birds sing. . . . I never had any eggs broke. . . . Paw caught a nice mess of fish today.*

Even those from whom we have no correspondence, most notably my great-grandfather Robert, emerge as fully developed characters thanks to the letters the women exchange. In one, Robert sneaks around the corner, nudging Hattie to take her chair and umbrella out to the rose arbor and sit a while. "Unhitch your irons," Robert tells his daughters when he decides they've been cooped up too long and need a walk in the woods and some fishing. In another letter, he has just attended the neighborhood masquerade party, where according to Hattie *he was a dude with those white pants a little straw hat and one of those little canes. Mrs. McMellien took the prize though.* In later years, Robert will pine for a visit from the grandbabies, and once they've come and gone, he will startle from his chair during supper, certain he has heard one of them cry. In letter after letter he dreams of the grandchildren and tells Hattie his dreams, which she relates to her daughters. *Paw said Baby Merrill was moast as big as Babe, he was so sad he moast cried to think he had not got to see him anymore before he got so big in long pants.* And one dark Christmas, with no money to buy gifts, Robert searches for a way to mark the occasion:

... Babe says we got along very well if we didn't have any Christmas. But Paw thought he would have to make some kind of a change so we would know it was Xmas so he shaved his mustach off and if he isn't a great looking old Christmas gift. He is moast as good looking as John Henery. Will have to quit now and go to bed. Up again—trying to get strait so can start the new year square. Hope you have a pleasant and prosperous year.

Trying to get straight, to *reconcile myself,* was a fulltime job for Hattie, especially in winter. December was her birthday month, but she rarely got a chance to celebrate, what with endless treks to the wood pile, endless stoking of fires, endless trips to the sand bunk to bury yet another piglet or chick. *Seems the good things are just not for me,* she wrote again and again. Hattie, the motherless daughter, the full grown woman with a child's heart, who by the end of this decade will mourn the loss of the Ohio River house as *the only home I've ever known.*

No matter that she and Robert have made a welcoming home out of a briar patch. No matter that Briarwood, though the most modest house in the township, was where everyone wanted to be, its tiny rooms "fairly rocking" with laughter, as her granddaughters would remember. Still, reading the letters and hearing the stories passed down, it is hard not to agree with Hattie's bleak assessment that the good things just weren't for her:

... You wanted to know when I was coming to eat onions with you but you know how it is if I leve for a minute the bottom falls out of everything. I went down to Mrs. A's the other day first time for about three weeks when I went I had 21 awfully nice little turks growing fine. When I came back 9 of them were gone, was only gone a few hours either. ...

... we carried water till we were blue trying to keep it from dying things are rather trying no fruit no garden just nothing; but one can die trying anyway. ...

... and the rats got 3 of my ducks and the pretty gosling it made me moast sick but we went after them and about tore up the place got one big old fat rascal and a small one. Ivan has put the ducks in a box and brings them in the room every since ...

. . . had another frackas with a weasel this morning he grabbed a chicken and run off. there was a nest of little baby rabbits in the garden. He got all of them. Seems like you have to watch everything night and day . . .

. . . the creek is up we had to move chickens sitting hens and one old hens coop washed her out and took some of her eggs, she would soon have hatched too, and the old Turkey hen left her nest the other day with her eggs all pipped they were cold when I found them but I mussed and fussed around with till I got 20. Then something got in and killed 20 of my biggest chicks so you see I am having a sweet time but a good deal of bitter with it. . . .

Across the county line, Hattie's elder daughter was also having a good deal of bitter with her sweet. Reading the letters Bessie wrote during the early years of her marriage, I hear her trying to talk herself out of the darkness, though she casts a veil over specifics, claiming *it has always been hard for me to put my thoughts on paper and then it would not always be safe anyway. I've no desire to start a conflagration of any sort . . . Well I must close now, as the "blue devils" are closing in again.*

Blue devils. Small eruptions of sadness? Or full-blown depression, like the depression that had plagued Bessie's grandmother Lucippa and perhaps Hattie as well? What did Bessie mean by "blue devils"? Was she borrowing from canto XV of Byron's "Don Juan"?

> Ah! who can tell? Or rather, who can not
> Remember, without telling, passion's errors?
> The drainer of oblivion, even the sot,
> Hath got blue devils for his morning mirrors:

Or had Bessie read the scathing tirade by one of her favorite poets, Lowell, blasting the sentimentalist's enjoyment of his own suffering, the man who walks his "pet sorrow, a blue-devil familiar, that goes with him everywhere, like Paracelsus' black dog"?

But Bessie was no sentimentalist. Even as a child she had leaned toward skepticism, and as the years passed, her skepticism threatened to grow into full-scale fatalism if she did not keep a tight hold on her emotions. As her mother would have phrased it, *Fate had not arranged things* as the young diarist of 1897 had imagined it should. Bessie had not had the chance to study astronomy, algebra, and music composition; had not made it to the Tennessee exposition; had not sung before appreciative audiences in high-ceilinged drawing rooms; had not gone on to high school or teachers' training; had not written books of "flora and fauna." The closest she got to the book world was the year she worked in Hammond. At twenty-four, Bessie had finally married, and Sant was a good man, though to Bessie's mind *O so confining* in his goodness!

And what of Bessie's most tender wish, what I believe to be Bessie's First Great Sorrow? Because she rarely spoke of the event, family accounts stop short of suggesting her emotional landscape during this time. "They were badly shaken, they never tried again," is what I heard growing up. And "Sant said he would never put her through that again." To never try again? What were those early years like for this not-so-young wife whose life was crowded with children—younger siblings, cousins, Sant's nephews and nieces, the children of friends and neighbors? Did Bessie wait expectantly, patiently, for her turn to come? Wait month after month for her body's rhythms, as regular as the moon, to shift? I see her hurrying to the bedroom closet, afraid to look but not being able to stop herself, afraid the stain would appear as it did every month. Month by month, year by year, the world refusing to grant what every woman should be granted. Even her own mother; after forty-four years of service, Hattie's body had still not let her be. Mere weeks after Bessie's wedding, one son still at her knee, Hattie held a squalling infant in her arms, a son that, had Fate arranged things differently, might have been Bessie's.

So, when after years of waiting and watching, the first heaviness finally came, the warmth and the heaviness in breast and belly, I imagine that Bessie was afraid to hope. Night passed to day and back into night and she kept her silence, lying beside her sleeping husband on the starched white sheets spread over the mattress stuffed with the feathers of geese whose carcasses she had plucked herself, as Hattie had taught her. Bessie lay in the dark, touching the almost imperceptible swell beneath her gown. As still as she could be. Not wanting to wake Sant, which was wrong, she knew, for the child was his too.

But she was not ready. This moment was her own, her hand resting on her belly, her mind playing out names: James, for Sant's father. Robert, for hers. Or one of the uncles? She scrolled down the list: Thomas, Benjamin, Lafayette, Harve, Harrison, Jeremiah, William. Or Charles. They could call him Charlie, after Uncle Charlie. Yes, she liked that. Charlie Cosby. Charlie Dale? Charlie Dale Cosby? And if it was a girl? O so many lovely names: Adeline. Aurora. Lady Aurora from "Don Juan." Anna. An alphabet of possibilities. Sant would have his own favorites, of course. And she *would* tell him, she was almost ready. Soon.

And Soon became Now, the glorious Now, Sant beaming, scurrying around her, beaming, and her flat belly rounding and Hattie sewing cotton wrappers with yokes and shirring. Days, Bessie filled jars with peaches and pears and sealed them with paraffin, lining the jars on the sill where the sun could pierce through them—"Like jewels!" Sant would say—and at night when the flutter kicks began, Bessie placed her hand on her belly and then Sant's hand, too, so he could feel what he could now claim as his.

Then one night, late summer perhaps, the windows open and across the white bed the white curtains billowing in, out, in, a stillness that stopped Bessie's breath. Even before her hand went to her belly, she knew. The curtains fluttered in, out, in, and Now became Then, and Then, Gone. Lying beneath the breathing curtains, she watched the weeks stretch out before her, white and silent. Nameless. She should have named her, marked her: Aurora. Anna. Not even a headstone—and why, she wondered now, all these years later, had she not insisted? Stillborn. Still born. Still.

◆

Some things we know only by their rustle. A small bird in a branch above our head, or a tiny animal moving through the woods, would be lost to us if it did not stir something up. Or leave tracks to mark its passing. Some trails, like the ghost scale signs that experienced trackers know to follow, dissipate within hours. The shine on the grass, dulling. The bent grass slowly, imperceptibly, recovering its spring.

Other tracks last a long time: blades of grass packed down, feathers snagged on a fallen limb, gnawed roots, leaf depressions, a broken twig.

There is nothing easy about burying an infant. My mother knows this, as did my grandmother Sylvia. If you are lucky, you get to hold the child one last time, memorizing details: the slight indentation on her chin, the swirl of hair on the nape of his neck. You name the child: Sylvia Sue, William Hayes. You purchase a headstone. Someone says a few words. In a few days you receive a sympathy card, another, a letter, a phone call. They are sorry for your loss, sorry you have to bear this.

To mourn a life lost to stillbirth or miscarriage is to mourn a life that was blown away like seed before it could be planted. You mourn not the child herself—the heart that had barely begun to tick, the blossoming petal of lung. What you mourn is what might have been. Unregistered grief, psychologists call what you are feeling. You know only that it hurts. "Better now than later," a well-meaning friend says, hoping to mitigate the loss. "Before you became attached." "You're young. You can try again," says another. "These things happen for a reason."

◆

October 18, 1910

Mrs. Bessie Cosby
Clarks Hill, Indiana
Dear Mrs. C.
You will be glad to hear we number 512 here, 300 paid up. You must have more confidence in yourself, then you will win others to have confidence, in Mr. L our Pres. Have you heard they are to give Mrs. L. a present on her return from Europe? Each member gives 5 cents.
Love from Your friend. Isabella Hurlburt

Bessie didn't save all her postcards—good heavens, she thought, who needed that clutter? But she saved the ones from Isabella, the first cards Bessie had ever received from Boston. This latest one was splendid, with a photo of the State House, New House of Representatives. The organization that Isabella Hurlburt was referring to was the American Woman's League, which Bessie had joined a few months before, during her June trip to the newly founded University City in St. Louis. She'd traveled alone on the train, mailing postcards to her mother and husband describing the glorious time she was having at the League's first national convention. Over one thousand delegates and guests, mostly suffragettes and Progressives, had gathered from all over the United

States. Some had even brought their husbands. Among other amenities, University City boasted a postal library, the Woman's Magazine Building, Art Academy, an Egyptian-style temple, and the People's University, which provided on-site classes as well as correspondence courses including the piano lessons Bessie would take advantage of once she returned home. There were parades, streetcar tours, dinners, speeches, exhibitions of pottery and ceramics, and a series of floats designed by young students of the Art Academy.

Of course there was a catch. Isn't there always? The American Woman's League founder and president was a man—E. G. Lewis, the publisher of the <u>Woman's Magazine</u> and the <u>Woman's Farm Journal</u>—and his membership plan dictated that each woman pay dues of fifty-two dollars or sell fifty-two dollars' worth of magazine subscriptions. This subscription business was what Bessie was avoiding during the months her Boston friend was writing to her, for Lewis's agenda was not at all what Bessie had imagined when she boarded the train for St. Louis.

Nor had she imagined the first sight that would greet her when she stepped off the train car. A sight she could not escape no matter which building she entered, which convention pamphlet she bought, which dinner she attended, which parade float passed before her eyes: the League's emblem, a visual representation of everything Bessie had failed to accomplish. What she had traveled three hundred miles, alone, to escape. Forget the vote, the workplace, cultural and educational opportunities for all. Even here, in the feminist-infused air of University City, the message was clear. Woman's Mission? A woman cradling a girl-child in one arm and a boy-child in the other.

Bessie's last postcard to her husband announced that she planned to head home early. I hope she decided to stay after all, to witness the final event of the convention—the launching of a huge gas balloon, suggesting the heights to which all women, mothers and others, would soon ascend.

CHAPTER

When my great-grandfather G. E. Sanders applied for membership in the Improved Order of Red Men, Washakee Tribe No. 408, Oxford, Indiana, he had no trouble confirming the eligibility statement included on the application, nor in filling in the first few blanks:

> I am a white citizen of the United States; have been a resident of this reservation for the last six months; I speak the English language; I believe in a Supreme Being; am sound in mind and body.

> Full Name: General Esau Sanders
> Occupation: Storekeeper and Carpenter
> Place of Birth: Greasy Ridge, Ohio

But when he reached the line "Condition of my wife's health is . . . ," I imagine that G. E. paused, lifted his pencil from the page, and considered: Golda Sanders was dead. Gone but not forgotten. Left two children. Bereft.

Pick up pencil. Start again.

Condition of my wife's health is? Deceased.

Fast-forward a few years. The children are gone—Vena married, Arthur heading to teachers' college. Time for G. E. to update his records for the IORR Insurance Fund. Did G. E. puzzle once more over the wife question, wondering if he should count Ada? No divorce yet, though divorce was definitely on the horizon.

Condition of my wife's health is? Vanished. Up and Left after Six Months. Took everything.

Well, not quite everything. Just everything of value, including the Sanders family piano. But not for long, according to my mother's recollection. Growing up, Juanita had heard the Ada stories, passed down from her father. Arthur had never gotten over losing his mother, let alone gaining a stepmother who, to hear Arthur tell it, was out to steal everything she could from G. E. Sanders. Ada should have known better than to mess with Arthur's father. Should have known her scrappy stepson would not abide such goings-on. And had Vena not been busy with a new baby and another on the way, she would have gotten in on the act, too.

As it turned out, Arthur managed the deed on his own, thanks to a neighbor's wagon borrowed for the nighttime retrieval raid at Ada's new place. So now the piano is back at the Sanders home again. Back where it belongs. Ada should have known better. You mess with one Sanders, you mess with all three. G. E. had always kept a close watch over Vena and Arthur, but their mother's early death in 1903 had lashed the small family even more tightly together, and G. E. *took great care,* as his uncle had admonished him, *in forming their character.*

Vena had her own ideas about forming Arthur's character. The young woman who had been *bereft of a mother* at fourteen had learned early on how to mother herself and her little brother. Never mind that Arthur was only two years her junior, he seemed younger to her, more apt to stray. Vena warned her brother to be *very saving* and to finish school so that he would *be fitted for this cruel fated world.* And though Arthur's dukes were always up, Vena knew the whole truth of Arthur. His little-boy past and his present self, the young man who still woke breathless from nightmares, certain that G. E. was dead and that he had been left, as he'd always feared, an orphan. And who was there to comfort him? Vena, the big sister who, as Arthur would remember, "was not afraid of the devil himself."

Although Vena was now a married woman with children, her bond with her brother remained arguably the closest bond she would ever know. *Confide in me what you will,* she writes to Arthur, *for I wanted someone to tell my secrets to once and did I not come to you and now I can sympathize with you.* By the spring of 1910, Arthur had much to confide. One morning, standing in front of the hardware store in Oxford, Indiana, he'd glimpsed a shapely, dark-haired girl who, as local papers would report in their marriage announcement eighteen months later, "by her quiet, genteel bearing has won herself many friends."

Genteel bearing aside, Sylvia Mounts was exceptionally good-looking, and Arthur decided on the spot, "if possible I will marry that girl." My future grandfather was only eighteen. Sylvia was nearly twenty-one, the same age as Vena, and had already known several suitors—Leonard, Ernest, Bob, to name a few. A neighbor named Earl Funk had even proposed marriage. "Wealthy landowners," was how Arthur described the Funks.

And as for my grandfather? "I was so poor it hurt," Arthur used to tell me.

"I thought he was cute," Grandma Sylvia says on the audiotape a friend made a few years before Sylvia died. "Strutting around town like he did. Twisting and strutting. With that curly brown hair. Oh, I liked him."

Within a few weeks, the moonstruck couple was begging Vena and John's buggy and horse for rides in the country. *Sure, you can borrow Old Dobbin if you promise not to spoon,* Vena commands in one letter. Arthur and Sylvia, promising not to spoon? What planet was Vena living on? *Remember the night we went to watch the comet?* Sylvia writes to Arthur, continuing:

> . . . *I didn't see any comet did you? John asked me if I remembered the first time I rode in their buggy. I should say I do. . . . I received a postcard from a girlfriend, a picture of shadows of two people hugging. There were never no shadows on the blind at Willie's because, you know?. . . . If you were only here we'd spoon, spoon, spoon. Not o.k. yet, but am not going to worry. . . . They all made fun of me when I came home said I looked like I had been on a drunk. Ha! I know I looked rather bummy. . . . I want to see you mighty bad, getting anxious to hug and squeeze. Oh! I'm bad! I know. But you love me don't you, SweetHeart?*

My grandparents' postcards fill one shoebox; their love letters, another. The salutations are a novel in themselves, or maybe a haiku novella, revealing the couple's swiftly growing intimacy: *Hello Boy, Kiddo, Dear Friend, Hey Kid* moving rapidly into *Dear Arthur, My dear Arthur, Sweetheart, My own Dear Sweetheart, Honey Boy, My own Honey Boy. My Own Dear Lover.* Sylvia sprinkles her letters with asterisks, virtual kisses ******* that *don't look much like real ones do they? Oh! For some real kiss-*

you going to do Sun? I don't think I will do any-thing, I will think of you for one thing though. Then next Sun. I hope we can be to-gether & (spoon) ≙? I will say "Bye X.Y.Z. X.Y.Z. very much,

Your loving S. H.

One of dozens of love letters from my grandmother Sylvia, aka S. H. ("Sweetheart") to her H. B. ("Honey Boy") in 1910, when my future grandfather Arthur was studying for a teacher's license at Valparaiso College.

es once more. Yours forever. ********* *Oh! It's simply grand to have a lover. And you are my ideal.*

If theirs was a whirlwind courtship, it did not feel so to the young couple, for *I have loved you Dear since before you were born.* By September, Sylvia was boarding at Vena and John's, helping out with their two young children, *talking to your imaginary self,* and plotting ways to join her Honey Boy, who had left to study for a teaching license. Valparaiso was the first tuition-free public university in Indiana, known as "the poor man's Harvard," though women attended as well. *I'm just so glad you are going to school*, Sylvia wrote, *that I could give myself a good shake when I am so foolish as to worry but I want to go too for you will know heap much more than I if I don't.* (The "heap much more" is courtesy of Little Sister Snow, a Japanese character in a book Arthur had given Sylvia.) ******* *These look like spiders but when I go to school I will learn how to make the picture of a kiss, won't I sweetheart?* Admitting that *it is not at all conventional but I can't help it can you?* Sylvia suggests that the two of them room together at Valparaiso, an idea that, to my astonishment, the churchgoing Vena champions in one of her letters. For by this time, Vena is convinced that the sooner Sylvia is with Arthur *the more satisfied and contented and happier she will be.* Besides, Vena does not want to risk losing her new "Sis."

Nov. 23, 1910

Arthur Sanders
Room 21, Stiles Hall
Valparaiso, Indiana

Dear Brother Arthur—
      . . . Lonesome you say, well that don't begin to spell the first part of lonesome for me. Sylvia went home this afternoon and I am almost in tears. . . . John and I certainly think they are hard to find like Sylvia. Baby Kenneth and Beulah think the same. . . . I think it great that I am to have so dandy a sister-in-law I have often wondered what kind I was going to have. . . . had a fine laugh on Sylvia last evening. I was taking a bath and changed my clothes and was running around here in my union suit and she said "You walk just like Arthur does" I ask her if she never noticed it before and she said "Tis the first time I saw you with pants on." I laughed till I cried and so did she. Well she said. I don't care. I always thought he walked so cute. I thanked her for the compliment on myself and then another laugh. See you was the whole thing on program that time. She ask me at whose funny brakes I was going to laugh at while she was gone and I told her she could make some in those letters she was going to write and I would try and keep up spirits . . . I must close suppose this will cost four cents. . . . From your loving sis Vena.

The envelope to this letter is missing, so I can't know if Vena's letter required a four-cent stamp. Most likely it did, as this brief excerpt *does not begin to spell the first part* of Vena's customary long-windedness. The dozens of letters she wrote to her brother, and later to Sylvia and their children, trail on for pages. *Mabe I can rub these lines across this ruff paper & tell you a few news,* she begins, charging forward until the *few news* grows to four pages, five, six, seven, and *was very sorry my last letter was such a buster and you had to pay freight I will try and do better this time.* The fact that *News are scarce as hens teeth* and *my paper is limited and must tell all with few words* does not slow Vena one bit. *I am sending a small newspaper, maybe I had better quit do you think so?. . . . I had to sharpen my pencil again to finish and now my paper is all gone. . . . Love from all I am ever your loving sister Vena.*

Sylvia often wrote to Arthur from Vena and John's home, reporting the household news. In this letter, Vena is playing "Silver Threads Among the Gold" while Sylvia writes, and though Sylvia would love to play those kinds of pieces too *I make sad failures but there is another day to try and do better.* Also, Sylvia has been practicing arithmetic, but *just can't get the hang of it somehow. . . . We studied the dictionary last night but my spelling does'ent prove it by any means does it?* Sylvia likes the poems Arthur clips from newspapers, and she has started clipping some herself. Yes, she has finished reading <u>Little Sister Snow</u>, but no, she hasn't reached the end of <u>John Halifax, Gentleman</u>, only to the place where John has fallen in love with Ursula. *Oh! do you think our ideals will ever be realized?* she asks Arthur, wondering what he thinks of "no testing of either's power over the other, in those perilous small quarrels which may be the removal of passions, but are the death of true love." Sylvia feels the author is right, *that quarrels <u>are</u> the death of true love. But Vena disagrees,* Sylvia writes, *says quarrels only make love stronger.*

Seems this is all news to Sylvia, these rules of engagement in passion and love. Arthur's books serve as a form of marriage tutorial, as do Sylvia's visits to Vena and John's. And though Sylvia spends time with the Cosbys as well, it seems there is nothing her older sister can teach her that she wants to know. After all, Bessie is nearly a decade older than Sylvia; Sant, two decades. Vena is almost exactly Sylvia's age, plus she and John have babies, adding another dimension to Sylvia's marital education. Rocking little Kenneth, snuggling with Beulah, are new experiences for the now-grown Sylvia, and she takes to them naturally. *I believe I've found my talent,* she tells Arthur.

◆

Sylvia's letters to Arthur, tucked neatly into the compact envelopes popular at the time, are bundled with ribbons that I untie slowly, carefully. Did she tie the packets herself? But no, my grandmother was not the recipient; my grandfather saved the letters. A strange complication, that so many of Sylvia's letters survive and so few of Arthur's. Did Sylvia hide them away somewhere, hoping to keep them from prying eyes? *Mother does not want me to go,* she writes from Briarwood, explaining to Vena why she cannot come for another visit. *She gets sad when I am away so long. . . . Oh that old South Wind is moaning around the corners and it makes "my heart bleed for lonely." . . . How I wish I could have the bearenness of heart that Little Sister Snow had. But people who love have much to bear, haven't they?*

Over the next months, Vena and Arthur wage a letter campaign to keep Sylvia in Oxford, apologizing to Hattie for their coaxing Sylvia to stay so long, and practically begging Hattie to let her come again. G. E. joins the campaign as well, concluding that Silvia, as he spells her name, is a fine girl. But Hattie is having none of it. Exasperated, Vena suggests to Arthur *you bring her home in a peanut sack and they wont know where she went and then we will keep her for keeps. I know if she was as small as her sister you could carry her in a peanut shell.*

Sylvia has long ago won her way with her father, for Robert is a pushover when it comes to his younger daughter's wishes. Bessie, too, has given if not her blessing then at least her nod. On a jelly-making day at the Cosbys, when Bessie asked Sylvia when she would be needing some jars of her own and Sylvia answered "most any time," Bessie did not even blink. Hattie is a harder nut to crack. *I haven't told her anything yet, Sweetheart,* Sylvia writes to Arthur. *What Mother says goes you know. I'm awfully anxious to know what that will be.*

Don't hold your breath, Sylvia. Hattie is not about to let you out of her sight, not for a while, anyway. But try to look on the bright side. At least your Sundays will be your own again.

At Vena's, Sylvia had been coaxed into attending church, but once she is back at Briarwood, all bets are off. One Sunday, she doesn't feel like going out in the snow, *but I know my lesson anyway and it's a sad lesson.* Another Sunday, she plays dominoes with Hattie and designs valentines with her little brothers, then carries her Hawkeye box camera down to the creek to take pictures. *I broke a commandment today,* she reports on yet another Sunday. *Stayed home to build a chicken coop. I mashed my thumb and lost my temper, but I have a chicken coop anyway.* Though she often jokes that she is too lazy for her own good, the Sylvia in the letters is always on the move. Hammering chicken coops, rescuing drowning chicks from the rain, digging potatoes with her father, hunting rabbits with Dale, hiking with her little brothers, butchering with Bessie, husking with Sant, butternutting with neighbors, fishing with her uncles, seeding and canning cherries until she dreams of them. In her busyness, she resembles Bessie. But unlike Bessie, Sylvia is aware of her body <u>as</u> body. *I think I weigh more than 117 lbs. now,* she tells Arthur. *They say my face is like the Full Moon. I wonder if it really does look like that! . . . . I went to town Saturday. Everybody I seen remarked about me being so plump. Oh! I'll tell you Sweetheart, you won't know me. . . . I put on my bathing suit and my legs felt about two feet longer and Oh! so much wider.*

Plump and wide, perhaps. Yet judging from the photos she sends to Arthur, photos taken with her Kodak Brownie Hawkeye, Sylvia delights in her womanly body. Here, she stretches languorously on the shore of Ottawa Beach. Here, she holds up a three-foot-long stringer of fish. In another photo, she leans her pretty face close to the face of her pet bulldog, Turk, who is *in disgrace once again, an egg-sucker. And you should see how he goes for the apples. Ha!* Physical energy pulses from Sylvia's photos and letters. When Old Kate breaks free of the barnyard and heads for the corn, it's a race for the wagon until Sylvia can finally get her by the nose and wrestle her to the barn. And Dobbin will know better than to try that turn-around again, for Sylvia *whipped his legs for him. I can manage him,* she tells Arthur, who though away at Valpo still finds opportunities to throw a punch now and then. *Sweetheart, you must not break any more chairs!* she orders. *Get him down on the floor and sit on him! If you can't do that I will send you one of my corn cakes or a biscuit and he will open his mouth very wide!*

My grandmother Sylvia in photos taken with her Hawkeye camera, circa 1910.
She caught the fish herself.

Weeks pass, months. *I can't remember when I have slept well and I
won't either until I can snuggle up close to Honey Boy and be content, contentment means happiness doesn't it?* Ask your mother, Sylvia. Thirty-
two years with the same man, Hattie should know something about the
sweet and bitter of it.

But no, this is your love chapter, Sylvia, spilling out in its own bit-
tersweet time. And just in time, too, as *I will die if I have to wait much
longer for it is getting very serious. U-Kno.*

Yes, we know, Sylvia. By now, everyone knows: *I was eating an apple
one day and told Mama to name it. She did. Guess who? Arthur. And I
counted the seeds, they said He Loves. Bessie wanted to know how soon, I
told her right away. She says, "Shoot! Aren't you going to wait until June,"
I told her no, that that would be too late to start anything and you should
have heard Sant laugh. Ha!*

◆

Dec. 29, 1911

G. E. Sanders
Oxford, Indiana

Mr. Sanders.

I am writing to thank you for your kind letter. And I do hope the new order of things will make you all Happy. But you don't know how hard it is to give my Darling away. She has always been the light of our home and when She is gone it will seem like it was broken up.

I trust it is for the best.

Respectfully,

Mrs. H. Z. Mounts

CHAPTER 9

January 20, 1912
Briarwood Cottage
Dayton, Indiana

Mr. and Mrs. Sanders
Oxford, Indiana
   Hellow there was a funny piece in the paper about you read as follows. I suppose you put on your old gray bonnet with the green ribbon on it and road up to dover for your golden wedding day. Thought you was in clover.
   Ivan Mounts.

Even at age twelve, Ivan could make a joke out of anything, and his big sister's wedding announcement in the local paper was too ripe an opportunity to pass up.

Sanders-Mount

Miss Myrtle Mount, daughter of Mr. and Mrs. Robert Mount, of Stockwell, and Andrew Sanders, of Oxford, were married yesterday at noon at the home of the bride's sister, Mrs. Stanton Cosby. Mr. and Mrs. Sanders are well known young people and have the best wishes of many friends. They will reside near Oxford.

Four lines of copy containing so many errors that any reader familiar with the Mountses would have scratched his head and wondered if indeed the couple's nuptials had been solemnized. Who is this Myrtle? Isn't the younger Mounts daughter named Sylvia? And I might be mistaken but isn't her fellow's name Arthur? And Bessie Cosby's husband is

Santford, right? When did Robert and Hattie move to Stockwell? Have they always spelled their name that way?

The other local towns' newspapers were more careful with their fact checking, though both misspell Sylvia's last name and Sant's first. The rest of the reported details are accurate. The bride has indeed "been much about" Oxford for several years and is well and favorably known, and the groom is indeed employed in the H. E. Bartindale grocery, which position he fills with much credit to himself. The guest list is accurate, too. Other than Bessie and Sant, the only attendants were the sister, brother-in-law, and father of the groom.

"Some more of my good luck," Hattie must have concluded, and who could argue with her? Modest as Hattie's dreams were, the Fates seemed determined to keep her from them. Eight years before, she'd missed Bessie's wedding in La Porte because she was about to give birth to another of Bessie's brothers. And though she had not wanted to give away her darling Sylvia, once Hattie saw that Sylvia's January wedding was inevitable, she began preparing for the festivities:

> *... Daddy shaved and primped up Wensday and I baked a cake and chicken—got up Thursday morning about 4 oclock and it rained and then rained some more and was so icy they could hardly get to the barn so we just set around all day like we were at a furnal felt like it too ... to make it more interesting, Turk howled. It was real livly, you can guess ...*

Hattie finally recovered from the disappointment of missing Sylvia's wedding, and within a year she was making plans for a late March train trip to Oxford, Indiana, where Sylvia and Arthur were now settled in what Hattie called their "little fairy castle." Nothing was going to keep Hattie from welcoming her first grandchild. Even if the town doctor might not allow her to assist with the delivery, she could at least hold the new one and maybe even name him. Or her. Though Hattie had the distinct feeling that her first grandchild would be a boy.

Then, as if fulfilling some Old Testament curse, the rains began. Easter Sunday storms that began in Ohio coursed into Indiana flooding towns and farmlands, knocking out bridges, breaking levees, leaving hundreds of thousands homeless, and claiming nearly four hundred lives. Not far from Briarwood, the Wildcat Creek overflowed its banks, taking the lives of two brothers who were duck hunting nearby. The next day in nearby Lafayette, a Purdue University student drowned in the Wabash River while trying to rescue two men marooned on a collapsed bridge. The river was rising six inches an hour, the city was dark, railroad tracks and houses had been washed away. The Main Street Bridge fell at 3:35 PM and by 10:00 that night, the river had crested at thirty-three feet, the worst flood in Lafayette history. Still the storms continued,

> *... raining a perfect torrent and the water creeping up on both sides and dark. I milked with the water coming in the stable till it was over my feet, we got the cow out and up in the yard, then coaxed the chickens out in frount pried a board in the wood house got two more that could not get out. Tore a hole in the roof of the cave and Dale went in on the ladder and got out some fruit then we drug things up from the barn as long as we could wade and it still kept on coming till it was the highest water that has ever been here it was up to the roof of the water closet with a creek running through the garden and the big creek clear up in the yard on the other side and still raining up over the bridge cannot get to from either side all the grade is gone from this side, I cant tell how awful it did look.*

By the time Hattie made it to Sylvia's little fairy castle in Oxford, her new grandson was several days old. Born April 1, Merrill Mounts Sanders was a fair-skinned, happy baby with curly red hair that would soon earn him the nickname "Red." He took to his grandmother from the start, and though Hattie had planned to stay two weeks or more, after a few days she began fearing what she would find when she returned home. On the train trip back to Lafayette, and later on the cable-controlled ferry the city had erected across the raging Wabash River, Hattie's worries continued. Had things, as usual, gone to pieces? She prepared for the worst.

When Hattie finally arrived at the depot, her neighbor Mrs. Anderson greeted her with a full report. She had stopped by to check on the Mounts men a few days before, and Dale had met her at the door, telling her "some folks think the women have nothing to do but he said he thought there were lots to do." The lots-to-do that Dale accomplished while Hattie was gone included setting a hen, getting kicked over by the cow, taking care of his young brothers, and churning *a nice roll of butter,* as Hattie later crowed in an exuberant letter to Sylvia. *He had everything spic an span . . . cleaned yard and made some garden so I am not complaining.*

Hattie shouldn't have been surprised. She'd taught her boys well, and her eldest son could manage almost any task set before him, including laundry, cooking, mending, and sickroom duties. Still, just shy of his thirtieth birthday, Dale was stalled between childhood and adulthood, tied at both ends like a stuck kite. He felt the stuckness most keenly when he was home at Briarwood. Like his sister Bessie, he took every opportunity to get away, and whenever the two of them could get free, they would head off in Bessie's buggy—to lectures, convocations, Chautauquas, and concerts. Not long ago they'd attended a local commencement, the kind that Bessie had longed for when she left common school. On the program that evening, a male quartet performed "Alice, Where Art Thou?" and "Annie Laurie," after which the school superintendent took the lectern, proclaiming the necessity of being active not passive. He told the story of the dreamer, who slept while all the opportunities of life passed him by. Dale worried that he might be one of those dreamers, that his life would pass before him like pages in a book, or, worse, like pages of the newspapers Pa studied each morning. On rainy days, Dale sometimes picked up the paper from the table where Pa had laid it, glancing at the local social announcements, the busy goings-on of the doers.

Then suddenly Dale was off again, on the train heading north to Wisconsin, where he was a doer not a dreamer. Sure, Aunt Mary was there as always. She and Dale still hunted wildflowers in the woods or along the roadside, and Dale still pressed the dried flowers inside the letters he sent to Bessie and Sylvia. More and more, though, he stayed with the men. Uncle Charlie especially but also Lafayette and Harve and Harrison and the male cousins, and all the young, strong men who crowded around them. In the photos Dale sent home, there they are, a tribe of young men—ice fishing, threshing hay, posing with hunting rifles, pitching teepees, smoking pipes, and stripping off their shirts for impromptu boxing matches, Dale's chest and shoulders thick with muscle he'd earned the hard way, back in Indiana, with his father.

But Pa was old now, Dale thought. Old and stooped. A doer sometimes, because he had to be. But more and more a dreamer. Sitting for hours beneath the rose arbor he'd built for Mother, reading the newspa-

My great-uncle Dale camping in Wisconsin with friends and cousins, circa 1905. Top photo: Dale is second from right in front row. Bottom photo: Dale is on left, boxing.

per or watching his pet crow. Stirring from bed teary-eyed, certain he hears the missing grandbabies crying. Well, Uncle Lafe has grandbabies too, Dale thought. But he sure as heck doesn't cry over them, he's too busy *doing*. Same with Uncle Charlie. Of course, Charlie is a lot younger than Lafe. A lot younger than Aunt Mary, for that matter, though of course Dale never brings this up. He thinks about it, though. He thinks about how odd it is that he and Uncle Charlie are just twelve years apart, closer in age than Dale is to his own brothers. Close as brothers, he and Charlie are. But not brothers. To Dale, that is the *most special* part about it.

The Cosby Ranch
Clark's Hill, Indiana
April 6th, 1913

Mrs. Arthur Sanders
Oxford, Indiana

Dear Sylvia:
    And so you are a "mother." I have been trying to get used to the idea ever since the day you were married but it doesn't seem to come easy. Somehow it sounds very queer. It is also queer that your son should resemble me, I thought those very young people were usually possessed of a florid complexion or does that merely refer to his nose? We are having a most exasperating time here waiting on babies, just as soon as one job is off hands, there is another to attend to with others expected momentarily and so much other work to be done until with it all I'm about tired and sick of everything. Lambs are coming three at a clip and there is a colt this morning and it is a pill.
    As ever, Your sister (and, in case Sylvia has forgotten her only sister's name)
    Bessie D. Cosby

Even when writing to family, Bessie kept her distance, often drafting letters on a slip of paper or a used envelope before mailing off a final copy, which usually began with an apology: *Though I think of you every day I know that is not enough. What you want is evidence isn't it? . . . It is perfectly scandalous that I haven't got word to you sooner but I've been trying to get myself properly composed and collected to write a rational letter but it is worse and worse this morning.* Bessie prized rationality and tried her best to collect herself before composing her letters. But when she was under stress, overly tired, or in the midst of tasks that threatened to overwhelm her, when she was unable *to get my wits together sufficiently,* Bessie was once again her mother's daughter, streaming thoughts together hurriedly, employing the equal opportunity conjunction "and" to link disparate ideas and events with no regard for a scale of mattering, though she occasionally caught herself—*and this sentence consists mostly of ands.* In these rare but highly emotional letters, Bessie is no longer stepping carefully outside herself to place her life's events in context. She is overflowing her banks, letting loose the torrent raging inside and out:

> *. . . such a mess of happenings I don't know where to begin telling . . . the hogs got the blind staggers and three of the best shoats drowned in the creek then I tried to raise two nice little sow pigs at the house and they both died and I didn't get a single chicken out of the incubator and the lambs began coming and the hogs got one and one ewe had an extra nice lamb and no milk for him, we worked with them both, did all we could fed the lamb on the bottle a week and then he died . . . and Mon. morning Sant went to hunt the little spotted cow and found her with a little calf but it was dead . . .*

Reading these letters, I can almost hear her stamping her little foot for emphasis. And I am happy to hear the stamping. When Bessie is stamping, she is most herself—*I pranced around here yesterday holding my jaw and wanting to bite anyone that looked at me but I soon got over it—that is, the toothache part. . . . I'll come over sometime maybe, though I may have to run away, but you know I'm very likely to do that anyway. . . . Sant sold our "Bet" all right so I'll have to walk for sure now. Ha! Don't care!* It's when Bessie's stamping ceases that I begin to worry. When she is silent, when she appears only as a brief mention in the letters of others, I know that the blue devils are closing in again. In the spring of 1913, shortly after she posted the *So you are a mother* letter to Sylvia, Bessie's letters suddenly stop, and her husband picks up the pen to write his first letter ever to his young sister-in-law. On the thin parchment paper, Sant's careful, brown-inked lettering stands out clearly, decorated now and then with a swirly flourish:

> *Hello Sis Sylvia—Excuse haste, I mean MaMa.*
>
> *How is Dad Arthur? Any gray hairs yet . . . Well I know you think we could surely come out, but I have engaged half a dozen since the first of Feb and not one has ever come yet so I just do every inch I am worth. Worked all day and half the night with our little colt and then lost it just the same. But if Bessie only felt real well I would be awful glad. She is practicing her music while I write. I love to hear her for I think she gets more enjoyment out of it than anything she has.*
>
> *I hear you are in the Bull business. I thought you would be a Bull Moose yet. Well if you cant make out this scribbling, just come over and I will show you a Mooser can read if he can't write. Now Sylvia be careful and don't get up too soon. Take good care of yourself and the little one and tell Arthur he must let his beard grow so people can tell which is the boy when he takes him uptown.*
>
> *GoodNight To All, Sant*
>
> *P.S. Bessie is pounding the piano, makes one feel like living any way.*

If Bessie only felt well? Yet she is practicing her music while Sant writes. Is she really too busy to visit her only sister and her newborn nephew, or has Sylvia's motherhood thrown Bessie into another bout with the blue devils? *Fate will buffet you about if you don't fight back,* she often writes. So maybe that's exactly what Bessie is doing, fighting back with one hand while pounding out a new plan with the other. Almonds, avocados, groves of lemon and lime trees, imagine! If all goes well, in a few years the three-acre plot in California will be theirs, thanks to the newly formed American Woman's Republic. Built on the ruins of the defunct American Woman's League, the Republic is, finally, an organization that Bessie can fully support. Last year a woman was sworn in as Republic president, and more than four hundred members signed the ratified Declaration of Equal Rights. Members are also joining the Woman's Peace Army, some even planning to attend the Peace Conference in Budapest. Budapest!

Of course such a trip is out of the question for Bessie, but she has done what she can, and now Sant is not only an official member of Roosevelt's Progressive Party but also onboard the Republic's Atascadero plan. Three acres isn't much, especially in comparison to the farm Bessie and Sant are working every inch they are worth to keep alive. But these three acres are in California, *The Land of Sunshine.* And who wouldn't want to be part of an agrarian utopia? Which is exactly what the Atascadero Colony will become, according to the "Option Fund Agreement" Bessie signed and mailed off just last week.

If the agreement's clause describing "an exclusive colony of desirable persons of the white or Caucasian race" registered with either of the Cosbys, no mention was made in Bessie's letters. Who, in Bessie's view, wouldn't want to be considered desirable? And if California was anything like Indiana, it went without saying that their neighbors would be of the Caucasian race. In 1913, Indiana was strikingly homogeneous not only racially but also in terms of religion and culture. Despite rapid population growth in cities like Gary, Terre Haute, Fort Wayne, Hammond, and especially Indianapolis, the percentage of Indiana blacks, like the percentage of Jews, Catholics, and immigrants, remained extremely small, especially in small towns and rural areas.

A decade will pass before the KKK arrives full force in Indiana, attracted in part by the Interurban, a sophisticated rail system linking Indianapolis to dozens of small towns within a sixty-mile radius. The same Interurban Bessie and her family used, the Interurban Arthur rode while courting Sylvia. By the mid-1920s, ordinary Hoosiers will be sharing Interurban cars with Klan recruiters looking to pull scores of like-minded men and women into their ranks, their efforts culminating in, among other events, a celebration on Mother's Day 1925 where Klan leaders call upon all men to honor our "glorious mothers as the only reliable source of counsel, sympathy, and courage in a man's life."

Like many phrases in the KKK lexicon, "glorious mother" will be lifted from popular culture in an attempt to appeal to ordinary citizens. Among my grandparents' possessions is an illustrated book titled The Glorious Mother, which Arthur presented to Hattie the year he married Sylvia. A perfect gift from one motherless child to another. "Each of us have now, or hold in loving remembrance, a glorious Mother," the preface begins, followed by poem after poem with titles like "Rock Me to

(Left) Cover of <u>Glorious Mother</u>, a gift from my grandfather Arthur to his new mother-in-law, Hattie, 1912. (Center) Deed to Atascadero Colony property, issued to Great-aunt Bessie and her husband. (Right) My grandmother Sylvia with her firstborn son, Merrill, 1913.

Sleep," "A Man's Mother," and "The Song of the Old Mother." Eighteen months later, in May 1914, President Woodrow Wilson signed a declaration for the nation's first official Mother's Day, and soon thousands of Americans were cranking up their newly purchased Victrolas to hear a tinny piano accompany 1915's most popular song, whose lyrics spelled out the word *m-o-t-h-e-r*.

◆

Tis a pity one has to be cooped up, Bessie writes to her sister. *But such is life, our lives anyway, and if we were not such weak creatures we wouldn't be mere victims of circumstance.* In the decade of the glorious mother, the three cooped-up Mounts women receive dozens of postcards and letters from friends, relatives, and neighbors, some of whom have pulled up stakes entirely. The Titsworths have moved to Albuquerque, boasting to Sant that Norman is *tanned now and looks like his own self again.* Mr. and Mrs. Ernest Carte write from Canada, where they now own *160 acres of nice land,* and a friend residing in Black Hills, South Dakota, reports he now has *100 akers of wheet, not a tree on this farm.* Arthur's aunt writes from Colorado and his friend Lansing from Bolivia, where he has found a job surveying, and though Lansing writes from *this forsaken country,* his descriptions of the mountains, plains, and brilliant sunsets would tempt even the most committed homebody. Vacationing friends post photo cards from the White House, from "Peaceful Valley" in Oklahoma, and from Long Beach, California, where Bessie's neighbor Mrs. Nantz is now *surf bathing,* now dashing off a note from "A California Bungalow" in Los Angeles, too near the Atascadero dreamscape to make her postcards welcome to the envious, exhausted Bessie.

May 24, 1915

Dear Sylvia

. . . I have been wanting to write for a long time and now it must be only to tell you that Sant's brother is dying and his father is likely to go anytime. It is a sad affair indeed. Riley has spinal meningitis, it is uncertain how long he will live but it surely can't be long and if he

goes Mr. Cosby surely will too. And here it is Mon. noon and not a soul
to help do one thing. There is no use saying there is, for there is no
dependence to be found in anyone. Well you will think I'm half crazy
from the sound of this and I suppose I am.
    With love Bessie Cosby

                                                        May 28, 1915
    My Dear Sylvia: Just a note to let you know that Riley died Wed.
morning at one o'clock. He is to be buried today at two.
    With love Bessie

                                                    November 9, 1915
    Sant's father has been in a terrible condition for some time now. .
. . We thought he was dying Wednesday morning, and we also thought
his mind was gone. It is all so strange and horrible I've gotten so I see
things myself.
    Your loving Sis

Sant's father hung on for a few more months, and according to Hattie, *it keeps Sant on the hump to do his work and be up there too. He looks*
so hollow eyed and tired. Bessie, too, is *worn to a frazzle,* for Mr. Cosby
relies on his daughter-in-law's help, claiming *none of the rest can do anything for him like Bessie can.* When Bessie can grab a minute, she scribbles to her sister *just a line to let you know something of the state of affairs*
with us and to ask, if you please, how they are with you for I don't know
any more about my people than if they were on the other side of the earth.

My people. Though Bessie lived close to Sant's family, spent holidays
with them, nursed them through illnesses and sat with them as they
died, she never considered the Cosbys her people. *My people* were the
Mountses and Meads—her parents, siblings, and the cousins, aunts,
and uncles in Hammond, Switzerland County, and Wisconsin. She
missed them all, especially Uncle Charlie and his growing family. Charlie's daughter Charlotte, the baby cousin in the teenage Bessie's diary,
was now a young woman, and she'd recently written from Wisconsin
to report that their family was *still on earth.* Brothers John and Stanley
were taller even than she was; Mettie, age thirteen, was almost as tall
but not, as Charlotte spelled it, *quiet as skinny.* Goodness, the persnicke-

ty Bessie must have thought, Charlotte had best get her spelling straight if she plans on heading west to become a teacher. She certainly looked like a teacher, standing there so stern and straight in the photograph Uncle Charlie had sent a few months earlier.

And a fine photograph it is, Bessie thought. What a striking family, Mary and Charlie and the four children—though they aren't children any longer, are they? Look how tall John and Stanley are, standing behind their parents and the young Mettie, who, Bessie noticed, was filling out to be bosomy and plump, so like Sylvia at that age. Strange, how features move about in families, landing here in one nephew, there in another niece. Aunt Mary's hands, crossed gracefully on her satiny dress, are elegantly delicate, with their long, narrow fingers. Mounts hands, like Pa's. And that black, shiny hair swirled carefully around her head. Bessie had always thought Mary the loveliest of Pa's sisters, but she is lovelier than ever in this photo. The promise of a smile bends her lips slightly upwards. She appears serene, calm, as if nothing could ever harm her.

Uncle Charlie is not exactly smiling, but his is as pleasant a countenance as Bessie can ever recall seeing on his face. In the photo, Charlie cocks his head slightly to the left, a pose his sister Hattie often adopts. Even a stranger would judge Charlie to be Hattie's brother. They have the same large, protruding ears, the same hooded eyes and cautious expression inherited from their mother Lucippa. But here is where it becomes clear that Charlie and Hattie had two different fathers. While Hattie has always been short and stout, and is growing shorter and stouter each year, Charlie is tall and lean—mostly leg, as Bessie remembers. She also remembers his large hands, and now, studying his family photograph, she is amazed at how long his fingers are, longer even than Mary's. They don't look like a farmer's hands at all. "Piano fingers," Bessie concludes. Yes, that's it. Uncle Charlie has piano fingers, like me. Why have I never noticed it before?

When Hattie received the photograph posted from Wisconsin, she probably placed it in a prominent location—on her sewing table near the indoor flower boxes or on the cabinet beside the kitchen window

Family of Charlie and Mary, connected to my family on both the Mead and Mounts sides: Charlie was my great-grandmother Hattie's half brother. His wife, Mary, was my great-grandfather Robert's sister. Their children were (back row, left to right) John, Charlotte, Stanley, and (front, center) Mettie Maud. Circa 1918.

where visiting neighbors could comment on the handsome family. "And how are Charlie's doing?" they would ask. Hattie knew only what she read in Mary's letters, as it had been months since she'd seen her brother's family. Hattie's doomed luck with livestock and gardens, compounded by money and health troubles, now keep her housebound most of the time. When a cousin invites her to Rising Sun, Hattie must decline, for *everything I have tried this summer has failed so I can't afford to go.* On the rare occasions when she can get away, *like it always is when I leave, things goes to pieces.* Returning from a two-day visit to Bessie's,

> *. . . found our Frisky dog dead and Babe rolling tumbling with high fever . . . I never set down when I came, just went to work to get him easy. As Byron used to say it just seems like I don't get one thing strait till something else happens whether you call it bad luck or another cooling off, anyway my little cow that I worked and sweated hard for came near dying and the little calf did die so we won't have no little Jersy to pet. Bessie's cow lost her calf too and the old sow ate two of her dollar hens and some of her pullets. Sunday too. This year I begin to feel a good deal like the Darkey when the lightning struck Just let it strike I am about calloused over anyhow . . .*

     . . . But one ought to be glad it is no worse. Worse, to Hattie, was what was happening to friends and neighbors—Holliday's barn burning down, their Canadian friend Ernest Carte struck by lightning and killed, the Packard's baby girl dying. And now Rhea Funk. Such a lovely girl, Sylvia's age, and gone so quickly. *Will be buried Sunday. Funeral at ten. It is a sad corner.* And one need only open the paper to know the terrible things the world is suffering through. All those babies drowned with their mothers, and some of them Americans, too. Would the Germans stop at nothing? Hattie hated to think this way, as some of her neighbors were Germans. But the Germans in Germany must be different, she figured. Who would sink a ship with mothers and babies on it? Wilson had best think of a plan, something short of war for that is the last thing this country needs.

     And if Aunt Phebe didn't start sending some good news for a change, Hattie might just ask her to quit sending any at all, as Hattie didn't know just how much more she could take.

Rising Sun Recorder, Friday 19 November 1915
DAN MEAD SHOT AND KILLED

Dan Mead was shot and instantly killed by Sid Sutton at Jasper, Alabama at 1 o'clock Sunday morning, Nov. 7. Mead was a boarder at Sutton's. For some time someone had been catching Sutton's chickens. Hearing a noise, Mead had gotten up and was on his way to the henhouse when Sutton appeared on the scene and seeing something moving at the top of the fence, he shot and the object fell with a heavy thud. Upon reaching it, Sutton discovered that he had shot his boarder.

Dan Mead. One of the little boys Hattie had lived with in her grandfather's home after her mother died, a boy Hattie had thought of as her brother. What was Dan doing at a boarding house in Alabama? He had a wife back home. Whatever the confusing circumstances surrounding Dan's death—"something moving at the top of the fence," "an object" falling "with a heavy thud"—by the time the news reached Hattie, Dan Mead had been dead twelve days. Too late for Hattie to wring her hands, to wonder. Or to make plans to travel south to help lay him to rest.

October 22, 1915

Dear Sister,

So you are about to start a "Kewpie" headquarters, better be careful, the inventor of the originals has them copyrighted. Sylvia my dear sympathy won't do you any good. You know if heartache would help in the very least, your case would be different this moment. I can only say as Uncle Mike Higgins used to say, "It's bad but it might be worse." Kiss Baby Merrill 'steen times on the back of his neck for his "Aunt-Bet" and tell him to write me some more pictures.

With love, Bessie D. Cosby

Whatever transpired to prompt Bessie to offer sympathy to her pregnant sister will remain their secret. In her little fairy castle in Oxford, Sylvia was one month shy of her due date, and *if we read between the lines there's more there anyway,* as she often wrote, it seems clear that the glorious mother was not feeling too glorious. If Hattie was aware of Sylvia's trouble, she gives no indication in her letters. And despite her fears that things will as usual *falls to pieces,* Hattie boards the train to Oxford to make herself of use. According to Arthur, the town doctor plans to give Sylvia a new drug. A German invented it, but Hattie can't remember the German name for it—the word is long and strange looking. Here in America, they call it "twilight sleep." The way Hattie understands it, the mother just floats away in her mind, like she is on a cloud. In one of the articles Hattie had read, a woman reported that when she woke up, a baby was lying beside her on a pillow and the nurses told her she had had it. But the woman didn't remember anything. She said that maybe the nurses were right, but that she couldn't prove it in a courtroom.

Painless childbirth? Hattie, mother of five, a midwife who has assisted dozens of women, is wary. To fall asleep and wake with no memory of what happened? Could that be good for the mother, for the baby? To Hattie, anything that seems too good to be true is probably just that, and she worries about what she will find. If anything happened to her sweet Sylvia, they would just have to dig the grave a little deeper and put Hattie in too.

January 7, 1916

Dear Sylvia:

   That day after you went away we were at dinner all at once Pa got up and hurried in the room then turned and came back. Thought he heard the baby and Bessie came near doing the same thing. I suppose Baby Leland is growing so fast he will be big old sassy and ugly when I get to see him again. How is Merrill is he getting to be a little man? Well take care of yourself and teach them the best you can. I will have to close and start dinner for those men will come in cold and hungry as hounds.

   As ever, Mother.

Those men. Cold and hungry as hounds. Since the day she married, Hattie's life had been filled with men and boys. The Mounts brothers in Switzerland County. The Mead uncles and Wisconsin nephews. And

My great-uncle Ivan, the tall boy in the back row, pictured with his school class in Oxford, Indiana, 1917, one year before he ran away to join the army at age 16.

now two grandsons—Leland had arrived fine, Fates be praised. Two grandsons who, if history held any lessons, would in time give Sylvia a run for her money. Goodness knows Hattie's sons still tie her in knots now and then, and with her daughters married and gone, she is the only female left at home to corral *those men:*

Dale, at thirty-two, mostly stays put at Briarwood, though he still lights out for Wisconsin with no provocation.

Wheezy with allergies and accident prone, twelve-year-old Babe sticks close to his mother, still her babe in many ways.

But fifteen-year-old Ivan Otto "Skinny" Mounts is no babe, and he takes every opportunity to remind his mother of this fact. Quick to make a joke, to pepper his language for effect, to bolt out the door with his rifle, Ivan has plans all right, none of which includes school. In photos, he is the black-haired boy in the back row, scowling. He wants to be anywhere but here. But Ivan is bright, he shows promise, and everyone—Hattie, Robert, Sylvia, Arthur, Bessie, Sant, Dale, and assorted friends and neighbors—has hopes for him. He will be the first Mounts child to go on to high school. To graduate. No matter the cost or sacrifice. Hattie hates the thought of putting him on that train to Sylvia and Arthur's, she'll miss her boy so. But if that's what it takes, so be it.

Ivan Mounts
c/o Arthur Sanders
Oxford, Indiana

Well old sweetheart I was glad to get your card and hear you got through allright. now you must just try your best and see how well you can do Babe just worry's and is trying to save up to buy Skinny something, you must do good when you have got a brother like that. I know it is uphill but keep trying. . . . Well it is snowing now, I will have to make a coat for the pig I guess . . . Pa just came in with a star Skunk. . . . We think about you every day and wonder what you are doing by with love Mommy

Dear Ivan,

. . . We have quite a variety of game today. Pa caught a carp and shot a hawk. Dale shot three squirrels and caught a possum. . . . Mrs. Mills stopped last week and asked about you said she was glad you were going to school in Oxford. Grandma Cosby and Mrs. Emma Cosby too that afternoon you went away. They were all glad to hear you were going on to school so you must live up to their good wishes and be worthy. Write to Mother. By with love

Dear Ivan,

Was glad you had a good time with those boys; just so they don't lead you into trouble. Pa and Harry went hunting and got 17 Squirrels. Babe poor boy had another bad accident today, he went up to the patch at Funks this morning with Pa and as he was climbing over the gate he caught his leg on a nail and tore a hole about 3 inches long and an inch or more deep right below his groin in his left leg. They done it up and Earl brought him home in the machine. . . . You must be careful and not get Sick. And write and tell me how you are doing. Don't be like so many of them, try and keep up with your class.
As ever, Mother.

In the Oxford school photo, Ivan again stands in the back row, markedly taller than he'd been the year before. Still scowling. *Teach them the best you can.* But sometimes, the harder you push the more they push back. So now, no school for Ivan? He's a man or so he thinks? *But that is the way it goes,* Hattie writes to Sylvia. *The harder they can hurt ones feelings the better they like it.* Well, at least my boy isn't twenty-one, she thinks. Won't have to march to town to sign his name on the dotted line. And Dale, thank heavens, is too old for conscription. Selective Service Act: They named that one right. Pass an act. Then select the ones who will die for, what? To keep the world safe for democracy? Well, at least they can't select my boys.

Had Hattie known what Ivan was planning, she would have grabbed him by the collar, sat him down in the kitchen, turned the oil lamp so it spilled its light across the table, and unfolded the letter Arthur had showed her. The birthday letter G. E. Sanders had received from *his* father not long before. A firsthand history lesson even the bullheaded Ivan would know to take to heart.

Mr. General Esau Sanders
Oxford, Indiana

Dear Son,

I was just thinking over my past life and It came to my mind that by some false report the Rebels was on their way to Washington D.C. and Our Regiment was ordered on a force march to intersect them before they got there, it was on Sunday and the first day of August 1864 just 52 years to day and as I have not got any Birthday Card I just thought write you a few lines to let you know about it and your Mother had Some one to write to me and Wanted me to Send her a name for you and I got the letter while I was laying in line of Battle and it was on Sunday on the 8th day of August 1864. But we had not marched many miles before our Boys began to fall in the Ranks by SunStroke and there was 120 of the Boys SunStroke that day and there was only Seven of our Regiment went in to camp Excep the three Regimental Commanders that was on Horse Back I was One of the Seven that made the march but we could not have made much of a fight with the Jonnies. Must close hopeing you may See many happy returns of this anniversary So long.
Zachariah Pendleton Sanders

"Read it again," Hattie would have demanded. "Out loud, Ivan, so we can all hear it. And now let me tell you the rest of Zachariah's story. He had brothers, just like you. They grew up together, just like you and Babe. One brother was a lot older, like Dale is to you. William, his name was. *Was.* Because never mind that he had a wife and five children, nothing would do but that he sign himself up, leave Ohio, and die somewhere in Kentucky, too far for any of his people to find him. Another of Zachariah's brothers, his name was Stephen, had followed his big brother out of Ohio. Signed up, just like he'd seen William do. And fifteen days after William died—are you listening, Ivan?—fifteen days later, Stephen died too, somewhere in Tennessee. Their people back in Ohio could not contain their grief but of course nothing would do but that Zachariah sign up too. Lucky for him the worst of it was sunstroke, though sunstroke, need I remind you Ivan, is no picnic either. Had Zachariah not made it, had he died like his brothers, there would be no G. E. Sanders, there would be no Arthur, there would no little Merrill or Baby Leland coming here to visit. Do you see how Fate arranges things? Now you think hard and long about your plan, little man. Think hard and long."

But of course Hattie had no idea what Ivan was cooking up, he and the Lecklitner boys. He watched and waited, hoping for a break. When Aunt Phebe's letter came, asking Hattie to please come down to Switzerland County, as Phebe needed her, Ivan knew that his mother could not say no to her aunt. And with Mother out of the picture, it was just a matter of time.

Cosby Ranch
Clarks Hill, Indiana
Dec. 12, 1917

Mrs. Arthur Sanders
Oxford, Indiana

Dear Sylvia:

It's no wonder you feel badly, so do we all. I felt sure you would learn about Ivan through the paper, that's the way I got the news. Mother came home Sat. night, came wading down from the depot at

half-past six in that bitter cold and snow carrying two heavy suitcases, but all enthusiasm over her visit and anxious to know how
everything was going at home and of course it was up to me, the least
capable of all, to tell her, but I did it and she said the last thing she
said to Daddy was "Pa take care of the boys, don't let anything happen to the boys while I'm gone." No wonder Pa had those awful nervous chills.

    With love,
    Aunt Bessie

CHAPTER  11

Briarwood Cottage
January 11, 1918

Mrs. A. H. Sanders
Oxford, Indiana

>*. . . Yes Sylvia the war certainly is straitning some of the boys out,*
>*those that they keep sending back in their boxes any way, only those*
>*that get broke and scattered to bad. I tell you they are getting thinned*
>*out around here with boys gone and hands all gone. Charley Mc.*
>*hand is gone, Funks & Joe Yundts. Nobody in where Redman lived . . .*
>*Ivan thinks they are to be moved right away but don't know where so*
>*don't know when I will hear from him . . .*

Hattie rarely scolded her darling Sylvia, but it is hard to miss her chiding response when Sylvia suggested that the war might be just the thing for straightening out boys like Ivan. A Civil War baby, Hattie had grown up hearing stories of her soldier uncles, learning early on what war can do to families. Her daughters had never felt war's consequences firsthand. What they knew was what they had heard—that "our boys" were fighting the Kaiser to keep the American way of life possible and the women at home could help out. While they waited for word from their soldier brother, Sylvia and Bessie and other Red Cross Ladies rolled gauze bandages, stitched Service flags, and exchanged newspaper clippings like "B-r-r-r. Knit a sweater to keep Sammy warm." A task which they promptly accomplished. They also knitted piles of wool socks, hoping to hear from their own "Sammy" soon so that they could send him some, wherever he was.

To Hattie, it seemed much longer than a month since her son had left, following the lead of older neighbors and friends. Some had enlisted mere months after Wilson signed the resolution. Elmer Rothenberger, for one, and Ada Clendenning's boy, who was just eighteen when he signed on. Hattie had thought the Clendenning boy far too young—his parents should have talked him out of joining. But of course there is no talking to grown boys. Or half-grown ones, for that matter. Sixteen years old, Ivan was. Lied about his age, of course, but a lie didn't change the facts. Sixteen. And barely a whisker on his chin. Well, Hattie thought, the harder they can break your heart the happier they are.

The new year of 1918 blew in hard and bitter—*winter in earnest,* Bessie wrote—and with Ivan gone to who knows where and Dale packed off again to Wisconsin, the aging Hattie and Robert had only thirteen-year-old Babe left to help out at Briarwood. Babe, the red-faced, smiling boy who by all accounts was allergic to the world. According to Hattie, *he has infection in his lame ear,* or *he has the snorts pretty bad as usual, have just been doping and putting him to bed and school starting tomorrow.* Not that Babe's attendance would have mattered much that winter, as the neighborhood school was closed first for an outbreak of whooping cough and then scarlet fever, *then the pipes bursted,* Hattie wrote to Sylvia, *then after that they had to stop for coal. Now they are shut up and all vaccinated for smallpox. . . . Pa has carried fodder on his back from way down in Philps field for 4 weeks and hauled wood on the handsled. Well, I am going to have dried rabbit for dinner so we will have to get it on.*

The pared-down family survives the winter mostly on "sugar-lasses" and dried rabbit, though Robert traps a possum now and then. They finally butcher one of the pigs, hoping to *make chewing and greesing for a while.* Hattie has been intending to send her daughters some of the treasures Aunt Phebe gave her, the dishes and linens she'd brought from Switzerland County the day she learned that Ivan had enlisted, but it's hard to keep her mind fixed on tasks, Hattie says, and nights *get pretty long some times. And getting longer.*

Weeks pass without a visit from Bessie and Sant, who are snowbound like everyone else. When the roads are finally shoveled and the mail can get through, Bessie posts a letter to her sister, wondering if Arthur has been exempted from the draft and if they've been able to get any fuel, and inquiring about Sylvia's sick babies—the whooping cough, no doubt, and too bad you don't have some of Mother's blackberry tod-dy. *We've been trying to go over home,* Bessie writes. *But everytime, January makes another assault.* Which just complicates Bessie's plans for the big sale they are arranging for Sant's mother. Now that her husband and older son are dead, Mrs. Cosby is closing down the family farm and sell-ing off her livestock. Does Sylvia want first grab at Mrs. Cosby's cow? Ac-cording to Sant, she's a daughter of the old cow and doesn't give much milk but like the old cow's, it is mostly butter. But the cow is wild and afraid of strangers, so Bessie doesn't know how in the world to get her to Sylvia. As for Bessie and Sant, they have only Belinda left: *She is spill-ing out lots of milk, it is such a pity . . . she lost her calf or rather we lost it, We left her out and the calf got down in the ditch and chilled to death. The biggest calf he ever saw Sant says.*

When Bessie and Sylvia finally hear from Ivan, first from Ken-tucky and then from steamy San Antonio, he thanks his sisters for the packages of hand-knit socks but *we haven't much use for heavy socks down here. I've got 7 pair.* In his characteristic "liars, thieves, sons-a-bitches" style, Ivan salts his letters with damns and hells. It's always a devil of a day, hot as hell, he's broke flat and what the hell's the matter with the girls back home, he wants some of them to *write him some dope.* He did hear from Cousin Charlotte in Wisconsin and *guess she has talked herself sick talking at patriotic speeches and dope like that. I guess she's certainly doing her bit.* Ivan's mother and sisters can barely keep track of his whereabouts; by April, Bessie has concluded that their soldier lad must surely be on foreign soil as so many of the local boys are. *Zena had a letter from her Hal over in France today,* Hattie reports, *and David is in Hospital again.* If this keeps up, *they will have them all after awhile.*

Soon, though, Ivan's letters catch up to his family—he's about to be shipped off to Long Island. But for now he's digging stumps in Morrison, Virginia, and on his day off he and his buddies camp along the James River making beds out of pine boughs. *Gee it was fine but damn it to hell it's been raining two days now* and his mess kit didn't pass inspection so no July 4 holiday for Ivan. He misses everyone but there's no chance to come home *until the damned Kaiser is dead. Tell little Merrill that Ivan is going after them old Germans allright.*

Back home, Hattie allows the holiday to pass unobserved. Long Island is too close to New York City for her comfort. Too close to the ports where they ship all those boys off. *What a glorious 4th it would be,* she writes to Sylvia, *if we could have the war ended. It seems like a mockery to talk about celebrating.* Throughout the long summer, Hattie continues her battles with the weasels and hawks, making trips to the sand bunk to bury the dead chicks. In September, when the draft age is raised to forty-five, Dale comes home from Wisconsin, and Hattie accompanies him to town to file his papers.

Meanwhile, the whole family is awaiting news about Arthur, who by all rights should be exempted, what with Sylvia and two babies to support. For now, he is drilling with the Home Guard in Oxford, anxiously awaiting the first "aeroplanes" that will be flying over from the air base in Rantoul, Illinois. *I was fully expecting,* my grandfather Arthur will write many years later, poking fun at his early ignorance, *that their wings would be in motion. That's the truth.* Bessie, too, was an eager sky watcher, complaining one day that there was *not even a plane to break the monotony.*

If Ivan's enlistment had broken Hattie's heart, by October 1918 she was counting herself lucky. Though *every one has their full measure of trouble* and *the Flu has about everything,* her loved ones had escaped the worst. Sylvia had had a bad scare, but not one family member was among the estimated ten thousand Hoosiers who would eventually die from the epidemic of Spanish Influenza that had begun in earnest a month earlier. And surveying the carnage of the past year's battles, Hattie had to admit that Fate could have arranged things a lot worse. To date, Ivan had not come home in a box. Nor had he been *broke too bad,* his parts scattered in some field in France. He was still here in the states, as far as she knew.

She'd saved the obituaries of the Clendenning and Rothenberger boys. She still thought of them as boys, though Elmer Rothenberger had had a wife. The Clendenning boy, though, was only nineteen. Hattie studied the French words on the obituaries, trying to sound them out: Aisne, Champagne, Châtillon-sur-Seine, St. Thibault. Those boys probably couldn't even pronounce the names of the battles they'd fought in, she thought, nor the cemeteries where they were buried. Buried among strangers, their families across the ocean holding tight to their grief and nowhere to put it.

Dec. 5, 1918

Dear Sylvia.
. . . I could have cried to think we always have to have such a time. One of my turkeys died that night too it shurly was a great day. pa is mending his socks and I am ironing. Have not heard from Ivan yet, just have to hope and wait I suppose.
Am as ever Mother.

Hope and wait. All that was left to do. Everywhere around her, people were celebrating the Armistice, but "am as ever" Hattie would not lift a flag or bake a cake until her boy was home. She'd saved all the newspapers, had read them so many times she'd memorized the headlines. The overseas boys were home already, so why, if Ivan was still here in the states, had he not written? Surely he was on his way home. Surely there would be a letter from him soon. Was he broke and scattered somewhere? Or sick to dying, like so many others? She'd seen the Red Cross pictures, all those boys on stretchers, their mouths covered in gauze as if that would keep the flu out. Hattie's heart seized up every time a car passed on the road, certain that it would stop to deliver a telegram with their name on it, though neighbors told her not to worry, only officers' families got that kind of treatment, the rest of them just got a letter. If that. A regular letter, no urgency demanded. Some letters didn't even arrive until after the funerals. That's what she'd heard.

So I imagine that when Hattie lifted the mailbox lid and saw the official army envelope, her knees gave out beneath her and she had to grab the post to keep from falling. Did she call out for Robert? Tear open the envelope? How long before her eyes could focus on the letter—"Dear Sir" it began, with Ivan's name nowhere to be found. Nor Robert's. Nor hers. As if they had no say, as if they were not the parents of this boy the army could not even bother to name. "Your Soldier" they called him. "Your Soldier." And you "an important member of that great Army of Encouragement and Enthusiasm which helped to make him . . ."

But wait. Wait a minute, Hattie. Take a breath. Wipe your eyes, *wipe off the weeps.* Your Soldier is coming home, "that spot in every man's heart no other place can fill." Or so says the commanding officer who signed the letter, boasting how proud he is of Your Soldier who has done his duty well. The army is returning him to you a better man, he says, with many fine qualities of body and mind which he has acquired in the military service, though his return will bring new problems for both of you to solve. "And in your hands and his, rests the future of our country."

Once she had recovered herself and could take the full measure of the letter in her hands—the arthritic, age-spotted hands that held the future of our country—Hattie must have smiled, then quickly covered her mouth as was her habit even when no one was looking, an attempt to hide her nearly toothless grin. She might even have laughed: no surprise that it took the whole army to make Ivan into a man, they surely had their work cut out for them. But no matter, he's coming back, her prodigal boy, and if they couldn't kill the fatted calf, they would butcher up something, or Robert would go up the woods for some four-legged fish and she would bake bread and rob the cellar of the last quince preserves and they would celebrate at Bessie's with all of Bessie's special things, the pickle dishes and sherbet goblets and all those fancy plates she'd ordered from Chicago. Was there time to get word to Charlie's? Surely they wouldn't want to miss the festivities, especially so near Christmas. *If* Mary could make the journey, what with her asthma acting up again. But Dale was still there in Wisconsin, so maybe he could help out with Mary and with the driving—he knew how to operate a Machine. And when they all got here, Hattie would trundle Mary and Babe into the same bed and they could wheeze in tandem until Dale could get them settled easy. *Come if you can,* Hattie will write. *There wont be many turkey dinners around but I thought would put the big pot in the little one and have a pot rost ... some kind of a rost if it is only to rost one another.*

Although no letter records the family feast celebrating Ivan's return, a few photos survive. In one, Ivan stands in full uniform, his arms clasped behind his back, a solemn expression in his eyes, those signature Mounts eyes with their downturned edges. His cap is cocked slightly to the right, and above his ears what is left of his thick black hair has been buzzed to military perfection. Despite his family nickname—"Skinny"—Ivan now appears fleshy enough to strain the fourth and fifth buttons on the regulation jacket. His form makes the hint of a shadow against the house.

But who is the soldier in the other photo? Wearing an identical uniform and striking an identical pose, though this soldier is smiling. No, wait, this is no soldier, this is a girl, a woman, her hair tucked under the army cap so that only a few tendrils peek out. Sylvia cuts a fine figure; Ivan's uniform might have been tailored expressly for her. Even her full breasts don't strain the buttons, and the blowsy chaps provide ample space for her hips. The younger of her sons has just turned two, and her hourglass figure has returned.

She'll lose that figure again before two more years have passed, though she cannot know this yet. Nor can she know the dark turns her life, and the life of her family and nation will take. The Sylvia in the photo lives only in the moment, with only herself, for this moment, to look after. So why not put on your brother's uniform, feel how it feels to be crisply buttoned down and capped, your frowsy hair swept out of the way, your hands free of babies and laundry? Feel how it feels to be a man returning home after a long time away, all your future before you, nothing to weigh you down.

◆

No matter how their roles shifted throughout the eighty years of their correspondence—working woman writing to teenage girl, childless aunt to first-time mother, restless traveler to stay-at-home grandmother—Bessie and Sylvia remained, *as ever, sisters.* Sisters who, to an outside eye, must have seemed as different as any two people could possibly be. No doubt Bessie and Sylvia encouraged this notion, as do most siblings, searching for ways to claim their own territory. I once read of a teenage boy who fashioned a partition down the middle of the bed he shared with an identical twin. And back in our family's station wagon days, my ever-resilient mother, looking to forge a temporary truce between her warring children crowded in the back seat (*Mom! He's hitting me, she's looking at me, he's breathing my air!*) divided that air with a calming sweep of her hand.

Wise parents are still sweeping hands through empty air, and decades hence their children will still be struggling to maintain their own breathable spaces. "Oh yes, I see the family resemblance," a friend says to us, and we bristle. For we have tried so hard to claim our tiny bit of the family map. "Oh, no," we answer. "She (fill in a sister's name here) is the beautiful one. Always has been. But she (fill in another sister's name) is the clever one, she can figure anything out." And, "Oh yes, he is the artist in the family. But he (fill in another brother's name) is the one everyone wants to be around, a social butterfly. Me? I'm a social moth." As if there is only so much territory in any family—artistic, intellectual, emotional, spiritual—and if part of that territory has been claimed, we'd better grab up another parcel before that one, too, is snatched from us.

So it goes. Nine times out of ten, when the subject of family comes up, most of us go straight for the differences, denying until we're red in the face (the same red-in-the-face our brother is famous for) every alleged family trait. The game holds for a while, each of us safe in the separate adult world carefully constructed to contain our own section of the inheritance. But throw all the siblings in a room together, as my siblings and I are often thrown, hand us each a glass of wine, watch us kick off our shoes and curl up under the same afghan, and then tell us we are not alike. Out come the lame jokes, the rude interruptions that aren't rude to us of course, the flat Indiana twang of our maternal grandparents mixed with the southern Illinois drawl of our paternals, and "Washington" becomes "Warshington," the corn on the cob a "roastin' ear" and the slice of bread a "poosher," a word that sends us into identical machine-gunfire guffaws, complete with nose wrinkles and goofy shoulder shrugs, our collective laughter veering off into sighs.

As I sort through letters that span a century, I am tempted to accentuate the differences among family members; for the most part, the distinguishing traits hold. Yes, my grandmother Sylvia was for the most part happy, upbeat, and capable of finding humor in any situation. Great-aunt Bessie was for the most part serious, meticulous, hard on herself and on others. Hattie was . . . and so it goes. But *for the most part* takes us only so far. Thus, cousins write to the outwardly stern Bessie, asking if she can teach them a new dance step, for no one can cut a rug like Bessie. And at a neighborhood costume picnic, the shy Dale dons a woman's dress and bonnet along with his buddies, who plump themselves in all the requisite womanly places to parade before Sylvia's Hawkeye camera.

Like their husbands, children, aunts, uncles, grandparents and grandchildren, the three Mounts women were complex, many-layered beings, and in their letters to each other, especially in the hardest times, each woman reveals her warring, inconsistent selves. As the women write, boundaries dissolve. They shape shift, taking on new identities as if attempting to make one whole woman from the disparate parts of three. When Bessie is in pain, Hattie soothes her; when Hattie descends into darkness, Sylvia lifts her out. When Sylvia needs reprimanding, Bessie delivers, holding nothing back. But when her little sister is despondent, Bessie steps over her customary wall to offer deepest sympathy, even while acknowledging *it won't do you any good, for if heartache would help in the very least, your case would be different this moment.*

Heartache? Sylvia's heartache? Sylvia the sweet child, the darling of the family, the "light of our home"? Heartache that the blue-deviled Bessie would be willing to absorb for her little sister, if only she could? In our collective family myth (for doesn't every family require such myths?) Sylvia is the most loving and loved member of the tribe, the warm, radiant center around which we gather. By her light, stories are told, poems written, quilts quilted, recipes handed down. My grandmother was one of those rare beings gifted with a child's sense of wonder and an unstinting attention to the present moment. Nothing was too trivial for her hand or eye to appreciate. And nothing—not cooking, cleaning, paying bills, entertaining neighbors—was so large and important that it could not be set aside for something small and important. Sewing doll clothes, saddling up the pony, hiking to the creek, teaching us grandchildren how to gather eggs or bait a fish hook or snap a chicken's neck.

Like most myths, the myth of Sylvia is rooted in truth. Study the poems she clipped from newspapers, read the hundreds of postcards and letters stored in her attic, and you'll meet the sweet, unspoiled child growing into the grandmother who, three decades past her death, abides with present-tense force in my memories and dreams. Yet when we *read between the lines there's more there anyway,* we come to know a woman as complicated and conflicted as her sister Bessie. Central to the Sylvia myth is the notion that she happily accepted whatever life handed out, that her world extended no farther than her own humble doorstep. Yet she often rode off alone on her horse, even into her sixties and seventies; once, late in life, she rode all the way to Indianapolis and back. And the same Sylvia who saved poems like "Be Kind to the Loved Ones at Home" and "The House by the Side of the Road" and wrote that *the country is the best place to be for contentment, don't you think?* became despondent when holed up in Briarwood too long.

Glad you are so happy in your little Fairy Castle, Hattie wrote to her daughter a few months after Sylvia's wedding, and for a while it seemed Sylvia's "Ideal Dream" had been realized. Arthur had passed up a teaching offer for a higher paying clerking job at Bartindale's Grocery. They'd set up housekeeping, planted their first garden, bought their first dog. Soon, Sylvia started attending euchre parties and quilting circles, and even joined the Modern Marthas at the First Christian Church—well, that must have been Vena's doing, Hattie suspected, as Arthur's sister had tried for years to pull Sylvia into church one way or another. But the Marthas have some nice programs, and maybe Sylvia would meet some new friends there. Lately, Sylvia has been complaining to Hattie that she misses the home place, misses her neighbors and friends, her brothers and Bessie. And though Vena can drive Sylvia batty sometimes with her long visits, now that she and John and the children have moved away, Sylvia misses them too, especially Beulah and Baby Kenneth.

Keep up your grit and think every day is another day gone, Hattie tells her daughter. Then, a month before Sylvia's first baby is due, Bartindale says the wrong thing to his young grocery clerk. *I knew if I stayed there,* my grandfather later wrote, *I would always be somebody's dog.* Arthur's alternative is a job eighty-five miles away in Terre Haute, which he finds to be *the worst place I ever struck, toughest place this side of Hades.* Though his letters to his wife and "kidlet" continue to be tender, as do Sylvia's to him, it is clear that financial troubles are straining the marriage. Writing from Bessie's home where she is staying with Baby Merrill, Sylvia reports that Sant can spare twenty-five dollars for three months. *He says he couldn't hardly let you have the whole amount he wishes he could. I will see Dale for the rest and send it Monday.*

Over the next few years, Arthur's father also sends money to the struggling couple, as does Hattie, who has pocketed some cash from egg sales and, later, from a small inheritance from Aunt Phebe. Though Arthur is far from idle during these years—he works on concrete gangs, construction jobs, on stationary balers, assembly lines, at restaurants, in grocery stores and pool rooms—the couple seems unable to stay afloat without help from their families. So when Bessie receives the disturbing news that Sylvia is pregnant for the third time, she answers with

I'm <u>mighty</u> sorry but I shall try not to worry because I know it is mostly an unprofitable pastime. I am puzzled to know why your experience shouldn't have taught you both more though. It seems to me it is too serious business to be careless or indifferent about.

What surprises me about this letter is not Bessie's attempt, if badly timed, to dispense contraceptive advice; Bessie had a habit of stating her opinion even when it wasn't welcome. What surprises is Sylvia's obvious anxiety over the situation. The glorious mother, the sweet daughter who had carried her baby sons on the train to visit their Aunt Bessie, their Aunt Vena, their grandparents and uncles and cousins—where has she gone? *I never here from Sylvia any more,* Vena writes to Arthur, *unless I call her and then don't seem she cares to talk to me she don't seem like Sylvia of old at home.*

One glance at the photographs taken in these years proves Vena's conclusion. In one, the Sanders sons, in billed caps and knickers, smile broadly, their young father in straw hat perched stiffly nearby. In the center of the photo, Sylvia, holding a black-haired baby girl, stares fiercely at the camera. *Yes,* Hattie chides her daughter in a letter written about this time, *I know it keeps one pretty busy to keep the bones from sticking out and keep clean but suppose you had 4 or 5 men to wash and mend for besides then it would be something like I had it when you was a baby.*

When you was a baby. But those days are gone and will never come again. No more Sylvia of old at home. "Oh I want to go home . . ." reads the most recent poem she'd clipped from the newspaper. ". . . I want to go home to my mother."

CHAPTER 12

Shumate Hotel
Williamson, W. Virginia
March 6, 1921

Mr. Dale Mounts
Route "E"
Lafayette, Indiana

Dear Brother:
   ... Hows everything along the Wildcat Creek? They sure do raise Hell along this river. The Tug River. Its supposed to be about the worst place in West Virginia. They always say the Tug never tells any lies. They mean by that, that theres so many people killed along here and I guess they throw them in the river but it never gives them up. Ha. A pretty cheerful place to be isn't it.
   They're having this trial here now and have 19 men indicted for killing 10 men up at Matwan. Don't know how they're going to come out.
   Most of the mines are out on a strike now and a fellow isn't safe hardly any place especilly an officer of the law. I had a battle the other day with some moonshiners Ha. Thought I was a goner for about half an hour. I sure burnt up some powder. I guess I got one of them didn't stay to see.
   I wish you wouldn't tell any body about this especially mother. I'm in the State police have been for quite awhile and these people up here like us like poisen. Ha. Ha. But just don't tell anyone about this. Say would like to know what you would take for that 38 pistol, Hostler and belt that I sold you. . . . I've got a brand new 32 automatic that

I'll trade to you if you want it because it isn't big enough for me to use up here. . . . If you decide to trade or sell wish you would send that blackjack along too. If you do send it you'll have to box that stuff up good and expres it. . . . Am staying here at the Shumate Hotel. Theres about twenty of us here. Have headquarters in the courthouse. Will probably be sent back to Glen Alum or some other mining town when this trial is over.

Well good-night tell everybody I said Hello.
Ivan.

January 22, 1922

Mrs. Sylvia Sanders
Oxford, Indiana
My Dear Sis.

Everything here rotten as ever. This is sure a Hell of a Country. Mud and rain guess that's all they seem to have here and trouble. Couldn't hardly get the horse through. I'm on duty 24 hours a day. . . . No my horse isn't a thoroughbred but never the less he's a plumb Damn Good one, a black with a white spot in his forehead. You bet they make the stuff at those stills. I think we'll have a hell of a time this spring again with these Damn Rednecks. From what I can hear I guess they'll shoot hell out of things. I don't care. I've got two rifles and plenty of ammunition and guess I can do my part.

Love, Ivan. Tell "Etta" I said Hello.

March 29, 1922

. . . Just got home today off a raid. Was in four counties. Made about 150 miles got about 4 stills but no men with them . . .

July 30, 1922

. . . Yes I think Bessie said something about Dale having a girl but I just thought she was kidding. And I didn't know anything about him having a "flivver." Darned if he aint got me skinned cause I haven't either one. Yea, boy that's the way I feel too enjoy yourself while you can. Damned if I can though. . . . Gosh, yes everything is in a hell of a fix. Don't believe it will last so awfully much longer though, hardly see how it can. . . .

As it turned out, the hell of a fix in West Virginia would last nearly a decade, exploding every few months in various counties. Not that it hadn't already blown several times: Bloody Mingo, the Matewan Massacre, violent skirmishes between strikers and non-union miners, between bootleggers and vigilante "volunteers" aiding State Police troopers like Ivan. West Virginia had long been infamous for civil unrest and feudal warfare, but 1921, the year Ivan joined the newly formed State Police, saw some of the most extreme altercations in the state's history. Ivan, like dozens of other young men eager to find work in the postwar economic crisis, reported to duty wearing his World War I uniform. Some of the recruits would not survive the four-month probationary period. Others would be dismissed for behavior unbecoming an officer, charged with offenses such as wanton destruction of property, arson, failure to retain neutrality during third-party altercations, and indiscriminate discharge of firearms. But Ivan Otto Mounts would retain his post, having been judged "of sound constitution" and "good moral character" and, most important to the demands of his job as a mounted trooper, an expert horseman.

Apparently no one checked Ivan's age qualification. When he wrote to his brother Dale in the spring of 1921, Ivan was more than five years shy of the minimum age (twenty-five) for a state policeman. But to his mind he was a man, fully grown, tested, and ready for action under the powers granted him under the Creative Act of 1919. As a member of the State Police, he could carry a firearm without a license. Arrest and detain persons. Assist local authorities in apprehending suspects. Execute summonses. Process criminals at court direction. Patrol forests. And aid his superiors in securing "the nationalization and Americanization of all foreign-born inhabitants." President Wilson had recently signed into law the Emergency Quota Act, a highly restrictive immigration policy that congressmen and their constituents had been pushing, in various forms, for months. Still reeling from the surge of patriotism following World War I, many Americans were outraged with the influx of immigrants they believed were responsible for falling farm prices and job shortages. Not to mention the radical "Red Menace" they imagined was waiting in the wings to undermine everything American stood for. The KKK had reignited its flame in 1915, and Klan publications like the <u>Fiery Cross</u> now blamed the nation's decline on Jewish businessmen

whose "foreign interests" threatened the U.S. economy and whose se-
duction of young Protestant women threatened the purity of the white
race. These publications also denounced Catholics, who, so Klan sympathizers believed, vowed allegiance to a foreign power (the pope) and
were trying to infiltrate the public schools. Soon, newspapers reported
the first accounts of violence and lawlessness by reemergent Klansmen.

◆

Carl Jung called it *adumbratio:* the umbrella, the veil, an "anticipatory
shadow" that hangs over the last days of a person who is close to death.
Aunt Bessie believed in it, too, but she had no fancy name for it. She just
called it "the shadow." She said that it lived behind the eyes and that if
you study the last photographs of a person, you will see it. In the last
photo of her son that Vena sent to her brother Arthur, twelve-year-old
Kenneth is in shadow, a frail presence leaning against a doorframe. Or
does he merely appear frail to our eyes, now that we know what is about
to transpire? A few weeks after the photo was taken, a distraught Vena
sent for Sylvia and Arthur, who left their two sons and toddler daughter in the care of Bessie and boarded the Interurban to Indianapolis.
The next morning, a postcard addressed to Bessie was delivered to the
Arthur Sanders home. Vena, the long-winded letter writer who often
complained that *news are scarce as hen's teeth* had more news than she
could squeeze onto the card. And none of it was good.

> *October 13, 8:30 PM*
> *Methodist Episcopal Hospital,*
> *Indianapolis, Indiana*

Mrs. Sant Cosby
c/o A. H. Sanders
Oxford, Indiana

Dear Bessie. Sylvia & Arthur came through fine but tired but still was
good to see them in all these sad hours of mine. I am almost desper-
ate, poor Kenneth is some sick boy. I can't tell in words, think it is a
brain tumor will know for sure this eve. & then they will operate, only
hope & they are very slim. Will drop card later. Vena

Bessie received the card about the time Sylvia and Arthur were stumbling out of the hospital after a sleepless night, dazed with grief but anxious to get back to their own living boys, who were just a few years younger than Kenneth. Than Kenneth *had been. Had been*? To use the past tense for a child? Unthinkable. It would be hours before Arthur realized that yesterday, October 13, had been his own birthday. All wrong. Wrong for me to have a birthday when my nephew will never have another one. The world is all wrong.

Can't tell in words. Hope are slim. Will drop card later.

No need to now, Vena, now that your sick boy is no more.

Adumbratio. The shadow. I now believe that it extends beyond the dying, that it casts its umbrella of darkness over living events, over whole years and deeds that, once they are finished and the veil is removed, we see in the bright clarity of the present.

Within the cache of family documents spanning a century, the mid-1920s is the most silent period. There is the stack of West Virginia letters from Ivan. Postcards from relatives in Hammond, Rising Sun, Wisconsin, and out west. The high school graduation announcement of Robert Wayne Mounts (after living in Stockwell with Sant and Bessie, Babe became the first and only Mounts sibling to attain this distinction). The marriage announcement of Ray Dale Mounts to Dora J. ("Ines") Floyd. The telegram from Charlie with the news of Mary's death. And the obituary of Lowell Kenneth Johnson, "aged 12 years, 5 months and 19 days," whose parents, Vena and John, and sister, Beulah, join "the host of relatives who mourn his loss."

But I can locate only a handful of letters from Sylvia, Bessie, or Hattie between 1922 and 1926. What accounts for the silence? Were the letters misplaced? Maybe they burned in the 1928 fire that destroyed one of Bessie and Sant's houses, which they had been renting out for extra income. Or maybe in their haste to pack up the South River farm, Sylvia and Arthur accidentally left the trunk they'd kept in the attic, the trunk Sylvia had admonished her children never to open, saying it belonged to a previous tenant.

If so, and if that trunk contained the missing correspondence, the women's letters might well have answered one of the most troubling questions of our family's history. But had the trunk been saved and the letters eventually passed on to me, the mystery of those years might have been solved too easily, before I'd even begun my search to recover the grandmother I so deeply missed. With each year since Sylvia's death, I had been losing the memory of the flesh and blood grandmother I had known: her easy, full-throated laughter; her strong, large-knuckled hands; her earthy scent. What was left was the *idea* of grandmother, a soft-focus composite of generic characteristics that applied to all grandmothers yet embodied none, least of all Sylvia Sanders. I wanted my grandmother back, my flesh and blood grandmother.

◆

My mother was born on November 11, 1924, while her brothers, ages eight and eleven, paraded through the farmhouse wearing paper hats and carrying make-believe flags. It was the sixth anniversary of the Armistice. Calvin Coolidge had just been reelected, America's farmers were experiencing a short burst of prosperity after years of falling prices, and my grandfather Arthur, who had recently sold a house in the town of Oxford to buy forty acres of farmland in Tippecanoe County, had set aside money for this day. Dr. Parker came from Oxford to deliver the baby. Arthur paid him fifteen dollars in cash, a feat he would brag about until his death, as he would brag about all his children, four of them now that this baby daughter had arrived safely on the earth.

Oh, but how to keep them safe? That is the thought that haunted Arthur. The death of Kenneth—Arthur's only nephew, and he'd loved him as his own son—felt as fresh today as it had two years before. Nothing they could do, nothing anyone could do, the doctors had said. Then why did Arthur still hurt so, still feel he could have, should have done more to ease his sister's grief? At the hospital, and later at the funeral and burial, Vena had wailed like an animal and scratched at the air, wild with terror, inconsolable. So perhaps it's best Vena couldn't be here today, as the joy filling the farmhouse might break her all over again—seeing the new one, hearing her first squalls. No, not squalls, more like bleats, Arthur thought. Feeble, lamblike bleats.

Besides, the little house was full enough. Mother Hattie was here, and Robert. Even Bessie had managed to get away, not an easy task in husking season, and the hired help not showing. As she entered the kitchen, her palm pressed against her jaw—were her teeth hurting her again?—Arthur wondered if this day might be hard on her, too, as it would have been for Vena. Did it pain Bessie to see her little sister once again become a mother? Bessie and Sant should have tried again, Arthur thought. "No," Sant had answered on the day Arthur asked, the first and last time the subject ever surfaced between the two men. "No," Sant had repeated, in the quiet, calm way he said everything, tilting his head slightly down so that the always carefully arranged curl in the middle of his forehead sprung loose. "I'd never put Bessie through that again."

Well, Arthur thought, such hopes were all in the past anyway, with Bessie forty-four years old and Sant Cosby nearly as old as Arthur's own father. Inside the farmhouse they were all bustling about, jockeying for position, to be the first to hold the tiny Juanita. "Yes, I'm sure," Arthur had told them after he announced the name he'd selected. "Yes. Juanita." Oh, let them think what they would, what if it did sound Spanish, it felt right to Arthur and he was keeping it. Hattie supplied the middle name. "A child born on Armistice Day!" she'd said excitedly. "A sign, and we must mark it."

Arthur agreed: a good sign. And wasn't it about time for a good sign, a new start? All that Oxford mess is behind us now, and the South River farm is coming along fine. It suits Sylvia, a country girl at heart. Or will suit her, once we get settled in. Of course, Sylvia hadn't wanted to leave Oxford and the friends she'd made there. "They are the best people," she'd protested. "The ladies do good things. They stand for what is right!" And, being Sylvia, she had stubbornly refused to release hold on her opinion, finally giving in only to keep the peace between them.

It rankles Arthur how the Kluxers pull people in, using the churches and bringing in speakers who could turn anyone's head with their talk, even his own father. And who knows what went on in the women's meetings? He knew only what he'd read in the paper, bits and pieces of that speech in Kansas City by—what did she call herself? The Imperial Commander. Yes, that was it: the Imperial Commander of the Women of the Ku Klux Klan. Gill was her name, a Miss Gill. And by all accounts, it had been a most stirring speech. "Every American woman is a queen," she had said. "The hand that rocks the cradle is the hand that rules the world." And, "We pledge our power of motherhood to America. Our knees can be altars of patriotism, and our homes shrines of idealism where liberty can be fostered."

Who could argue with such sentiments? That was how the Kluxers reeled people in. Thousands of people, hundreds of thousands. Everywhere you looked, another meeting, another rally, and Sylvia leaving out for evenings with her lady friends, coming home late, her dark eyes bright with excitement, her lips silent when he pressed her for details. That was part of the intrigue, he figured. The silence, the secrecy. Any brotherhood—and maybe sisterhood, too, Arthur reasoned—required some measure of secrecy to set it apart, to bind one heart to another.

The rituals and the passwords, Arthur well understood, so he'd never questioned Sylvia on that front. Just as she'd never asked him what happened inside the lodge. "Red Men?" Ivan had once joked when he saw Arthur suiting up for meeting. "I never seen any red men heading into that lodge. You sure it ain't the Improved Order of White Men?" Four Palefaces were to be initiated that night, so Arthur had been in full regalia—wig, headdress, tomahawk, leathers—a sight that apparently just lit Ivan up with laughter. Had Ivan been anyone other than Sylvia's brother, Arthur would have taken him to task for the remark, then launched into a full-scale explanation: how the Improved Order of Red Men was the oldest fraternal organization in the country, formed from the original Sons of Liberty to revere and preserve the customs of the American Indian. Ivan was a kidder, any way you sliced it, and would never have sat still for the facts anyway but would cut right to the chase, hungry for details Arthur would never have divulged even had his oath to the Tribe allowed it. Besides, he couldn't risk being late for meeting, not on Adoption night, and it would be a late night, too, what with the staking and rescue, the revelation of signs and passwords—as a third degree Warrior, Arthur had much to teach the Adoptees. The last time, he'd nearly bungled the job, mixing up the complicated hand gestures, but the Senior Sagamore had let it pass uncorrected. The Sagamore was a Grange member, too, like Arthur, and must have realized right away that Arthur had given the Grange handshake by accident. A forgivable slip, considering all the years Arthur and his family had been in the Grange, Arthur having progressed nearly to the seventh degree, where the secret work of the Grange was coded and controlled.

Not that Grange secrets didn't get out now and then, what with all the children involved, though Arthur was fairly certain neither of his boys had ever divulged the Grange passwords or signs. Nor, he was sure, had Sylvia. For though she found laughter in nearly everything—joking was as characteristic of the Mountses as their black, straight hair—she took promises seriously. She was careful where she pledged her allegiance, but once she pledged it, she was loyal to the end. Which is what had worried Arthur about the Oxford doings, why he'd taken drastic measures to get them away from all that. But would it matter, finally? The Klan was everywhere now, east to west and south to north. According to Dale, even that little scrap of a Wisconsin town where Sylvia's cousins live has a Klan meeting place, right there at the junction. And the rallies! Every time you turn around, there's another one, bigger than the last.

Studying the microfilm documents and the local newspapers of the time, I must agree with Arthur's assessment. From California to New York, the Klan of the 1920s boasted some of the largest and most spectacular events ordinary citizens could ever hope to see. There was something for everyone; Klonvokations were family affairs. Ku Klux Kiddies rode on floats and marched in parades. The Tri-K Klub, the all-girls' order established by the Women of the Ku Klux Klan, had its own robes, rituals, drum corps, and marching bands. The Junior KKK, for boys only, sponsored basketball tournaments, picnics, and father-and-son nights. An estimated fifty thousand people from Illinois, Ohio, Michigan, and various cities in Indiana gathered in Valparaiso for the "monster" rally that had been announced on the streets of small-town America, after the Fiery Cross first heralded it in an ad in the spring of 1923:

KU KLUX KLAN
and the Women's Organization
Home Coming and May Festival
Saturday, May 19th
Valparaiso, Indiana
ONE DAZZLING DAY OF DIVERSIFIED DELIGHT
100,000 KLANSMEN THE WOMEN'S ORGANIZATION
GIGANTIC—20 Brass Bands—Free Acts—Colossal
A Big Barbecue
High, Tight Wire Walking, 100 Feet in the Air—Wild Broncho-
Busting—Outlaw Horses—Imported Texas Cowboys—National
Speakers—200 Horsemen—Evening Fire Works—Illustrated

Parades—Visit Valparaiso University—The Sand Dunes—See the
Calumet Region
ALL DAY   ALL NIGHT
On the Lincoln Highway, Yellowstone Trail and Liberty Way
ALL ROADS LEAD TO VALPARAISO, MAY 19TH
You are Welcome to Our City

I imagine that when Arthur heard news of the Valparaiso rally, as he
very likely would have, he was extremely disturbed. The Klan in Valparaiso? As it turned out, the rally was nothing compared to the plan the
Klan was cooking up for Valparaiso University, Arthur's *alma mater.* And
because of what my grandfather had learned there, he even knew what
alma mater meant: nourishing mother. Which is exactly what Valpo
had been for this motherless boy. No matter if you were "so poor it hurt,"
as Arthur often described himself. If your marks were high enough and
you could raise money for room and board, you could attend "the poor
man's Harvard." That was the beauty of Valpo, its singular distinction.

And hadn't Valpo been good to Arthur? In the great halls he'd studied literature and ethics, listened to learned professors and guest lec-
turers. He'd even saved his school notebooks, and sometimes on rainy
evenings when the chores were done and the children bedded down,
he would take the notebooks out of the glass-front cabinet and review
them. One of the notebooks, labeled "Arthur H. Sanders. Pedagogy
Class. Room B. 1:00 PM," contained some of his favorite quotations from
Oliver Wendell Holmes and from John Holland's "Prayer of a Nation,"
wherein the poet calls upon God to "give us men . . . who possess opin-
ions and a will." Another quote, from an unnamed source, summed up
perfectly Arthur's own convictions about the value of education: "To be
at home in all lands and in all ages, to gain appreciation of other men's
work, and the criticism of one's own home."

Well, so much for my alma mater, he thought. In the end, it didn't
matter to Arthur that the deal had not gone through. What was shame-
ful—to Arthur, unforgivable!—was how close the Kluxers had come to
creating a Klan Kollege "free" of the "scum o' the melting pot." "America
for Americans" was their plan, to make Valpo into "a bastion of Ameri-
canism" composed of "hundred-percenters," none of the "refuse of other
lands" threatening to pollute "pure American blood." If such foolishness

is what this great nation has come to, Arthur thought, then maybe it *was* time to exercise criticism of one's own home. Where would this foolishness stop? Not in Oxford, Arthur had concluded. Not even in Lafayette, home to Purdue University—to Arthur's mind, the pinnacle of learning in these parts. But not even Lafayette's mayor could stop the Kluxers. Their pockets were deep, and now even the fairgrounds belonged to them. The Tippecanoe County fairgrounds!

Arthur couldn't take on the lot of them, but he could do what he could do. What he *had* done, for his family. Yes, they would all miss their Oxford home, but Sylvia would get used to being out here in the country, especially now that she had a new one to tend to. And a pretty one she was, too, if a bit scrawny. Oh, but Juanita would fill out, Arthur thought. Would take on the rounded form of her mother, still the most beautiful woman he'd ever known. Even now, propped up in the iron bed in her oldest bedclothes, her black hair wild and tangled from the hard labor and her dark eyes shadowed with exhaustion, Sylvia managed a laugh— over something Hattie had said, leaning down to her daughter—smiling with that crooked half-smile that still took his heart to pieces.

◆

Once Dr. Parker had left and her mother was freshened up, four-year-old Barbara was allowed in the bedroom. Over and over, whispering to herself, she practiced the new name: Juanita Armista Sanders. A big name, Barbara thought, for such a tiny baby. Now, finally, Barbara would have a sister to play with, to keep her company on those long days when her brothers were away at school or out in the fields. Barbara was plump and outgoing, her straight, shiny black hair—Mounts hair—cut in the bowl style of the period. She was a cheerful child, not given to nightmare imaginings. One daydream, however, haunted her. The context was vague, major pieces of the narrative missing, but the details were clear: white robes and pointed hats, a wooden casket, and the lisping sibilance of women's voices.

It would be many decades, after the death of Sylvia, before Barbara's ghostly images coalesced into one clear memory. Her little sister would carry no such images. Juanita *would* remember, as a child, overhearing bits of conversation about why her father had moved the family from

Oxford the year she was born. Not only was he anxious to buy a farm; he was also eager to remove Sylvia from "some influences that were harming our family." The subject of the 1920s would resurface now and then over the next several decades, and during our family's visits to Indiana, I would occasionally catch snippets of my grandparents' discussions. Arthur was an opinionated, articulate man who often wrote impassioned letters to the editor of the Lafayette <u>Journal & Courier</u> on one topic or another, and over the years I'd become accustomed to my grandfather's dinnertime orations. Grandma Sylvia had, too, as far as I could tell. She would sit quietly with her arms folded across her breasts and her chin jutting upwards as she listened, nodding her head. But on one particular night, when my grandfather's voice modulated from a tone of general annoyance to one tinged with high emotion, as if he had some intimate stake in this issue, I noticed a change in Sylvia. I don't remember any discussion of G. E. Sanders, though Arthur had to have been aware of his father's involvement; the focus that evening was on Sylvia's actions. Apparently my grandmother had been involved in some things "she shouldn't have been involved in," that she "did not fully understand."

That was when Sylvia erupted. "It wasn't like that. That's not what it was about at all. We did good things, we stood for what was right!" As was usual with my grandmother, whose sentences were few and carefully chosen, once her last word was spoken, the world stopped for an instant, and only her smile or conciliatory shrug could set it back in motion. When I reach into memory, the defiant thrust of Sylvia's chin and the set of her clamped jaw are as present to me as her generous spirit, her hearty laugh, and her earthy, sweet scent. In dreams, I fall into her softness, am surrounded by her warmth, but when I look up, her lips are stitched shut, a tight line that puts an end to further discussion.

After that night, the subject of the 1920s never resurfaced in my presence while my grandmother was alive. And her death might have put an end to the matter, had not several events combined to complicate the mystery. First, shortly after my fortieth birthday, my mother began sending me dozens of family letters and documents, a collection that would continue to grow over the next several years. The first letters to arrive were Sylvia's, documenting my grandparents' courtship and the early years of their marriage. As I lifted each carefully folded letter from its yellowed, crisped-with-age envelope, I felt, for the first

time in my life, that I was entering Sylvia's thoughts and feelings, looking out through her eyes, the eyes of a young woman. Reading the letters, I longed to be at the kitchen table at Briarwood, sitting across from
the lovesick Sylvia as she composes yet another letter to a young man
named Arthur (*I have loved you Dear since before you were born*). Or
working beside her near the banks of Wildcat Creek, both of us having
skipped church yet again to attend to more pressing matters (*I mashed
my thumb and lost my temper, but I have a chicken coop anyway.*)

The second event, concurrent with my reading of the first box of
letters, was my discovery of Kathleen M. Blee's scholarly examination of
the Women of the Ku Klux Klan. Although <u>Women of the Klan: Racism
and Gender in the 1920s</u> is a nonfiction book, complete with statistics
and tables, it held my attention as few novels have. From the first chapter on, I felt as if a door were creaking open just out of my view, shedding
thin strips of light across the page. This was all news to me. Until this
time, my assumptions about the Klan were based on my limited knowledge of the original KKK of the Reconstruction era and its reincarnation
during the Civil Rights era, both movements fueled by white suprema-
cists employing violence and terrorism to accomplish their goals. And
though I knew that various women's auxiliaries had been connected to
the Klan, I'd always assumed that their members were southern women
working alongside Klansmen, and that their primary focus was intimi-
dation of blacks.

I had no idea that a radically different Klan had flourished throughout the United States during the 1920s, and that an estimated five million people all over the country joined its ranks. Nor did I know that
between 1922 and 1925, Indiana was the center of the Klan's power, its
state membership estimated at between one-quarter and one-third of
Indiana's native-born white men; for some communities, estimates run
as high as forty or fifty percent. But what surprised me most, studying
Blee's book along with several other scholarly texts, was how strongly
involved Indiana women were in the Women of the Ku Klux Klan. With
each page I turned, scenes appeared in my peripheral vision, scenes
drawn from Aunt Barbara's recollection of masked images, from conversations I'd overheard between my grandparents, and from the bare
facts disclosed in Blee's book. My mind was spinning with possibilities:
Could it be? If so, what difference did it make now? *Let the dead Past*

bury its dead, as Sylvia, quoting Longfellow, had written in her letters. Let it go.

The third event occurred during a visit to my parents' home in the winter of 1993. I had recently begun an extended writing residency at an Ohio university a few hours' drive from my parents' home in West Lafayette, Indiana. Located between the university and their home is the National Archives of Ball State University, which houses original documents and ephemera of the WKKK: photographs of rallies and parades, catalogs of the group's paraphernalia, newspaper articles, pamphlets, and other Klan-related items. Since I had been unable to let the dead Past bury its dead, I used my residency breaks to continue my research into the WKKK, stopping at the Ball State archives and then continuing my journey over Indiana country roads on my way to West Lafayette. As a child visiting the Circle S farm and Briarwood, I had traveled many roads like these. But it had almost always been summer, the landscape open and inviting: white farmhouses, freshly painted barns, blue skies, fields green with soybeans and shoulder-high corn.

Now, the fields were brown with stubble. The leaden sky hung low, making the farmhouses appear small and forlorn, *fairly screaming with loneliness,* as my grandmother had written. Not even the smoke rising from the chimneys could warm the view. As I drove, scenes from Blee's book flickered at the edges of thought, until, by the time I crossed the Tippecanoe County line, the thousands of faceless Indiana women that Blee had described—white, Protestant, native-born, middle-class farmers and shopkeepers and teachers—were as present to me as the farm women alive in my childhood memories. Women who patted my head and smiled at my achievements, who sat up late with dying friends, who sacrificed time and money for those in need. Women who huddled around quilting frames, who shared the potluck of their gardens' bounty—squash casseroles, pickled beets, new potatoes drenched in butter. With each mile, I felt I was driving not only from east to west but from summer into winter, from present into past, from light into dark. Is it possible, I wondered, steering the car into my parents' driveway, that behind the shield of lap quilts and the fan of euchre cards, these women were remnants of the 1920s sorority of "hundred-percenter" Hoosiers? Possible that they held secrets I had never guessed?

CHAPTER

The Women of the Ku Klux Klan was officially chartered in 1923 in Little Rock, Arkansas, following the lead of right-wing and nativist women's organizations in the South, Midwest, Northwest, and Ozark regions, organizations such as Queens of the Golden Mask and Hooded Ladies of the Mystic Den. By this time, the Klan had been active throughout the United States for several years, and though the KKK would remain linked in many ways to the newly chartered women's organization, the WKKK was founded as a separate entity, asserting itself as "by women, for women, and of women." Many of its founders, though they espoused the tenets of the KKK, protested their exclusion from its ranks, pointing to social and political inequities between the sexes. Yes, both organizations agreed that "our glorious mothers" were powerful forces in society, the prime shapers of the values of home and family that were the foundation of a strong America. But to at least some of the WKKK leaders, those beliefs did not equate with the belief that motherhood was the ideal fulfillment of a woman's destiny. Running a household and taking care of children was, plainly and simply, work. Work that should be respected and rewarded. An eight-hour day for mothers? So suggested one of the major Kleagles in her Mother's Day address to approximately eight thousand people.

Within a few months of its inception, the WKKK boasted chapters in thirty-six states, much of its strength centered in Ohio and Indiana. It is impossible to know for certain the extent of any secret society's membership, but according to Blee, "historians estimate the total membership of Indiana's WKKK as a quarter-million during the 1920s, or 32 percent of the entire white native-born female population of the state," and other women who were never officially initiated sympathized with the cause. Many Indiana chapters formed in and around Indianapolis, not only because it was the regional headquarters for the Klan but also because the Interurban rail system linked the city to dozens of small towns, enabling WKKK recruiters to move easily from one town to another. Although women from all areas of the state joined the WKKK, many of the rallies were held in small towns. And while rural women remained active in the organization despite their geographical isolation, those living in small communities had more opportunities to socialize with "like-minded" women.

Like-minded women and men were the norm in small town Indiana during the 1920s. In 1920, the population of the entire state was approximately ninety-seven percent white and ninety-seven percent Protestant. Cities like Gary, Evansville, and Indianapolis were more heterogeneous than smaller ones, and their populations of blacks, Jews, Catholics, and immigrants, though representing a minority, still wielded some power against the white, Protestant, middle-class front. And though racial and ethnic tensions were common in certain pockets of large cities, physically threatening acts by Klan members were few and far between in Indiana, especially in comparison to the violence that erupted in neighboring Ohio and Illinois. Indeed, according to scholars of the 1920s Klan movement, most notably Leonard J. Moore, whose Citizen Klansmen: The Ku Klux Klan in Indiana, 1921–1928 appeared in 1991, the same year as Kathleen Blee's book, overt racial and ethnic conflict played a small role in the day-to-day workings of the Indiana KKK and WKKK. And even in states where Klan-related violence was reported, such encounters were more likely to occur between Klan and anti-Klan forces, bootleggers, or local police than between Klan members and minority citizens.

This is not to say that individual Indiana Klan members did not employ violent, bigoted rhetoric or project an ominous image that strengthened the KKK's reputation as a vigilante force, a reputation sometimes backed up with acts. Certainly many Kluxers harbored deep-seated feelings against "the other," openly expressing their belief in racial segregation, quotas for immigration, and anti-miscegenation laws. Still, though some KKK and WKKK members succeeded in threatening the livelihood of minority citizens, the majority of their energies were spent not in fighting "the other"—by which they meant Jews, Catholics, immigrants, and blacks—but rather in defending what they saw as their rightful place in society. The movement of the 1920s Indiana Klan, according to Moore, was in many ways a populist movement that "concerned itself not with persecuting ethnic minorities but with promoting the ability of average citizens to influence the workings of society and government."

Where to find these average citizens in 1920s Indiana? Recruitment meetings, as well as Klavern meetings, were held in private homes, YMCAs, YWCAs, lodge halls, campgrounds, and various community centers. Although one might expect that the KKK would hold its meetings in secret, this was not always the case. I recently discovered among my family's possessions a mouse-nibbled, stained copy of the official program of the Fourth Imperial Klonvokation, which had convened in Chicago in July 1928. Its events, lasting three days, were held at the Eighth Street Theatre, the Midway Masonic Temple, and the Grand Ballroom of the Palmer House. All forty-eight states were represented at the Klonvokation, along with Alaska, the District of Columbia, and the "Canal Zone," and judging from the program's contents, members made no attempt to hide their identity. Unmasked faces of Grand Dragons, Kludds, Kleagles, Klokards, Klaliffs, Klabees, and other Imperial representatives appear on the program's pages, along with the names of their family members, the names and denominations of their home churches (all Protestant), and a list of each leader's fraternal affiliations, which included membership in the Masons, Kiwanis Club, Shriners, Elks, Knights of Pythias, Woodmen of the World, Odd Fellows, Loyal Order of Moose, and—of course, I think as I scan the lists—The Improved Order of Red Men.

And here, tucked inside the pages describing the progress of the Indiana "realm," those "energetic Klansmen who have weathered the storm and will press forward victoriously with the principles they strive for," is an Invisible Empire card bearing the signature of G. E. Sanders of Oxford, Indiana, and another card certifying that "the bearer whose signature appears here has been found worthy of advancement in the mysteries of Klankraft and has been passed to K-Trio or Knights of the Great Forest." Issued on the 16th day of July, 1928. Four years past my mother's birth, five years past the time G. E.'s son had packed up his family and left for Tippecanoe County. Had G. E. tried to convince Arthur to join? And, failing that, had my great-grandfather suggested to Sylvia that she might want to stop over at his church one evening and listen to a fine lady speaker?

Protestant churches were important centers of social life in small Indiana towns, and some recruiters, especially recruiters for the WKKK, held organizational meetings in churches. Why not? On the surface, churchwomen and Klanswomen of this time had much in common. Their agendas, in some cases, appeared to be identical: visiting the sick and grieving, raising money for orphans and widows, establishing homes for unwed mothers, and distributing holiday gift baskets, for starters. On the political front, members of both groups crusaded against gambling, pornography, liquor and other vices, and lobbied for child welfare legislation.

But any like-minded community has a dark side. Even, or perhaps *especially* when that community purports to be clothed in light. The light of insularity, of inclusion (which cannot exist without exclusion), of resistance to the "other," however distant or symbolic that "other" appears to be. Thus, while Klansmen and Klanswomen donated Bibles and flags to public schools, they also urged compulsory Bible reading led only by Protestant teachers, campaigned against the teaching of German and the use of Catholic encyclopedias, boycotted Jewish businesses, and pushed for the firing of Catholic schoolteachers, among other actions.

Most Klan activities, however, were directed toward solidarity, the building of the organization's ranks by appealing to the social and domestic needs of members and sympathizers. It's not difficult to imagine 1920s Protestant churchwomen skimming over the pages of the Klan-sponsored Fellowship Forum's racist and xenophobic articles, searching for "household and health hints for all the family." Beneath headlines like "Protestant Hosts to Invade Rocky Mount for Monster Klan Rally," you could find answers to questions like "In making quick breads, how much baking powder is needed for each cup of flour?" or "Where can I get a book about linoleum?" or "What would you suggest as a nice plate lunch for a home recruitment meeting?"

Knowing what I now know, it seems probable that my grandmother attended at least one recruitment meeting, if not in Oxford then in one of the other towns in Benton County, which had an extremely strong Klan presence during the 1920s. Was she officially initiated into the WKKK? It would have been a financial hardship for the cash-strapped household to manage the ten-dollar application fee. And if Sylvia owned any Klan-related items, I've found no evidence of them, not the WKKK robe and helmet nor any item a prominent dues-paying member might have ordered from the classified ads placed in the Fellowship Forum or the Fiery Cross. Things like KKK mystery spinning charms, AKIA (A Klansman I Am) fountain pens, or sheet music of "Kluxer Blues" or "The Face Behind the Mask." I do recall seeing, in my grandparents' house, sheet music with titles from the Fellowship Forum's catalogs—"The Church in the Wildwood," "You're a Grand Old Flag," and "The Old Rugged Cross" among then. But these well-known songs, though performed at Klan gatherings, were not Klan-specific; they were tied to the everyday life of most Hoosiers of the time.

That 1920s Klan rituals borrowed so shamelessly from prevailing traditions was one of the most essential elements of the Invisible Empire's strategy. At rallies and cross-burnings, members sang the same songs my grandparents sang at church services or around family campfires. The same songs I would sing, decades later, as part of a Baptist youth group, along with hymns filled with militaristic imagery: "Onward Christian Soldiers," "The Banner of the Cross," and "Stand up, Stand Up for Jesus," among others. In Vacation Bible School, we 1950s Protestant children pledged allegiance to the same American flag the Kluxers had saluted; we also pledged our allegiance to "the Christian flag, and to the Savior for whose Kingdom it stands" and to "the Bible, God's Holy Word," which we sometimes called the "Sword of the Spirit." Bible, flag, cross, sword: four of the seven ritualistic symbols of the Klan. A fifth symbol? Water. Water, as in baptism. It appears that the only symbols we Protestants did not share with the Klan were the robe and the mask. We might pledge our allegiance to our nation, our God, our Bible, and to the Sword of the Spirit; we could even be baptized into a new spirit and body, and into a new Body of like-minded believers. But we could not make ourselves invisible.

◆

WKKK recruitment tactics were mild for the most part, offer-ing women the chance to belong to a "high-minded, patriotic" group: "Women of clean American ideals" was the appeal of one such recruit-ment announcement. But sometimes the tactics went beyond offering and urging; women who were reluctant to join could face ostracism from friends and family members who were part of the organization. This possibility would have disturbed a woman like my grandmother. Beneath her independent, devil-may-care façade was a woman prone to feelings of loneliness. And while Sylvia was physically brave, her cour-age demonstrated in acts such as leaping onto a skittish pony's back to steer him out of harm's way, or amputating her pet dog's leg to save him, the woman revealed in her letters is hardly fearless, and the child inside the woman, sometimes terrified. In a journal entry made shortly before her death, my grandmother recalls some early memories:

> .... *There was a hill in front of the house and I would go out when the neighbor girls came to the top of the hill and coax me to come closer of course I don't like to think they meant to hit me but they would throw rocks at me and then I would run for my life back to the house then they would laugh. To this day many many years later I am still afraid of a rock in the hands of someone whom I thought was going to throw it my way.*

Although Sylvia feared these girls, she also craved their acceptance, despite her assertions, expressed in a 1910 letter to her future husband, that *Girls are not that true to one another no matter how good friends they are. Possibly I am wrong but it has always seemed so to me. If girls told me some gossip about you I would just think they were scheming a little for themselves.* However unpopular the stereotype of gossiping women may be today, its reality was clear in the day-to-day workings of the WKKK; the organization's self-described "poison squad of whispering women" was just that. Members in Indiana and elsewhere launched sophisticat-ed campaigns of rumor and gossip, warning "true Americans" to avoid certain individuals and establishments. Members distributed handbills and printed announcements in church bulletins, endorsing political candidates sympathetic to the Klan.

In many ways, Sylvia was the ideal candidate for the WKKK's propa-ganda. Not only did she meet the outward requirements for admission, being a native-born, white, Gentile, Protestant woman over the age of eighteen (a woman who also happened to live, at the time, in a county with one of the highest percentages of Klan activity in the state) but she also possessed inner qualities that would have predisposed her to embrace the organization's teachings. These qualities included a strong sense of patriotism, a concern that the nation's economic and moral decay was due in part to foreign influences, a single-minded devotion to home and family values, the need to be accepted into a society of "the better people" coupled with a fear of exclusion and social loneliness, and a fierce streak of independence fueled by a yearning for equality between the sexes.

As for Sylvia's sister? Anything is possible, of course. If an estimated one out of three white, native-born, Protestant woman in Indiana joined the WKKK, and thousands of other women, perhaps tens of thousands, supported the Klan's platform, what makes me believe that Bessie did not participate as well? First, Bessie, unlike her siblings, was a lifelong Democrat, as was her mother, Hattie; Klan members, like the majority of Hoosiers, were overwhelmingly Republican. Second, though Bessie was no doubt aware of the Klan's workings in nearby towns, she appears to have been too busy helping Sant work their farm and care for his aged mother to trouble herself with local goings-on. Finally, apart from her brief foray into the American Woman's League, Bessie had never been a joiner. Sewing circles, euchre parties, church suppers, quilt takings, all the places where women gathered to laugh and talk, to pass the time, could not compare to solitary hikes in the woods or cemetery, bird-watching expeditions, or evenings spent with seed catalogs and charts of Egyptian hieroglyphics. The older Bessie got, the more difficult it was for her to remain part of the social scene. And, good heavens, I imagine her thinking, what is the quarrel against Catholics and Jews anyway? And immigrants? Where would this nation be without immigrants? As a young woman working in Hammond, she'd witnessed *all manner of men* working together.

All manner of men would have included, for Bessie, the blacks that she'd encountered on her many train trips, as well as the sharecropper children who lived near the Old Mead House along the Ohio River. Bessie had grown up in Switzerland County; her little sister Sylvia, who had been born in central Indiana, had had fewer opportunities to associate with blacks. Like many rural and small-town whites in the 1920s, Sylvia had rarely seen a black person except from a distance, perhaps while traveling by train to her uncles' homes in Wisconsin. Late in her life, she told me that she'd been "in close quarters with a colored person" only twice: once when Arthur invited a preacher to their home for dinner, and once on the train to Texas when she came to visit our family in the 1950s.

Thinking back over Sylvia's stories, I keep imagining an alternative history for my grandmother, a different road her life might have taken had she been given the opportunities that higher education, or extensive travel, might have afforded. Would exposure to books, lectures, and the ideologies and cultures of other lands have created a different Sylvia, a woman less susceptible to the lures of a nativist, exclusionary organization? Perhaps not. Though it is tempting to believe that higher education broadens the aperture of one's world view, the record of the Indiana Klan suggests otherwise. Many leaders, members, and sympathizers of the 1920s Klan were well-educated men and women. Alongside evangelists, financial opportunists, temperance organizers, farmers, and shopkeepers, there were also ministers, nurses, physicians, social workers, and teachers; one of the most prominent organizers of the Indiana WKKK was a teacher who had graduated from Valparaiso University, my grandfather Arthur's alma mater and the school that Sylvia had so desperately wished to attend.

Still, I can't shake the notion that education might have altered the course of many men and women who were drawn into the Klan's influence. Around 1920, it appears that someone in the Mounts-Sanders family, probably my grandfather Arthur but perhaps Uncle Dale or Aunt Bessie, traveled to Indianapolis to hear a lecture by a distinguished Negro, a Mr. David Manley. (I discovered Manley's 1919 biography, <u>From the Jungles of Africa to Indiana Central University</u>, among our family documents.) Manley's African name had been Ndapy, and his brief biography, penned by his sponsor, a Christian Endeavor minister, told of Ndapy's early years: his boyhood in Sierra Leone, his journey to America in 1919, and his then-recent arrival in Indianapolis, where he was about to begin his college studies. Four years later, the author would publish an updated version of the biography detailing Manley's much lauded four years at the Indianapolis-based college, including serving as editor of the school magazine and president of the literary society. "I believe," the author concluded, "that the students of Indiana Central College are more cosmopolitan in their views of the world . . . because this black man from across the sea has been among them for the past few years."

Of course, I thought. Of course Manley's presence would have influenced these students. Yet the more I studied Manley's biography, alongside Klan documents of the time, the more I saw Ndapy's reputed acceptance by his fellow students not as an indicator of "cosmopolitan. . . views of the world" but rather as yet another expression of the dominant culture of the time, the same culture that allowed the 1920s Indiana Klan to flourish. Yes, Ndapy (as Manley) succeeded in the new world to which he'd immigrated. But how much of his success depended upon his assimilation into the Protestant white man's world, and upon his ability to relinquish his own personal and cultural history? A history more rich and complex than his fellow students at Indiana Central University might have believed possible.

To imagine it, I open the Manley biography and place it side by side with Bessie's geography text bookmarked at her favorite page: "Map of the World." In my mind, I step inside the parlor Sant has refurbished for her. I walk across the polished floor to the library table. Spin the globe. Land in a secluded pocket of Sierra Leone, circa 1895, just a few years before Bessie sat in Kyger's classroom, fancying the world as one large ball spinning. Half a world away, a young woman from "the hottest Grand Division of the Earth" is paddling a canoe up Africa's coast, a baby strapped to her breast. Thus begins a story even the imaginative Bessie could never have conjured, locked as she was in her own spinning world. The child at Fatima's breast is the son of a Sierra Leone chieftain who recently died a hero's death in battle, but not before he named his son. "Ndapy," he announced to his young wife, and Fatima was not surprised, for she knew the meaning of the name: "a fight." One day, the proud father vowed, this boy would be the most powerful Mohammedan chief in all of Africa.

But Fate, as Hattie would have said, did not arrange things as Ndapy's family had planned. After a sixth-month stay in the "society bush" where along with other boys he was initiated into the Sierra Leone tribe of men, Ndapy arrived with his mother in Shenge. Here, the destitute Fatima released him into the care of the United Brethren Mission,

(Left) My grandfather Arthur's notebook from Valparaiso University, 1910. (Right) Biography of David Jayn Manley, 1919, discovered in the family archives.

whose teachers gave him a new name, a Christian name. Soon, David was living in a mission school dormitory like dozens of other orphaned African boys with new, Christian names, who were now sleeping in English beds and eating with spoons from individual bowls. If all went well, if he worked hard and stayed out of a trouble—not an easy task for the scrappy, mischievous David—he could finish school and become a teacher who would, if the missionaries got their wish, "train those neighbors in the dark lands . . . who will take the light."

Thus wrote Manley's white, Protestant sponsor from his desk at Indiana Central University, just five or six miles from the 1920s head-quarters of the <u>Fiery Cross</u>, the Klan's major publication and the self-proclaimed "only Protestant newspaper in the Central West." Could any two institutions be more different from each other? At first glance, I thought not. After all, here was a young black man who had not only been accepted into a white, middle-class, Protestant college during the heyday of the Indianapolis-based Klan's resurgence, but had flourished in that world. Klan members writing for the <u>Fiery Cross</u>, though they might not have questioned Manley's right to flourish, made it clear that the "negro . . . should develop in his own realm." A realm like the Tuskegee Institute, perhaps. For even the <u>Fiery Cross</u> writers maintained that "the negro can go to the top within his own race." Provided, of course, that he is "under the tutelage of the white man."

And is tutelage so far removed from sponsorship? If Ndapy had refused to give up his African name and his religious heritage, would he have made it <u>From the Jungles of Africa to Indiana Central University</u>? Probably not. Not in Indiana in 1923, the year of David Manley's graduation and the year before my grandfather Arthur moved his young family out of Benton County. Within another year, candidates with the Klan seal of approval would win not only many mayoral and sheriff contests in Indiana but the governorship as well, and Arthur and Sylvia would be settling into their new farm in Tippecanoe County, preparing to welcome a new baby into their lives.

◆

On the last night of my 1993 visit in my parents' home, Aunt Barbara came by for supper, followed by Uncle Merrill, the elder of my mother's two brothers. The younger brother, Leland, had been dead for several years. Since I'd last seen the widowed Merrill, he'd grown a mustache and sideburns, and though he was about to celebrate his eightieth birthday, Merrill's hair still held the same reddish cast I'd known since my childhood. "Red," I thought, recalling the boyhood nickname mentioned in my grandparents' letters. Merrill didn't know I'd been reading letters written even before his birth. *I have known you Dear since before you were born,* I was thinking, but being his niece, of course I did not say this. Instead, we sat in the living room drinking coffee and reminiscing about the past—what were our earliest memories? When I brought up the subject of the 1920s Indiana Klan, I expected Merrill to answer in the negative. In all the years of listening to my uncle's storytelling, I'd never heard one hint about the Klan.

"Oh yeah, sure," Merrill replied casually, as if I'd asked him what he'd had for breakfast this morning at Bob Evans. I grabbed the arms of the rocker and leaned forward, then rocked backwards, trying to act nonchalant. "Sure, I remember a couple of things," he continued. "One time Leland and me went to the bakery to get something for Mother—I was about nine, Leland was maybe seven—and the baker chased us out. He kept yelling, 'You little K-K-K-ers, you get out of here!'"

The baker? Why would he chase you out? My mind was reeling.

"Another time, the whole family rode out to the country one night. It was real dark, I remember that. We rode for a long time in the dark and then suddenly there was this great light. A giant cross on fire in the middle of a field! Hundreds of people were there, it was very exciting, lots of long benches set up—I remember because I was jumping on them, leaping from one to the other, and I fell and hit my head."

The children, I thought. *Of course. The biggest events always included the children.*

"That's all I remember, my head hurting, and the cross burning, and all the people. We didn't stay long. Dad took us back pretty quick." Merrill took a breath. "After that, I never thought much about it," he said, turning to face Barbara. "You were real little then, probably too little to remember."

Merrill was right. Barbara didn't remember the cross-burning. What she remembered was another scene altogether. Holding onto her mother's skirt, trying to hide behind it. They were in a church. Someone had died, and people were crying. Mostly she remembered being afraid—of the masks, mostly. Her father wasn't there, and she was afraid.

If the funeral Barbara recalled had been for a WKKK member, it is quite possible that few men were present that day, perhaps none. Though men as well as women attended WKKK funerals and burials, some members took the WKKK charter literally when it declared itself "by women, for women, and of women." Klanswomen often served as pallbearers and eulogists at WKKK funerals, just as they performed christenings and baptisms of babies and small children. Children were an important part of the Klan's outreach program, so it's no surprise that Merrill and his little brother hadn't wanted to leave the campground that night. What child would want to miss out on such a sight? Not even the Chautauquas and state fairs that Aunt Bessie took them to could compare to the Klonvokations and Klan Karnivals they'd heard about—balloon rides, Ferris wheels, brass bands, lighted torches. Certainly more fun than riding in the grocery wagon with your father through the dusty streets of Oxford, as Merrill and Leland often did.

As I listened to Merrill and Barbara, and as I watched my mother's face trying to absorb her older siblings' stories, my mind was divided. I wanted and didn't want to know more. When I'd first begun my research, I'd been propelled by curiosity, plain and simple. 1920s Indiana: another intriguing aspect of history I'd known nothing about. Later, as I sifted through clues, piecing together the crazy quilt of historical fact, half-remembered conversations, and instinct, the granddaughter in me receded and the detective came forward. All I wanted was to solve the riddle. As if a riddle like this can ever be fully solved. To this day, I am certain only that my great-grandfather G. E. Sanders was a card-carrying member of the Invisible Empire of the Knights of the Ku Klux Klan, and that his daughter-in-law, my grandmother Sylvia, attended Klan-sponsored functions and sympathized with the Klan's causes, and that her involvement was strong enough to precipitate her family's move out of Benton County.

That winter evening, sitting in the living room with Sylvia's children, what else was I feeling? A mixture of shame, titillation, and the kind of perverse pride that accompanies the revelation of any secret to which we claim part-ownership. I also felt exhausted, used up. Worse, I felt I had used up my grandmother, allowed a splinter of past experience to embed itself into my memory of her, to infect the totality of her long and complicated life. If strangers learned what I had learned, would they judge my grandmother harshly? They would not have a lifetime of moments with Sylvia to balance the scale.

Yet I needed this chapter of my grandmother's life story, in part to tip the scales of *my* memory, which had, since Sylvia's death, been weighted heavily on the side of mythological reverence. It is easy to love a composite grandmother; harder, yet ultimately more freeing, to love a flesh and blood grandmother, individually and particularly flawed. As I am individually and particularly flawed. Had the circumstances of our lives been reversed, had I lived Sylvia's life and she mine, one day she might well have written an account of her maternal grandmother Rebecca, who along with a quarter-million other Indiana women, was drawn into the Klan's circle of influence.

"I cannot point to one decisive moment" (I hope Sylvia would have written) "when things changed for Grandma Rebecca. Many forces, external and internal, must have been gradually pulling her toward this point. No, point is not the right word. I imagine her crossover to the other side as more of a slide, a transition so natural and easy that she slipped into it as into a comfortable bed. The other side was not the other side at all. It was made up of kindred spirits who spoke her language, voiced her fears, and promised the solace and community she sought."

If, as the adage goes, the road to hell is paved with good intentions, then hell must be larger than we've ever imagined, each of us having laid at least one paving stone. It might also be smaller than we've imagined, dwelling within the secret regions of every head and heart. If hell exists, perhaps it is not a lake of blazing fire at all. Perhaps it is a cornfield, dotted with barns and farmhouses and country churches, the white steeples pointing toward a clear summer sky. If a woman as generous, highly principled, and down-to-earth as my grandmother could be drawn toward an organization like the WKKK, then anything is possible. Whatever the locked trunk held, I believe Sylvia was right in forbidding her children access to its contents. She was also right in saying that the trunk had belonged to a previous tenant. By that time, the Sylvia *of old at home* would have been no more. That Sylvia had moved out, moved on.

The story of any event in a family's life—the birth of a daughter on Armistice Day, for instance—is also the story of those who were not present. On the day Juanita was born, many members of the Mounts-Sanders tribe were missing from the scene. Arthur's sister Vena and her husband, still shell-shocked from their son's death, had moved to Detroit, leaving Kenneth's pony for Barbara and her brothers to ride. Up in Wisconsin, it was hunting season, and Sylvia's uncles and cousins were cleaning their rifles or tromping through the dense woods or stretching deer and wolf hides over the poles in Lafe's yard.

Everyone, that is, except Sylvia's cousin Stanley, who was busy tending to his own new one. Stanley's wife had just given birth to a little girl, and how Grandpa Charlie would crow the news to his sister Hattie the next time he saw her. "Your boys better get busy," her brother would say whenever he came to Briarwood for a visit. Hattie would laugh and give it right back to Charlie, reminding him about Dale's little daughter but keeping her feelings to herself. It was nobody's business what her sons did with their lives. Nobody's business but their own.

And they did have business, all three of her sons, business that kept them from the Armistice Day celebration. Babe, the youngest, was helping Sant and Bessie with the husking. Ivan was still in the West Virginia mountains along with other state troopers, saddling up his horse for a moonshine raid or another miner's strike, or dragging the river for some poor soul—a suicide, or a victim of vigilante violence. Hattie's eldest son, too, was absent from the celebration, for Dale now had his own family to care for, a fact that still jolted Hattie whenever it came to her mind. Dale, married! Who could have guessed that, at nearly forty, Dale would find Ines, one of the prettiest girls in Lafayette, no less, and make himself into a husband, then a father. Hattie and Robert had fully expected Dale to stay forever as he had always been, making his continuous loop from Briarwood to Wisconsin and back to Briarwood for the rest of his days, setting up camp with his cousins along one lake or another, disappearing for months at a time doing whatever it is that grown men do in the wild country of Wisconsin, and then, as quickly and mysteriously as he had left, returning home to them, usually in the middle of the night. Hattie would hear the click of the door, the thump of boots—one then the other—then the squeak of the stairs above her head as his heavy feet made their way to the sleeping loft, Robert turning beside her beneath the quilt to whisper, "Our boy's home." And Hattie not correcting him, not reminding him that their *boy* was already home—Babe, at twenty, had never left—and that this wanderer returning in the night was a *man*. Their fully-grown man. She did not correct Robert, for her sons—all three of them, wherever they were and however old they got—were still her boys and always would be.

It made no sense, Hattie thought as she tucked the blanket around the baby Juanita and handed her over to Bessie, who had just appeared at Sylvia's bedroom door. No sense at all, this worry she held for her boys. All the nights she startled awake, Robert sleeping beside her, with thoughts of her sons. Especially Dale. She could not clear her mind of him. Hard as it had been to give up her girls—Sylvia, especially, for Bessie had seemed grown-up, grown-away, almost from the beginning—hard as it had been, Hattie did not lie awake worrying for her girls. A girl remains her mother's daughter even after she becomes someone's wife. But to Hattie's mind, a son is lost to a mother the moment he takes a wife. Which is the way it should be, must be, isn't it, Hattie wondered. Isn't this the ending any mother would hope for? Her son to find a beautiful wife who gave him one of the prettiest baby girls Hattie had ever laid eyes on—a doll, Clara was, a porcelain doll. And how Dale doted on her. A happy ending. Then why the worry, the dreams that poke through her sleep? Hard as Hattie tried, she could not sweeten her thoughts on the situation. A mother knew when things were awry in her children's lives. And something was awry in Dale's.

◆

Bessie signed the Easter card with her usual *As ever, your sister Bessie D. Cosby* and returned to her large, sunny kitchen, where the warm eggs were cooling on the counter. She would decorate the eggs the old-fashioned way, Mother's way. Bessie had taken extra care in peeling the onions. She needed to keep the skins as whole as possible, easier to drape on the eggs that way, especially for Barbara's little hands. Hard-boiled was certainly not as healthy as soft, Bessie thought, but one could not properly decorate a soft-boiled egg. Where was that child, anyway? Those children of Sylvia's just turned a deaf ear whenever it suited them.

A few feet away, in a crate that Sant had placed beside the stove, the new biddies were peeping and squeaking. Bessie did not generally approve of keeping chicks in the house, but the hen had given her no choice. And after all the trouble Bessie had gone to: burying the dead ones, making the trip to the hatchery, choosing the liveliest, healthiest of the batch. To what end? That hen had refused them outright! Had Bessie not rescued the chicks, the hen would have pecked them to death. There was no dependence to be found in anything.

And where was that child? Probably in the cellar again, or upstairs in the sewing room. Bessie had best find Barbara before she woke Grandma Cosby from her nap. *Mother* Cosby, she corrected herself. Over and over, Sant had asked Bessie to please call her *Mother,* but the moniker did not come trippingly to her lips. Bessie had a mother, and Sarah Cosby certainly wasn't Hattie, not by any stretch of the imagination. She was eighty years old—for goodness sakes, Bessie thought, old enough to be my grandmother! And Lord knows she dressed like a grandmother. High-top shoes, long dress, bonnet: black, black, black. And on Easter, too!

Had Bessie gone looking for Barbara, it might have taken some time to find her, for the home of Santford and Bessie Cosby was large and rambling, and a four-year-old could find many places to hide. Downstairs, a library table built by Bessie's father dominated the parlor, its massive, carved legs salvaged from an old piano that Robert had found someplace or other; he was always inventing ways to reclaim what would otherwise be lost. Bessie was grateful for her father's effort, as she needed all the book space she could find, but she preferred the modern, Mission-style furniture she'd first seen at the 1910 convention in St. Louis. That's where she'd found the oak-and-leather chairs, the only two chairs in the parlor. Good taste, Bessie had observed, was not synonymous with clutter, and she liked the feeling of openness, especially in a reading room. One needed space to absorb all that flowed into one's mind through the books. On the small table by her chair was The Rubaiyat of Omar Khayyam, which Sant had given her as a wedding present twenty years ago, and which she had lately been rereading. Persia was a long way off, over one ocean and many smaller seas, and an open view was necessary to bring the vision close. A long, unobstructed view across the parlor and out the window to the slice of blue sky.

Sometimes, of course, openness must give way to practicality, so, according to my mother, her aunt's dining room held a limed oak table with three leaves, eight straight-backed chairs, and an open cabinet that Bessie's father had built to house Bessie's special china, her pickle and sauce dishes, the lidded soup tureen from which she spooned her Christmas Eve oyster stew, and the decanter for the homemade elderberry wine reserved for special occasions. And of course there was the tall bureau with drawers for silverware and linens—damask tablecloths, lace doilies and runners, napkins creased to perfection. More than once, Bessie had discovered Barbara with her small hands raised high to an open linen drawer, an experience that, decades later, Barbara could easily recall, for Bessie's ironing was "a work of art," and Barbara loved running her hands across the "satiny" napkins.

Strange and marvelous, the things children remember, the moments that hold. While the grownups are bustling about, scrubbing and pouring and tossing and muttering, the child is blinking at the wonders: sunlight ricocheting off the button jar; the play of dust motes above the window sill; the soft thrum-thrum of Bessie's Spanish guitar; Uncle Sant before the wavy mirror, twirling a thick strand of dark hair around his index finger and then releasing it, creating the perfectly centered forehead curl that Barbara will study throughout the day, amazed at how it keeps its shape.

Downstairs off the main entry hall was Grandma Cosby's room, and Barbara knew better than to bother her. Grandma Cosby was old, very old. Like someone from a storybook. Barbara thought it strange that someone as old as Uncle Sant should have a mother, and that she would live in his house in her own little room with her own stove, her own washstand with a pitcher and basin, her own rocking chair and (here Barbara giggled) "chamber pot." That was Aunt Bessie's name for it. Barbara's aunt was fond of fancy words and "employed" them (another one of Bessie's big words) whenever she got the chance.

A central staircase divided the roomy downstairs from the upstairs, its polished banister irresistible to any child who had a mind to slide down it, something Bessie chided against even while she tacitly allowed it. Upstairs, the railing looped nearly a full oval, creating an open hallway from which four large bedrooms sprouted, their floor-to-ceiling windows curtained in white lace. One bedroom held a rug loom and a dress form that little Barbara often dressed in Bessie's clothes, placing a hat on the neck stump to complete the costume. This was great fun while it lasted, but Barbara must always remember to close the door behind her when she left. If she didn't, if she forgot and left the loom room door open, the sight, as she later climbed the stairs, would startle: the late afternoon sun slanting through the blinds and across the ghostly form that seemed now—yes, look, it moved again!—to be watching from the corner. Watching, waiting. A ghostly, robed figure, faceless beneath the floppy hat. Something snapped in Barbara's memory, then a heart-pumping leap to close the door, a sudden turn at the top of the stairs where she took the steps flying, finally spilling herself into the safe, cool hallway. Beneath the stairway, her toys and books waited, stacked neatly. No shadowy figure here, no blinds casting crisscross shapes across the floor. She was safe, Aunt Bessie just steps away in the kitchen.

And here, across the room in the sweet-smelling parlor, was, to Barbara's eyes, the deepest wonder of all. The smooth, polished keys, the repeating pattern of black above white. There was a high tinkle of sound at one end of the piano and a low rumble at the other, and Aunt Bessie could put the high and low together to make songs, her hands moving fast or slow, then her voice pushing up through the middle of all that sound as if she were part of the piano.

In this particular moment, Bessie has left her task at the deep sink to search for her niece, untying her apron as she turns the corner into the parlor, where she finds the little girl standing by the window, her straight black hair glistening. Without even a nod, Bessie pulls out the stool, sits down, and pats the space beside her. Barbara scrambles up, scooting as close as she can without getting in the way, for Aunt Bessie's hands must be free and her feet too, to press and release the pedals that open and close the sound and sometimes make an echo. Some days the notes are fast and light, and Barbara sits up tall, swinging her legs along to the words. But not today. Today, the notes are slower, heavier, and Barbara feels a sad song coming. Aunt Bessie's low voice grows even lower, deeper. She bows her head close to the keyboard as if in prayer:

> Pickaninny comin' home today
> Cryin' cause him little heart am sore

The song from down south, Barbara thinks. Down south in Indiana where Grandma Mounts lived as a little girl. Not the Wabash River but a bigger one, one that Barbara has never seen. She looks up at her aunt, focusing on her mouth—such a wide mouth, Barbara thinks, for such a small lady. Barbara has heard the song before, many times, and it always makes her sad. Because the pickaninny is sad. Barbara doesn't know what a pickaninny is, but he has a mama and he is sad. So Aunt Bessie is sad, too. Her voice dips low, lower, and her mouth turns down at the corners while she sings:

> Mammy in her lap
> Take her little weepin' chap
> And say in her kind old way

Here comes the part Barbara knows by heart, since Bessie always repeats it again and again, each time softer and sadder, until by the end it is hardly more than a whisper:

> Don't you mine what the white child say
> Don't you mine what the white child say
> Stay on this side of the high back fence
> Stay in your own backyard.

◆

An early June morning after a night storm, the rain barrel brimming. Below the barrel, the sodden grass has already laid itself down. A small girl who one day will become my mother stands in the barrel, the rainwater chest-high. One arm splashes in the water, the other wrapped tightly around a small black goose flapping to get free. The girl's mother is inside at the kitchen sink, wiping a basket of warm eggs matted with feathers and feces. Sylvia's hands know this daily task, the stubborn braille of bumps and dots her fingers read, freeing her eyes to witness scenes through the window. For a moment, Sylvia sees not as a mother but as a photographer, and if she thought the moment would last she would dry her hands and hurry to get the box camera she keeps on the top shelf of the Hoosier hutch.

But a scene this perfect will not hold. The sun will move, a cloud shift, the child's bare shoulder ripple in a shiver that breaks the pattern of light. So my grandmother chooses to stay at the sink, her hands in the egg basket, her eyes memorizing the details: the child's smooth, white shoulder; black hair encircling a white face. Close up on the lashes, feathery and black, on the small head thrown back in laughter as the child splashes with a black goose in water silver from the shed's reflection.

Then Sylvia looks away. A ruffle in the tall grass or the kitten's tail switching—*something* steals her focus for an instant—and when her eyes shift back, the picture is moving, a series of black and white images sputtering like the first silent movie Sylvia ever saw. Black wings flutter, the child's arms fly up, the barrel rocks. Wings flutter again, the child's arms flail, the barrel rocks, the child's mouth opens in a scream silenced by the pane of glass separating her from her mother. The child lunges, and in the flurry of the moment the barrel rocks one more time then falls onto the grass, pouring onto the goose the black-haired child and all the silver water.

Perhaps the child wondered at the backward twist of the goose's neck, and the stillness. "I remember the rain barrel, the goose, I remember splashing. That's all," my mother says to this day.

One of the blessings of childhood is its distance from adulthood, the long, vast landscape of forgetting. Many years later, when my mother writes about the experience, which must have been traumatic—her first close-up look at death, and she its unwitting accomplice—the details will be reportorial, rendered without emotion. For though Juanita was the child to whom the event happened, she was not the one moved by the event. In this way, the goose story, though it happened to Juanita, does not belong to Juanita. Like so many events that happen to young children, it belongs to the parents and grandparents, the aunts and uncles and older siblings. Those who remember. And make stories out of the rememberings.

So, let's give the rain barrel story back to Sylvia, who watched it happen and locked the details inside her memory until her daughter was ready to hear them.

Barbara, my mother's older sister, can keep the shoulder blade story, though she would gladly give the story back, as she had never meant to hurt Baby Juanita, she was just trying to help turn her on the blanket. To this day, she can still hear her sister's screams that lasted all the way to Lafayette while Barbara sat alone in the back of the deep-seated touring car.

Hattie, dispenser of toddies and cordials and poultices, deserves Juanita's illness stories—the old fashioned red measles and the dreaded whooping cough that ravaged the little granddaughter who had just learned to walk, and who, if she survived, would have to learn to walk all over again.

As Hattie had predicted, Juanita did have to learn to walk all over again, and, like her Aunt Bessie when *she* was a child, little Juanita escaped whenever she got the chance. One spring morning when she was barely two years old, Juanita followed her father outside where he was loading a calf into a crate to be taken to the sale barn. He carried her back into the house, thinking that was the end of her shenanigans.

The rest of Juanita's story belongs to her father, for whom the experience acquired the quality of myth over the decades of telling and retelling. So, go ahead, Arthur. Tell it in your own words, the words you wrote seventy years later:

> . . . *Just as I was backing up toward the highway, I heard a tiny little cry. I grabbed the emergency brake, turned off the ignition switch, looked down and saw my little frail daughter on her back, and that hind tire on both of her knees. In less than it takes to count one, two, I vaulted over the left side of the car, spread my feet past her, lifted that hind wheel, stood on one foot and slid her out from under that wheel. Something greater than you and I. She looked up as if to say "Daddy, you won't hurt me." I grabbed her in my arms and ran to the house. In writing this, the tears flow until I can hardly see to write.*

Does Juanita have no childhood story only she can tell? No memory that has not been witnessed, interpreted, corrected, told and retold by those larger and older? Nothing of her own?

Wait. Something is floating up, rippling the surface. Something my mother never wrote about, talked about.

It comes first as a scent—smoke, curing meat. Smokehouse? Then a taste. Salt. Salt-cured air. Salt tears. On her lips, and on the soft shirt pressing warm against her. Her own tears on the warm soft shirt holding her close, and a deep voice saying, "It's okay, Juanita. Aunt Ines didn't mean it. Clara isn't hurt at all, it's okay." A hand wraps tentatively around her head, pulls her closer: "You'll be okay." Juanita has never cried like this, no one has ever scolded her so harshly before, but now Uncle Dale is saying she will be okay, so she will. She pushes her face deeper into the warmth and wipes her eyes. Looks up into Uncle Dale's face. He is crying too.

The smokehouse is the final scene in Juanita's remembering, and it takes some effort to rewind the scene and splice it together with all the scenes that came before. She and Barbara had gone to Ines and Dale's farmhouse, on a big hill out in the country. It was always a treat to go to Uncle Dale's, especially when Mom and Dad left them for the whole day—no chores to do, just play. Mostly the girls wanted to see their cousin Clara. She was so pretty and sweet, and wore such nice dresses that Juanita and Barbara both wanted Clara for their own. But she was exactly the age to fit perfectly between them, so they had to share her. Today they were playing Blind Man's Bluff, a game that Juanita had only recently learned. It scared her a little, reaching out in the dark to tag someone.

But it was fun, and Clara was laughing and having a fun time, too. Now it was Juanita's turn again, and once the blindfold was tight around her eyes, she began to spin and swirl and reach out—and then a cry, was it Clara? By the time Juanita could get the blindfold off, Aunt Ines was there, grabbing Juanita's arm roughly and screaming at her. No adult had ever screamed at Juanita, and Ines was screaming mean things too, saying that Juanita was a bad girl, that she had hurt Clara, that she would never be invited to their farm again.

Whether Juanita ran to the smokehouse to get away, or whether Uncle Dale saw what was happening and intervened, Juanita cannot remember. What she remembers is the smoky sweetness of the salt-cured air—a smell she would always associate with comfort—and the closeness of her uncle, the way he held her while she cried her heart out for the first time ever. It would be many years before Juanita understood that Dale's tears were not only for his niece, they were for himself, for everything that he knew was about to come. Within a year, Dale's little family would leave their farm, and within a few more years they would be "breaking up house" as Hattie called it. And Dale would store at his sister Bessie's what was left of his things—not much, for Ines had taken most of the household furnishings. She had also taken Clara. And Ines made good on her promise. Though Dale had been right—Clara wasn't hurt at all, just startled from being knocked off balance onto the grass—after that day in the smokehouse, Juanita and Barbara never saw their cousin again.

◆

Uncle and niece. Uncle and nephew. Forget the other familial loves for a moment, and focus only on these connections, each a small, arrow-pierced valentine with room for only two names: Ivan and Uncle Sant. Kenneth and Uncle Arthur. Juanita and Uncle Dale.

Dale and Uncle Charlie.

Dear nephew, begins the last postcard I can trace between the two. *When the time comes to say goodBy your always in a hury to get away so miss you, all ok from uncle Charlie.*

When the unfamiliar car stopped on the lane beside Wildcat Creek and a stranger began walking toward the log house, I imagine that my great-grandfather looked up from his newspaper. It was June, Robert's favorite month, and he rarely missed a chance to sit near the arched trellis where yellow roses climbed, sending their fragrance in all directions. Maybe his pet crow was perched on his shoulder, as it so often was. Maybe he called to Hattie, working the raised garden beds wearing one of her everpresent sunbonnets. As the stranger approached, Robert could see an envelope in his hand. Did Robert sense what the envelope held? Telegrams rarely bring good luck, at least not those delivered to Briarwood. That much, Robert Mounts knew.

> *Menomonie, Wis. 10:20 am, 6/27/26*
> *Mary passed away Saturday four pm. Come if possible tell the others funeral not before Tuesday answer if coming.*
> *Charlie*

The news had not been entirely unexpected, as Mary's asthma had been worsening for some time. But for Robert, this was a hard blow—his first sibling to die, and his closest sister. How does a person ready himself for such news? Beautiful Mary. He still thought of her as beautiful, though of course, as with the rest of them, age had had its way with her.

Still, Mary would always be his baby sister, no matter what the pictures show. In the last photo of them together, Robert's last visit to Wisconsin, Mary stands with three of her eight Mounts brothers. Her eyes look sunken—her mouth, too. Like Hattie, she'd lost most of her teeth by then. But on this afternoon, posing with her older brothers,

Mary isn't feeling her age. She's smiling. Her long hair, thinning but still shiny, has been pinned up hastily into a bun. She's wearing a handmade apron, its bodice fastened with two pins to her blouse. They must have just finished dinner, and a fine dinner it would have been, for how often did Brother Robert make the trip from Indiana to see them? As was his custom for any gathering, however informal, Robert wears a white shirt and black tie. On this day, he's buttoned a work shirt over the dress shirt. For warmth, perhaps, or in solidarity with his Wisconsin brothers, who are less formally dressed.

All three men wear hats that shadow their eyes: Robert wears a perfectly creased fedora with grosgrain trim; bachelor Harve (supported today by a walking stick), a slouchy number that dwarfs his stooped form; Lafayette, an engineer's-style billed cap. Each brother has a white mustache, but, as is the case with their hats, each mustache is distinct, suggestive of each brother's character. Great-grandpa Robert's is the trimmest, the most carefully groomed, his aquiline nose sharply defined above it. Harve's droops down the sides of his face, accentuating the deep dewlaps on his cheeks. But Lafayette's mustache is a wonder to behold. Thick and white, it dominates his face, filling the space between nose and chin so that only a bit of lower, pouting lip protrudes.

He's proud of the mustache, you can tell. Proud of just about everything about himself. Nearly seventy, older than his brother Robert but still sturdy as a tree trunk. Trapper, hunter, herbalist. Lafe to his family, Leif to the neighbors, Swedes and Norwegians mostly, who spell his name the way they hear it. Hell, let them spell it however they want, he thinks, it makes no matter: Lafayette Mounts, married to a woman young enough to be his daughter. Pearl was—what? Sixteen when they married. Or was it fifteen? Well, it was a New Year's Eve wedding, that much Lafe remembers. But that was thirty years ago. Lafe, father of four. Six if you count little Harry and Bessie, the two they'd buried those first years.

In the photo, Lafe wears only a light vest over his shirt. If it were winter, he'd be covered in fur, a coat and hat made from the pelts he hadn't been able to sell. Deer, wolf, fox, squirrel. But this is a mild day, late summer, so a vest is sufficient. As soon as they're finished posing—for his brother-in-law Charlie's camera, most likely—Lafe will say his goodbyes and scramble off to check on his ginseng and goldenseal, which he's sheltered with a teepee covered with grapevines. He'll feed the hunt-

My great-grandfather Robert with three of his ten siblings, circa 1924. Left to right: Mary, wife of Charlie; Robert, Harve, and Lafayette.

ing hounds and fill their water bowls from the rainwater trough he's fashioned from a split hollow log. He's proud of that trough, too. Let the neighbors say what they want—"Work isn't the Mounts brothers' long suit"—Lafe knows how to make do. He looks the camera straight in the eye as if daring it to blink first.

◆

Once Robert had handed over the telegram to Hattie, she was able to put it all together. Robert's face. His tears. She studied the words on the message, noting the two periods. Periods cost extra, she'd read that. Most people just wrote "stop" to separate their thoughts. "Stop" was free, no extra charge. But Charlie had paid extra for the periods. Mary, gone? This is a sad corner. Mary had been like a sister to Hattie.

But *like a sister* is not the same as *sister,* and even as she held the telegram, even before she untied her sunbonnet and headed back to the house, Hattie's grief was already taking a different shape, more akin to worry. Worry for Charlie. But then she'd always worried about her little brother. The motherless boy who'd been taken from her when he was barely two years old had never been far from Hattie's thoughts, and even after the two siblings had reunited, for years she kept a close watch over Charlie, until she no longer needed to.

For Mary Mounts had come into the picture by then. The fact that Mary was Robert's sister was a welcome bonus—double connection, double joy. Exactly the kind of woman Charlie needed, old enough to serve not only as wife but in many ways as mother and sister to Charlie as well. Mary was Charlie's ballast, providing weight and balance to his days. He hadn't had much luck farming in Indiana, and Wisconsin was even a tougher go, but with the chickens Mary raised, the cows they milked for butter and cream, the pigs they butchered and the large garden she kept, they managed. Mary was the eldest of the Mounts daughters, and Mother Mounts had taught her well. So I imagine there was always bread rising in a pan, a quilt-in-progress on the frame, a pile of mending beside Mary's chair, and on the walls of the farmhouse a few mementos from her dead parents' home in Switzerland County, perhaps the hair picture Mother Mounts had woven so long ago.

But Mary was gone, Hattie reminded herself, and now who will keep Charlie tethered to home, to work? With his farm situated like it is, way back in the hollow, who knows what might go on? So many men in the Valley drink too much—that, Hattie knew—and liquor was never good for Charlie. Hattie longed to see her brother, but she and Robert were getting too old to make the trip, and how could they afford it? She would send one of their boys, but Dale and Ivan had wives now, responsibilities. And Babe? Hattie's youngest son just wasn't suited to the wilds of Wisconsin. Babe was a homebody through and through.

As the months passed, then one year, two, worry for Charlie occupied more and more of Hattie's thoughts and dreams. His increasing silence disturbed her. Was he still mourning? Lost in his grief? Hattie tried not to think of the worst, though the worst would not surprise her, for Charlie's youngest daughter and her husband had recently broken ground on the Valley Bar and Grocery, and, well, isn't that exactly what Charlie doesn't need? Hattie didn't know all the details, but she knew enough to worry.

So, what a relief to see her brother's car pull into the lane at Briarwood one summer evening. The driver's door opened and out he came, unwinding his legs to their full length. He stood to stretch. It had been a long drive, a hot one, too, but Charlie was dressed for visitation: dark bowler hat, three-piece suit, white shirt. In the photo, he stands tall and erect, arms akimbo. White cuffs peek out from the jacket, drawing attention to his large hands with their long, slender fingers. Charlie's face, though, is shadowed under the hat's brim. There's a suggestion of a chin, a section of nose, but the eyes appear to be missing. It's impossible to read his expression, to guess what he might be thinking. And no letter survives to describe his last visit with Hattie and Robert, only the postcard he mailed to Hattie once he'd returned home to Menomonie, with its printed message:

> As the sunshine paints the flowers
> A gay and lovely hue
> So life is made much brighter
> When I remember you

And, on the back of the card, his scrawled message to his sister:

> *Arrived home Sun 2 PM no mishaps found Everything all rite thrashing and silo filling rite away so will be busy for some time, dry here all is well will rite soon as I can*
> *Charlie*

As it turned out, all was not well. Charlie had not told Hattie that he had taken out a three-thousand-dollar loan to keep his farm alive, nor had he told her that he had not been entirely alone since Mary's death. When Pearl moved in, and under what conditions, is unclear, though the 1930 census lists her name beneath Charlie's. Pearl, who had turned fifty that year, was still married to the ancient Lafayette and would remain married until Lafe's death years later, long after the tragic events at Charlie's played themselves out. Their community was small and tightly knit; people knew each other's business. Was Charlie immune to the rumors? Was Lafe? Lafe, who was now living with his son and grandchildren just a few miles away? And what did Charlie's son and his wife make of the situation with Pearl and Charlie? Most likely, Pearl was already gone, the case closed, long before Stanley and his family arrived.

Whatever reservations Stanley might have had, the plan went forward: Stanley and his wife and children moved in with Charlie. Times were tough all around, and it made sense to combine their efforts to bring the dying farm back to life. But although the two men persisted, working side by side for nearly three years, their dream died almost as soon as it was born. And if a man's home was his castle, whose castle was this? Charlie's? Stanley's? Who would make the hard decisions, take the blame? Charlie was stubborn, proud, volatile, and Mary wasn't there to fix things, to act as mediator between father and son. Yet her ghost must have haunted them both, making them yearn for simpler, happier times. Would they ever come again?

Stanley's eldest daughter, though quite young at the time, still remembers the months leading up to the tragedy. Yes, she explained to me, the pattern was predictable. Every night after the family had finished supper, Stanley's wife would gather the children together and take them upstairs, but the children could still hear the quarreling between their father and grandfather—voices rising, tempers flying, sometimes a crash as furniture was knocked over, smashed against a wall. No doubt their mother protected them from the details of the arguments, as she would later protect them from details of the August day that would alter the family's life forever. As her daughter explained to me, their mother "did not talk about the event as I remember, because it was something she didn't <u>want</u> to remember."

What were Charlie and Stanley arguing about? The loan that Charlie had taken out? The machinery and livestock that Stanley was accumulating and moving from the farm, insisting that he had been doing more than his share and that he deserved something in return so that he and his family could start fresh? Did they fight about Pearl? Was Charlie's temper fueled by liquor? Or was their trouble no more than the primal, ancient violence that pulses in the blood of most fathers and sons, but in the case of Charlie just kept pulsing, pulsing, until there was nothing to do but allow the rage to rise to the surface and finish its job?

No family member claims to know the answers to these questions. All we really know is what nearly everyone in the Valley seemed to know at the time: Trouble was building between Charlie and Stanley. Trouble so fierce that one summer day, Charlie's daughter Mettie went to her father's house while he wasn't there and gathered up all the firearms she could find—the hunting rifles and the shotguns. She might have gathered the knives and hid them as well, for according to local rumors, Charlie had had a bad history with knives and fighting, a history written in a deep, diagonal scar across his torso. But that was a long time ago, his daughter must have reasoned. Certainly Dad had mellowed since then. Things would blow over between him and Stanley.

Still, you could never be too sure. Better safe than sorry.

Had Hattie known the extent of the trouble in Wisconsin, she would have moved heaven and earth to reach her brother. Certainly she sensed something wrong, as Charlie's letters and postcards had stopped arriving many months before. The last she'd heard, things were fine. Better than fine. Stanley and his wife had moved in with Charlie and would help him farm the land. Hattie couldn't wait to tell Bessie. This is the way it should be, she thought. The way it used to be. Everyone pitching in together, being a family. And how wonderful for Charlie to have children around him again—four little ones, counting Stanley's newest, his first baby son.

Although Hattie tried to stay in touch with Charlie (*Dear One, Are you still among the living?* her customary greeting) too many miles separated their households, and the Indiana clan needed to care for those closest to home. The last few years had been filled with calamity. Bessie and Sant's house in Stockwell, which they had been renting out while they worked their nearby farm, burned to the ground in a mysterious blaze; shortly thereafter, Sant's only remaining brother fell off a ladder and died from the injuries. Meanwhile, the Great Depression had hit home in full force, and Arthur and Sylvia's sons left for Detroit in search of work. Soon, Arthur was laid off from Ross Gear plant, where he had been working to keep the mortgage on the South River farm paid.

Arthur followed his sons to Detroit, standing in line at factory after factory while men were turned away—"by the thousands," my grandfather would later recall. Men who slept outside the hiring offices so they could be first in line in the morning, some covered only with newspapers to keep warm. Arthur was fortunate enough to find temporary work at the steel mill, and though the family struggled, he and Sylvia managed to hand over the mortgage money each month to a banker who promised to make payments directly to the mortgage company. They never doubted the banker's integrity. Why would they? "An honest man is the noblest work of God," Arthur often quoted. Besides, the family had other concerns. The heartache of Dale's situation, for one. His marriage with Ines was strained, and if anything happened, what would become of their little daughter?

◆

Summer in Wisconsin's Lucas Valley is a green, magical time. Maples and red oaks are lush with foliage; irises and tiger lilies dot the hillsides. Soon, fall mornings will dawn cool and clear, and local hunters will start preparing for the black bear trials. Until then, there is August to endure, and some Augusts are hotter than others. The August of 1933, for instance, with its clammy torpor, its interminable afternoons unwinding into evenings like a slow-motion film even the cows can't stir themselves to watch. Mornings offer scarce relief, the first waves of heat already rippling outside the barn. Inside, the Guernsey and Brown Swiss switch their tails and blink their eyes against the assault of murmuring black flies. The cows have been milked hours before, at first light—by Charlie, probably, his large, practiced hands pulling and squeezing until one bucket, then the next, is filled then emptied into large metal cans, which are now cooling in the springhouse, awaiting the arrival of the milk truck.

The morning of August 17, 1933, found Emil Finder where it had found him every morning for as far back as he could remember, his Chevy truck having made the milk route so many years that it seemed to know the route by heart. That terribly hot morning, a Thursday, the truck made its way up the rutted road to Charlie's farm. Perhaps one of Stanley's little girls ran out from the house to greet Emil. One daughter would remember that it was so hot that day, her mother and Aunt Mettie were sitting outside in rocking chairs, trying to cool off. Maybe Stanley's wife waved at Emil from the front porch, holding in her arms her baby son. Emil's own new son had been born just a few weeks before. Hard as it was raising children—Stanley had four, Emil five—both men probably imagined that one day they would look back on these days as the happiest of their lives.

As for the trouble between Charlie and Stanley, everyone seemed to think it would blow over; these things always do. Stanley greeted Emil when he arrived, and after they'd loaded the milk cans into the truck, Stanley asked Emil if he would bring the truck back later in the day, as he needed to move some last things to the new place he and his wife had rented. Emil agreed. He'd be back as soon as his route was finished.

Where was Charlie when the milk truck arrived that morning? Perhaps mucking out the stalls in the barn, or in the cornfield checking the stalks for earworm. Maybe across the field at the Valley Bar buying groceries, or helping himself to a drink or two from the lean-to still. He might have been at the bank in Menomonie, trying to get another loan to carry them through the season. Or maybe Charlie was out in the yard all along, Byron's *blue devils* glaring from his *morning mirrors,* and when he saw Stanley and Emil talking, he figured Stanley really was going to do it, take the last load of furniture and machinery. Is that when Charlie went to the pump house to check on the shotgun? To be sure it was still there, hidden along with the shells he'd stashed, for you never know when you might need protection—from a wolf, a wild hound, an intruder. Not since he was a boy in Switzerland County had he been without a gun, and he wasn't about to be without one now. A man without his gun, why, what kind of a man was that?

Decades past this moment, people will still be arguing over what happened. Some say that Charlie and Stanley had words over Pearl having lived at Charlie's. Some members of the Indiana tribe surmised that Stanley was a drinker, was cruel to his wife and children, and that Charlie had finally taken matters into his own hands. No evidence supports this notion, as Stanley's surviving children remember the man they still call "Daddy" as kind and affectionate, and Stanley's widow, before her death at age ninety-four, declared to them that Stanley never drank at all. Perhaps the Indiana Mountses were confused. Maybe they'd heard of Charlie's older son's alleged mistreatment of *his* wife, and somehow they'd mixed up the two stories. Certainly they would have been desperate to latch onto anything that might explain the terrible events, including the story circulating around the Lucas Valley that while he was packing to leave, Stanley tried to remove Mary's ancestral "hair picture," claiming that it was "of the Mountses" and so belonged to him and not to Charlie.

The full truth of what happened, we will never know. But a few facts are clear. At some point, Charlie went to the pump house and got the shotgun. A single-barrel shotgun, which, of course, requires reloading. How many shells did he take? Enough to do the job, certainly. But did Charlie know what that job would be? Perhaps he thought only to scare Stanley, to coerce him into staying. Or maybe Charlie knew that the end had finally come, that there was nothing left for him here in the Valley. Maybe he thought to take only his own life, to exit this world on his own terms. Or maybe he didn't think at all. *The mind has a thousand eyes. And the heart has but one.*

The only eyewitness was Emil Finder, who, according to his children, never spoke of that day. Certainly Emil wished he could have foreseen the tragic outcome. But he was just a neighbor trying to help out. Even if he had seen Charlie hurrying from the yard and toward the pump house, Emil could not have known where that action would lead. Like Stanley, Emil probably had his back to Charlie when Charlie returned, "approaching close," as the news account will later claim, moving quickly no doubt, his long legs striding, the decades of hunting experience kicking in, pure instinct, reflex—click latch, break open, load, relatch, pull hammer, sight down barrel, pull. After Stanley fell, Charlie started to reload, and though Emil hurried toward him to stop what he feared was coming next, Charlie was too quick—instinct, reflex—and within seconds had thrown himself to the ground, repositioned the shotgun, and, holding it as far from his body as his long arms would stretch, turned its barrel to target his own heart.

When it was over, two bodies lay on the ground beside the truck: father, son. But in terms of family connection, many more than two individuals died on that August afternoon. When Charlie killed Stanley:

He killed his own son.
He killed his dead wife Mary's son.
He killed the husband of Margaret.

He killed the brother of Charlotte, John, and Mettie.

He killed the father of Lorraine, Patricia, Valerine, and the baby, his namesake Anton Charles.

He killed the nephew of Hattie, Robert, Lafe, Thomas, Benjamin, Harve, Jeremiah, William, Lavina, Laura, and Harrison.

He killed the cousin of Bessie, Dale, Sylvia, Ivan, and Babe Mounts, and dozens of other relatives scattered in Indiana, Wisconsin, California, and throughout the country.

The damage was beyond repair. No wonder Charlie reloaded. He must put an end to it, now. Except there is no end to such a story. For when Charlie killed himself:

He killed the surviving husband of Mary;
the father of Stanley, Charlotte, John, and Mettie;
the grandfather of Lorraine, Patricia, Valerine, and Anton Charles;
the brother of Hattie;
the uncle of Bessie, Sylvia, Dale, Ivan, Babe and . . .

How many other strands unraveled that day? I imagine the Mounts hair weaving lying in the farmhouse yard. Or tucked inside a bureau, to be found months or years later, once the house had passed into other hands. Did a stranger retrieve it? Was it lost, destroyed, sold to an anonymous antique dealer? If the weaving survived, on whose wall does it hang now?

Ah! who can tell? Or rather, who can not
Remember, without telling, passion's errors?

News of the shootings traveled quickly around the Valley. Charlie's surviving son arrived to identify the bodies of his father and brother. The county coroner signed the death certificates, ordering no inquest. Dazed family members, careful to keep details from the children, planned separate funeral and burial services. Bessie's cousin Charlotte, the baby in Bessie's diary pages, received the news at her home in California, but for whatever reason, did not make the trip for the funerals of her father and brother. A few days later, on a high hill of the Lucas Cemetery, Charlie was buried beside Mary on their family plot, beneath the family stone that Charlie and Mary had purchased years before, along with several burial spaces reserved for their children and grandchildren. Stanley's grave was dug far from his parents', in the center of the cemetery, aligning Stanley with a new tribe, his wife's people.

Down in Indiana, the news arrived at Robert and Hattie's log house on the edge of Wildcat Creek. If "news" is sufficient to hold all that was delivered that day. "It broke them," is my mother's take on the event. "A double tragedy, both sides of the family." *A siege of sorrow,* Hattie would have named it, lying beside Robert on the feather bed, the August night alive with the treet-treet of field crickets and the click of katydids, Hattie's mind rolling backward, over the miles and down the years, Charlie and Stanley and Charlie and Mary and Charlie and Hattie, the years unrolling, Menomonie to Briarwood and down to Switzerland County, to the Old Mead House beside the river, and still it rolls, her mind, the river, the crickets scraping, scraping their song, soon school would start and Hattie would present her calling cards to her new chums, and Brother Charlie, wherever he was, would be wearing long pants and starting school, too, and one day soon he would make it home, washing ashore like the lost boy in <u>Christmas Day at the Beacon</u>. Hattie would be watching from the upstairs window and see him there, bobbing at the edge of the river, and she would call out to Aunt Phebe and the two of them would rush to the bank and wade in deep, not caring if they ruined their good slippers, and they would fish Charlie out and bring him into Grandfather's house where a fire was blazing, like the fire in <u>Christmas Day at the Beacon</u>, and Hattie would never let him out of her sight again.

CHAPTER  16

The first and only time I saw Aunt Bessie cry was the night I played Lottie Moon. The production was <u>Her Lengthened Shadow</u>, a sentimental playlet about a missionary who had died half a century before. I was fifteen, the same age as Lottie Moon when the play opens; in the hour it took to perform the play, I would age fifty-seven years. Bessie rarely attended church with our family, but she came that night in Santa Ana, California, to see what all the fuss was about. My mother had sewn my costumes. Someone else's mother had applied the pancake makeup and, during scene changes, penciled in lines between my eyes and on the sides of my mouth. I remember lifting my eyebrows to create forehead furrows, and smiling crazily, unnaturally, to form craters around my mouth so that she could guide the eyebrow pencil into the depressions. In the last scene, when a special lightbulb cast a shadow across the stage, signifying my death at the impossibly old age of seventy-two, I heard gasps in the audience and knew I had played my part well.

After cold-creaming the years from my face, I walked out to the family station wagon, parked at the edge of the church parking lot. My parents and siblings, who'd been waiting for me, responded with almost universal praise, but Bessie was uncharacteristically silent, facing straight ahead, her hands clasped tightly in her lap. I climbed into the back seat beside her. Though I was a petite teenager, I sat higher in the seat than Bessie, who, try as she might, could never quite keep herself erect; a crooked hip tilted her body to the side. Bessie was smaller than any grownup I knew, but her hands were disproportionately large, marbled by dark, prominent veins and mottled with age spots. And now, smack-dab in the middle of the Lottie Moon memory, I am stopping to do the math: 1965; Bessie was eighty-five years old. Tears were sliding down her face. Tears? I had known Bessie all my life, had slept in the same room with her, the same bed, had even loved her in my selfish, adolescent way. But I had never seen her cry.

I leaned forward and tapped my mother on the shoulder. "What's wrong?" I asked. I often talked *around* Aunt Bessie as if she weren't there. My mother turned from the front seat and calmly shook her head as if to silence the question. But Bessie had heard, and she turned to me, her eyes rimmed with red. "You looked so old," she said. "It hurt to see you look so old."

Hurt? Aunt Bessie hurt? But I was just play-acting, couldn't she see that? Or did she think I was making fun of her, mimicking her gestures? Now, looking back on that moment nearly fifty years gone, I believe I finally understand. Watching me, Bessie must have glimpsed the old woman I would become, and this glimpse threw her headlong into a future she was not ready to accept. Like the child Margaret in the Gerard Manley Hopkins poem, who appears to be grieving for the fallen leaves, Bessie was actually grieving for herself. She was mourning what would not be. The autumns she would not live to see. The nieces who would grow old without her.

D. C. Mead, Jr.
1152 Summer Street
Hammond, Indiana

My Dear niece Hattie,

This is a rather dark day for me to do much writing but Ile try to scratch off a few lines so you will know that I am still hanging around in the way. As usual for the last couple of weeks has been pretty tough hanging on have been having the epigaptic or Distemper or som other dang deseas, but maby I have about wore them out they gave me a pretty good fight but I kept pretty well oiled up and kept sliping away from them so I think I have them whiped to a stand still . . . I don't get any news from the West, I guess I am a forgotten saint you know when you nothing els to do you do a lot of thinking that is the way with me that is all that I have to do is to think. I was thinking about brother Ben and wondering if was among living yet or not and I do not know how to find out.

Well how is things down at Bryer Wood and the Wildcat is the creek frozen over so you can get a mess of fish through ice, gee my hand is cramping now I recon that Dale thinks am one big fiber I tried make good but always some good excuse. Excuse this paper, my well wishes to you are just the same as if it was written on the finest of paper. Good luck to all and best wishes to all as ever Uncle Clint.

Uncle Clint Mead's letter, composed on the back of a newsprint circular advertising "Men's Work Shoes at 95 c," "Fleece-lined Canvas Gloves for 4 c," and "1933 Topcoats valued at $65 for $17," is one of only several family documents surviving from the 1930s. Hattie, who saved practically everything, had not saved the Oshkosh newspaper article headlined "Kills Son With Shotgun." Nor did Hattie save the court papers her son Dale no doubt brought with him after his divorce was final and he'd moved back to Briarwood. Best to put all of that out of her mind—the terrible things that Ines had said about him. Well, no matter now, Hattie thought. Dale is home again, though still more gone than not—visiting friends, setting up camp, sending postcards when the mood strikes him. *Better not look for him until we see him,* Hattie writes to Bessie, who fears that Dale is drinking again and that the blue devils she has fought for so long are assailing her brother as well.

But who has time to worry? With Mother Cosby still in their care and their California ranch plans looming further away than ever, Bessie and Sant have moved to a new farm in Clinton County and are furiously trying to set things in order. In Bessie's letters of this time, she labors alongside Sant, toiling round the clock to keep the hogs, cows, chickens, and lambs alive and thriving. Sometimes a sheep *denies her lamb,* as Bessie describes it, and the lamb has to be fed with a bottle.

And of course there are always somebody's children to keep for a day, a week, a month, however long Bessie can convince them to stay: Ivan's children, Sant's nephews, or Sylvia's daughters. My mother recalls long visits at Bessie's Clinton County farm, its large, rambling, vine-covered house set far back from the road, near a long stand of trees. The house had two sets of stairs, allowing for a separate entrance for itinerant hired men, who never seemed to show up when needed. A deep porch encircled the house, and Juanita remembers a lamb named Debby "trip-trapping around that big porch and baaing like a spoiled baby." Mostly, though, Juanita recalls the walks she took with her aunt, long hikes that wore the child out, for the tiny, wiry Bessie could tromp for miles without pause. Hikes to nearby cemeteries, where Bessie pointed out headstones and told stories about the people who were buried there. Hikes in the woods, where Bessie taught the names of trees and plants, flowers and birds, an education that continued in long letters she sent to her young charges: *A red-bellied woodpecker (the red isn't on his belly, that is so you can notice it, it is on his head just like all the other woodpeckers) came and sat in the old Balm-of-Gilead tree and scolded and scolded and of course you couldn't blame him, now could you?*

The visiting children helped with chores when they were asked to, but none could keep up with Sant, nor with Bessie, whose flurry of activity never seemed to slow. She often complained that she hadn't gotten more done, yet in one set of letters written over a few weeks' time, Bessie reports that she has canned tomatoes, put up forty-three quarts of blackberries, twenty-three glasses of blackberry jelly and thirteen glasses of apple jelly, washed two quilts and a blanket, made apple butter, baked four loaves and two pies, canned pears and fixed some pickles, made some piccallili, dug sweet potatoes, is about to boil down seven gallons of cider, and (even as she writes) there is a batch of ketchup on the stove to be finished tomorrow. But, wait, Sant has just announced he's *manuring out the cellar,* so Bessie decides it's time for her to get in on the act, too: *I want to white-wash a little, make it smell better, remove some of the mold of ages past.*

The mold of ages past was not something Bessie put much store in. Cemetery prowling was one thing—that qualified as history, and of course history should not be forgotten. As Hattie and Robert's eldest child, Bessie was the chief repository of the Switzerland County stories that stretched back to the Civil War and even earlier. But when it came to her own life, Bessie was forward thinking. "Why look back?" she often said. "It only makes you sad." And as for the letters and postcards and birthday cards and knickknacks that her mother and sister seemed unable to relinquish their hold on, enough! Unnecessary clutter ties you down, and Bessie needs to be free to take off at a moment's notice.

Which is why she keeps her suitcase packed at all times, just in case. No California trip for now. But who knows? Any day, a neighbor might stop by on his way somewhere—Indianapolis, St. Louis, Chicago. Chicago! Bessie has not given up on seeing the World's Fair. The double-towered Skyride alone would be worth the price of admission. Imagine flying in a rocket car two hundred feet above the Rainbow City! Twenty million visitors already for the Century of Progress Exposition. No Woman's Building this time, but she'd heard that the House of Tomorrow has an automatic dish washing machine and refrigerated air cooling throughout. What would they think of next?

Bessie has no interest whatsoever in Sally Rand's silly fan dance or the blind xylophonist or the human pincushion. And could it be true that they are exhibiting live babies inside incubators? Now why would someone pay good money to see that? She'd read that one little baby in the Ripley Odditorium—a "preemie" they were calling her—weighed four pounds seven ounces. What was newsworthy about that? Bessie had not weighed nearly that much, and she'd survived quite well, thank you. Maybe if they exhibited those little Dionne quints, that might be worth a look. Imagine, five little girls, each smaller than the next. Well, that is the way of the world, Bessie thinks. Those who are meant to survive, do.

◆

"I'll never forget the look in her eyes," my mother tells me. "It was the first time I'd ever seen such pain." My mother was nine years old the spring of 1934, and when she got home from school that afternoon, her big sister Barbara told her what had happened—how the doctor, with his black bag and black hat, had come as soon as he could but it was too late. Juanita went up the stairs quietly, up the long stairs of the rooming house in Battle Ground, Indiana, to the two rooms she and Barbara shared with their parents. They'd moved from the South River farm only a few weeks before, the farm that had been Juanita's first and only home. But they'd lost it somehow, Juanita didn't understand exactly; it had something to do with the bank. Juanita had hated to leave her school and friends, but she was excited she was going to have a new sister or brother. Finally, she would not be the baby anymore!

"Come spring," Dad had told her. Had Juanita been older—as old as Barbara, who was in eighth grade now—she might have wondered why her mother was the only mother in their circle of friends who was about to have a baby. In April 1934, Sylvia Sanders was just shy of forty-five years old. Her first granddaughter had been born last month, up in Detroit, which meant that Juanita was now an aunt. Imagine that, Juanita thought. Only nine, and already I'm an aunt: Aunt Juanita. And now it was spring, and the baby that Juanita had been waiting for had been born today: William Hayes Sanders.

But he was dead now, and Mother was very, very sad. Juanita put her book satchel down on the table and stood for a minute outside her parents' door before entering as quietly as she could. Her mother did not stir, did not raise her head from the pillow. When Juanita bent down to the bed, Sylvia rolled over, turning to face her. That is when Juanita saw her eyes, hollowed out with pain and a darkness so deep that Juanita thought she would fall into it. If this was not Sylvia's First Great Sorrow, it was the first witnessed by her young daughter, a moment that Juanita would remember for the rest of her life.

Recently, when I questioned Aunt Barbara about 1934—the loss of the South River farm, the months in the rooming house while Grandpa Arthur searched for a new home for his family, the death of her baby brother—she surprised me with her tears. Barbara, at age ninety-one, does not cry easily. "It breaks my heart, still, to think of it," she answered. She'd never fully understood the foreclosure details. All she knows is that her dad had made his monthly mortgage payments on the farm for twelve years, ever since they'd moved from Oxford. Barbara believes, though she can't be sure, that Arthur paid in cash, to someone who worked for the bank. "It was a terrible year," she said, "in every way. But Mom and Dad always shielded us, so I don't know everything that happened." She remembers the move to Battle Ground, and later the many trips, by horse and wagon, to move the family's possessions to the farm out on Tyler Road. "The new place was awful. Broken windows. Burdock, waist-high." The plaster walls, she recalls, were scarred with large black marks where the former tenants struck matches, "to light their cigarettes, imagine that. And Mom was so sick," Barbara continued, her voice now thick with emotion. "All that winter before the move, and all through the spring."

By the time Juanita entered her parents' room, her brother's body had been removed. William Hayes Sanders had come into the world, and left, too quickly for even Hattie to get there. Vena and John, receiving the news at their home in Detroit, offered the plot next to their son Kenneth's grave in the Justus Cemetery in Oxford, Indiana. Two young cousins who never knew each other would be planted side by side: Row 11, Column K. When news of the baby's death reached Bessie, she must have remembered her own First Great Sorrow so many years before. Or had that memory lost its weight, pressed against the horror of the past year? Charlie and Stanley, both gone. Sylvia and Arthur's farm. And now, a baby to bury. Could things get any worse?

Of course they can. They always can.

J. E. Mead
1152 Summer St.
Hammond, Ind.
April 26, 1934

Dear Cousin Hattie:

Father was struck by an auto yesterday and died last night at 9:00 o'clock the funeral will be Saturday at 2:30.

Call Mrs. Carson and see if they are coming to the funeral and if they are they will probably bring you up and Cousin Robert.

Struck by an auto? Uncle Clint? After all he'd done to keep *well oiled up and slipping away from all those dang deseases?* Clint, the last brother of Hattie's dead mother, the last uncle to have known Hattie as a child. No more "Dear Niece" letters would arrive in the mailbox at Briarwood. Hattie was no one's niece now.

When all those who knew you as a child are dead, what happens to your history, to all those lives you lived?

◆

Juanita always enjoyed her time at Aunt Bessie's, but after a few days she was homesick for their new farm, which they'd named the Circle S, for "Sanders." She missed Prince, the spotted white and brown pony that had belonged to her cousin, a little boy named Kenneth who had died before Juanita was born; she would ride Prince to neighboring farms to visit her new friends, or over the hills to fetch the cows when it was time to milk. Mostly, though, she missed her mother and sister. Missed coming home from school to the smell of bread, still warm from the oven, and Mother slicing it for her, and asking about her day. They'd sit at the table and sew or read by the light of the coal oil lamp, just the two of them—and sometimes Barbara, too, when she wasn't with her friends or working at the Sweet Shoppe in Lafayette. Most often, though, it was just Sylvia and Juanita *holding down the fort,* as her dad wrote in his letters to them. Juanita missed her father, but Arthur had been gone so much these past few years—to Dearborn, Detroit, Indianapolis, wherever he could find work—that Juanita had gotten used to his absences. Like she'd gotten used to her brothers being away.

Although the second Sanders farm was nothing fancy like Aunt Bessie's place, the Circle S had finally begun to feel like home. When they'd first arrived, after those weeks in the rooming house, after her mother had lost the baby and finally started feeling better, the young Juanita could not believe what she saw. Could not believe that this would be their new home. Filthy walls, cracked plaster, yards overgrown with briars and weeds, broken-down fences and debris left from the previous tenants who, no doubt, had had to leave in a hurry like so many others that year. *The farm was a sorry place when we got there,* Juanita wrote in an eighth-grade composition a few years later. *We had to begin again.*

And begin again, they did. The ledgers and notes that Arthur and Sylvia kept those first few years record every cent paid to keep the Circle S standing. Taxes, insurance, deed recording. *Paintbrushes for house $3.00; paint for barn roof $3.15; plaster and putty $1.75; shingles and weatherboard $9.45. Repair for window glass $5.50. Rhode Island Reds (20) at 9 cents comes to $1.80. Buff Rocks (90) at 11 cents comes to $9.90. New Idea chick mash. Brooder house equipment. Ground corn. Chick fountains.*

Sylvia and Arthur, like most good parents who value the memories they are planting within their children, kept the worst from them. No need for Barbara and Juanita to know how close to the edge the family was teetering. Reading through the ledgers is like prying open a nailed door into my grandparents' most difficult times. Every job is record-

Public sale notice for animals and implements from the foreclosed farm of my grandparents, Arthur and Sylvia, 1934; a page from the "Breeding Record" of their farm animals.

ed, every task my grandparents hustled up to make it through those years. Selling eggs, milk, cream, butter, cottage cheese, sorghum, bread, cakes, and pies. Rendering lard, filling silos, sawing wood, threshing beans, stripping cane, cutting corn, shredding corn, husking corn, hauling straw, hauling clover, grinding oats, digging potatoes, frying chickens, carding wool, shredding fodder, putting up hay, butchering hogs. Mostly they worked for neighbors and friends—the Oberholtzers and Van Nattas, the Sheehans and Emricks—and were paid "real money." They sometimes bartered for goods and services, but usually they paid their neighbors outright: *White sow of Charles Taylor, $15. Veal calf of Morehouse, $12.* Once in a while, a relative's name appears in the ledger. On June 21, 1936, they paid Hattie ("Mrs. Robert Mounts," the column reads) eleven dollars for a heifer calf. Hattie would happily have gifted the calf to her daughter had she been able to, but everyone had bills to pay, even Hattie. Even Bessie. *I hate to think of selling the lambs,* Bessie wrote to her sister. *But we can't sell anything else it seems, and we must have the money to apply on the mortgage the first of the month. Mortgage. What a disagreeable sound it has! And I imagine there are worse crimes committed in the name of mortgage than selling lambs.*

Besides financial ledgers, my grandparents kept a livestock breeding record, its two columns charting the elapsed time from "service" to birth. Some animals were listed by name—Big Ruth, Petty—but most were merely described by their most salient features: Big Hampshire Sow, Young Grey Mare, Old Goat. With all the breeding and birthing going on in these pages, it's a wonder that Juanita never witnessed an event from either side of the ledger. But according to my mother, Sylvia and Arthur guarded their youngest child from such barnyard goings-on, and to this day my mother swears that she never once witnessed animals mating or giving birth. Indeed, for years she seemed to have no firm knowledge of what animals—or people, for that matter—did with each other when they were alone. Of course she'd seen movies, so she knew about kissing, and certainly some of the older children at school told tales, so by the time she entered high school, Juanita had puzzled out most of the details. Still, like most young people, she'd never linked these details to her own parents' lives, until one spring evening when her mother came storming across the field and into the house, slamming the screen door behind her.

It was an unusually warm spring evening, and Juanita had invited a friend from school to stay overnight at the farm. Arthur was working out of town again, so only Sylvia and Juanita and Juanita's friend were home, sitting around the kitchen table eating a cold supper. Juanita guesses that she was wearing one of the dresses she'd sewn to earn her

4-H badge, though it's possible she wore a ready-made dress that Barbara had bought with her earnings from the Sweet Shoppe. Sylvia and Arthur had recently advertised cattle and lambs for sale, and in the past few days several people had come by to have a look. That evening, as the two teenagers and Sylvia sat at the table, a man knocked at the side door, asking to see the livestock. Sylvia left with him and they made their way out to the back field. Within minutes, as Juanita and her friend watched from the window, Sylvia came stomping across the field, past the cow barn and the outhouse and the chicken yards, her arms crossed firmly across her large bosom. She turned the corner into the garage, disappearing from their view for a moment before reappearing, slamming the screen door and huffing into the room, red-faced and vehement.

"Do you know what that fellow said to me?" she cried.

The girls turned from their perch at the window.

"He said," Sylvia began, staring hard at the girls as if they might be partly responsible, "'Do. You. Want. To . . .'"

The words hung in the silent, heavy air. Two seconds. Three.

"Neck."

Sylvia crossed her arms tighter across her breasts. She lifted her chin, set her mouth into its thinnest line. The girls were stunned silent. Not at hearing the word—they'd heard of "necking"—but at hearing it from her mouth. From a *mother's* mouth. Another few seconds passed. Long enough for meaning to settle, for the unseen scene to play itself out in Juanita's mind: Mother and a man. No, not Mother. *Sylvia* and a man. Sylvia Sanders. A woman, approached by a man. The fact that my grandmother chose to announce the encounter to her daughter is another layer of the story, as is the fact that many years later, Juanita chose to tell the story to me. Did she think it was time I released my hold on the *grandmother* Sylvia so that the whole Sylvia could come forth? Emphasis on *grandmother*, Sylvia's default position.

Yet to the man, Sylvia was no one's grandmother. No one's mother. Maybe someone's wife, but that someone was away for the evening so why not try and see how things might go? She was a shapely woman, after all, with an easy smile, an easy laugh. Not young, of course, but young is overrated when it comes to nights like this.

Can we ever know our loved ones, all their separate and warring selves? Or understand what role they played in someone else's story? Or must we always edit their lives to complete our own? I recently discovered, tucked inside Aunt Bessie's copy of A. E. Housman's <u>Last Poems</u>, a dried flower staining the page with several shadows of itself, and beside the flower, a torn, folded slip of paper I now open carefully. Bessie's unmistakable handwriting: *XXXVII, I did not lose my heart in summer's even,* and then the rest of Housman's poem, copied word for word.

The purpose of poetry, Housman once said, is to "harmonize the sadness of the universe." And if the stories about the poet are true—that he fell in love only once, with a heterosexual man who could not or did not return his love—then Housman must have had much sadness to harmonize. "I publish these poems," he writes in the preface of the 1922 edition, "because it is not likely that I shall ever be impelled to write much more." Yet he did. "I did not lose my heart in summer's even" does not appear in the pages of <u>Last Poems</u>. It appears in <u>More Poems</u>, published in 1936, after Housman's death. Which means that when Bessie copied the poem and placed it in this book, she would have been at least fifty-six years old, Sant at least sixty-eight. I love that <u>More Poems</u> can appear after <u>Last Poems</u>. Last does not have to mean forever.

CHAPTER

Dr. M. L. Harshman
Colfax, Indiana

Dear Mrs. Cosby,

Thanks for the check. I could say more about the drug bill if I could see the total hospital bill. Remember Sant received many drugs & food by venous route and took almost nothing by mouth. If you're over this way stop in and I'll be glad to look it over for you.

Sincerely yours, Martin Harshman

Dr. Harshman was a trusted family friend, so Bessie paid his bill promptly. The bill from the hospital was another matter altogether. Bessie was not accustomed to dealing with hospitals; neither she nor Sant had ever set foot in one until it became clear that there was no choice. Sant, the hearty, strapping Swede who at age seventy-two still worked his fields with plow horses, who had exceeded the life expectancy tables of the time, who had outlived his three siblings, and who, if his mother's longevity was any indication (Sarah Cosby had died the year before, at age ninety-two) should have lasted at least long enough to travel with Bessie to California and draw out plans for their orchard, could hide his illness no longer. The prostate cancer that Sant had silently soldiered through for months, perhaps years, had spread to his bones, and the resulting pain was—and I choose the word carefully—excruciating. Excruciating: as in *crux, cross,* torment beyond imagining. Decades later, his niece Barbara will recall her January 1941 visits to Home Hospital in Lafayette, remembering how difficult it was to witness the "dire pain Uncle was in."

In. When an illness like Sant's reaches its final stages, grown so large and strong that you cannot contain it, the pain is no longer in you. You are in it. Those gathered around you may suffer, but they cannot climb inside the pain with you.

What *can* they do?

Offer homemade toddies and poultices, as mother-in-law Hattie does. Knock at the door of your hospital room like the lovely, dark-haired nieces, Barbara and Juanita, who appear in their bright winter coats still dusted with snow, trailing the clean, crisp scent of January wind. Sit quietly at your bedside like your brother-in-law Dale. Or bustle about like Bessie, stirring up the dust of life, making small noises against the silence. And then, in the next moment, against the cries that rise from her husband's mouth. Yes, Sant is still her husband, she must keep telling herself that, though so mightily changed that in these moments he seems to belong to someone else entirely, to some other world he is crossing into, a world into which she cannot follow.

Not that Bessie believes in some other world, not the kind the minister talks about. *Is* talking about, on and on, as she sits in her library parlor crowded with neighbors, friends, and relatives, her mother on one side, her father on the other. Hattie reaches for her daughter's hand to calm the fluttering, and Bessie looks down at the funeral card in her lap:

> In Memory of Santford M. Cosby
> Born Kirkpatrick, Indiana, September 3, 1868
> Passed away Lafayette Home Hospital Jan. 8, 1941
> Services held at home Jan. 11, 1941 10:30 a.m.
> Interment Salem Cemetery

Now the minister is reciting Tennyson's "Crossing the Bar," a poem someone selected while Bessie was busy with other details. Bessie never much liked the poem, though at least it comes at death from an angle. No outright mention of heaven, or God for that matter.

It feels strange to sit—it's been days since she's just sat—and Bessie keeps thinking there must be something she should be doing, something she's forgotten to do. Her mind travels down the list: Babe has fed the animals, carried in wood, stoked the fire in the kitchen. She's stacked her best dishes buffet-style on the table and retrieved from the cellar the cherry preserves, all she could spare, but even with the pies and casseroles the neighbors keep bringing, will there be enough to feed everyone? And now here's Mother's hand again, patting, and all around Bessie, people are standing, bowing their heads for the benediction. Out of the corner of her eye, she watches as the young men slip out, one by one, the six she finally chose. She'd agonized over each name on the list, not wishing to slight anyone. Pallbearing is an honor, yes, but also a job, plain and simple. Each man has to bear his share of the weight. Sant's brothers are dead, but she wouldn't have chosen them anyway. Too close a relation. That is asking too much. As for her own brothers? Out of the question. Sant might not have been their brother by blood, but you'd be hard pressed to convince them of that.

Best to skip a generation, opt for youth and strength: four of Sant's nephews and two of his friends' sons. Close enough but not too close. You can't have a man going down on one knee, or choking up just when it comes time to lift.

◆

Dear Sis,

Well Bessie thanks for your letter and I know you have had plenty to do besides write letters. I really don't see how you got through the winter. But I guess we're tough Eh? What's the matter with Mother is it her hip or a cold or liver or what? Tell Everybody Hello! and Keep your <u>CHIN UP</u>!

Love, Sylvia

The two Mounts sisters were indeed tough, and, luckily, their roughest patches never hit at the same time. By the time Bessie answered Sylvia's letter in the spring of 1943, it was Sylvia who needed cheering. The financial problems that she and Arthur had suffered through all their married life had intensified. No matter what they did, they couldn't seem to get ahead. Arthur had finally found work sixty miles south in Indianapolis, leaving Sylvia to manage the Circle S farm alone. *Shall we buy the sheep?* Sylvia wrote to her Honey Boy, care of the YMCA, where Arthur was rooming to keep expenses down:

... The int. & prin. at the court house will be due the 15th and is $122. It doesn't have to be paid right on the date so I thought I could take this money I have and with the hog we have to sell yet mabe we could buy part of the sheep anyway. I <u>could</u> sell my chickens if I had to. I am going to pay the oil man $5 today which will take all my change but it will be that much anyway. . . .

Still, Arthur and Sylvia were determined that at least one of their children would go to college. *Will be no exemptions for Juanita's education,* Sylvia wrote. *I guess they want all the boys in the army and all the girls in the factories.*

The following weekend, while driving back to Indianapolis, Arthur blew out both front tires and had to travel the last fifteen miles on the rims. When he finally made it to town, he began his quest to buy new tires, not an easy task. *Damn the dictators any how,* he wrote to his wife and daughter, then crossed out *damn* and replaced it with *censored.* The "dictators" were the ration board controllers, and Arthur tangled with them for the next several months while they refused to grant a requisite for new tires.

Obviously, the dictators didn't know Arthur Sanders. Still as scrappy and proud as when he was a boy, he finally told the controller off, adding, "Well, I'll just quit farming, then, as I need tractor tires too."

"Oh, no, we don't want you to quit farming," the controller answered, weakening.

But it was too late. Arthur's mind was made up. He closed the Circle S farm, for the time being anyway, and took a factory job in Lafayette. Juanita had started at Purdue, and she loved it so much that her parents decided they'd do whatever they could to keep her in school. The three of them moved into a small apartment within walking distance of campus, where Sylvia found kitchen work at a nearby restaurant. "I hated seeing her peeling kettles and kettles of potatoes," my mother remembers, "but it helped contribute. It was what she could do."

As she tells this story—an episode of Sylvia Sanders's life I never knew until now—sadness crosses my mother's face, and I imagine Juanita as she was then. Beautiful as many co-eds are at that age, but more distinctively beautiful, with her thick, blue-black hair and those famous Sanders eyes, her father's eyes, deep-set, with an exotic, Asian cast. Youngest child of Sylvia and Arthur. Youngest daughter of a youngest daughter, and, like her mother, the darling of the household. Yet unspoiled enough to understand what her education was costing the family.

My mother completed one year at Purdue; twenty-four years would pass before she entered another college classroom. She took a job at Bell Telephone, then at the Aluminum Company of America, where she was the first woman hired in the timekeeping department, working three different eight-hour shifts, in consecutive weeks. The night shift was the hardest, she remembers. Still, Juanita Armista Sanders, named for a peace her grandmother had prayed would hold, considered herself lucky. Neither of her brothers had yet been drafted, and her brother-in-law and uncles had thus far escaped injury. But so many were hurting. Every day brought more bad news. Her fifth grade teacher had died overseas. Then a high school classmate's plane went down in the English Channel, and when his fiancée heard the news, she killed herself. *Killed herself.* Juanita had never heard of a woman committing suicide. Men, yes: Great-uncle Charlie. But a woman killing herself? Over a man? Is that what love did to you? Could losing someone hurt that much?

◆

The rough draft of Bessie's letter to Hirrell is scrawled in pencil, complete with the numerous cross-outs, arrows, and edits characteristic of Bessie's letter writing process:

> *Well Hirrell I need a helper much more than I did when you wrote me but now which would you prefer to do? Climb up in the hay mow and fork the hay onto the barn floor, climb down for it down the chute, go down stairs and fork it into the racks for the cows and horses and carry more to the sheep and feed the chickens and carry corn and slops to the hogs and sort about a bushel of corn and chop it for the cows and maybe go to the field and husk some and clean the stable and milk, or do the house-work, carry coal up from the basement, etc?? I can't do both but I am trying to. My brother was drafted and left the 26th of Oct. with the crops still in the field and no one to help me at all.*

Sant has now been dead nearly two years, and although Bessie is determined to keep the Clinton County farm alive, with her brother Babe out of the picture, her choices are dwindling. Nearly every neighbor and relative of serving age has already shipped out. One Wisconsin cousin is serving stateside; another is unaccounted for. Luckily, Brother Dale is too old for service—he's working up north on the railroad—but Ivan is somewhere in England, and no telling when he'll be back on home ground.

Bessie is afraid her nephew Leland will be next, and Sylvia is beside herself with worry. She writes to Bessie that her new son-in-law—Barbara has recently married—is deferred until November, but according to Sylvia *he feels pretty badly. He doesn't want to go but he doesn't want any one to think he is yellow either.* Not that Sylvia would consider him yellow. Not anymore. The young woman who three decades before posed jauntily in her brother's uniform, who wrote to her mother that the war might be just the thing for straightening those young men out, is now praying that her own son won't have to serve. *Well I guess I can rave all I want to,* Sylvia writes, *and it won't help any or do any good.* She knows that even if Leland isn't sent overseas where the worst is happening, there's no guarantee he will stay safe. One of Sylvia's friends, Mrs. Giles, *just lost her boy in a bomber crash in Idaho or Wy. She is very bitter about it and there doesn't seem to be anything to say to her.* Idaho? Wyoming? It's easy to understand Sylvia's confusion, both places being so removed from her life in Indiana that they might as well be Germany or England.

To set the record straight: The bomber crash that killed Mrs. Giles's "boy" occurred in a hilly area northwest of Glenrock, Wyoming. All ten soldiers aboard were killed. Staff Sergeant Eugene Giles Jr. hailed from Lafayette, Indiana; the others, from Texas, Oregon, Ohio, California, Massachusetts, and North Carolina. None came from Wyoming. *Like so many, many others,* as Bessie writes to Hirrell, they had been *caught up in this awful upheaval called War and set down in an entirely different environment.* Bessie wonders if this has been Hirrell's fate, as well, if perhaps this letter she is writing might not even reach Hirrell.

Who was this correspondent, and what relationship did Bessie have with Hirrell? My search turned up no records for this person, nor did relatives or family friends recall anyone by that name, male or female. A variation of Harold or Harrell, Hirrell is an unusual first name, even for a man, and almost unheard of for a woman. Besides, would Bessie have written to a woman to suggest she might be a "helper" on the farm? Not likely. More likely, I concluded, Hirrell was a man. A married man, perhaps, as Bessie closes with *Hope this finds you both well and as happy as anyone can be in these trying times.*

In 1942, a sixty-one-year-old widow, especially one as flinty and opinionated as Bessie, was an unlikely candidate for romance. Still, the possibility isn't unthinkable. Although Bessie had never been a beauty, her small, wiry body had aged well, and when she wasn't suffering from her blue-deviled moods, she was a lively, spirited companion. Earlier in my search, I had discovered a black and white photo postcard of a music duo, "Howard and Dec," both men wearing the wide-lapelled, wide-leg suits popular in the late 1940s. Howard, sporting a bow tie and a too-wide grin, sits at a piano. Beside him, a tall, dashing man supports a double bass, his left hand fingering the frets, his right index finger poised in mid-pluck. The back of the photo is addressed, in a confident, loopy script *To Bessie, a wonderful person, with the wish that we may have a long, long friendship always. Think of me once in awhile, will ya? Love, Dec.*

Love, Dec. So maybe Bessie did have male admirers, late in life. Men she met on her travels, perhaps. But what of the letter to Hirrell, written so soon after Sant's death? Whoever this person was, male or female, married or unmarried, it's clear that Hirrell and Bessie shared a long history—of birdwatching, literature, and correspondence. In the draft, Bessie answers that, yes, she has indeed read Thoreau's <u>Walden</u> and wonders if Hirrell knows the essays of Henry W. Van Dyke. As was her custom, Bessie apologizes for her late reply: *I have answered your letter (in my mind) many times, even dreamed of some things we might do together and get a lot of pleasure out of it.* If Hirrell was a man, I wondered, what was the nature of their friendship? Did Bessie ever mail the letter she had composed so carefully?

Then, a few months ago, I discovered a letter signed "Hirrell" folded carefully into a forgotten hatbox, along with other artifacts from Bessie's life. Hurriedly, I skimmed the letter, anxious for clues. Much of the letter reads like a birder's life list, the names and numbers of birds that have appeared in Hirrell's yard: two cardinals, three chickadees, three titmice, four downy woodpeckers, three flickers, one Carolina wren, ten doves, one hundred sparrows, ten starlings, one hawk that occasionally picks up a sparrow or dove, and one owl, which Hirrell found dead just last night. At one point Hirrell, apologizing for not *being gifted with a fine power of speech or a keen intellect,* seems to be laboring to impress the bookish Bessie, describing *a flicker peeping out of a hole*—or *a squirrel asleep on a limb*—or *a chickadee hunting for spider's eggs.*

I finished the letter, refolded it neatly, and placed it back in the hatbox. Hirrell was no man, but a self-described "lady of leisure." Married to a man named Hayden. My mind had left on its own journey, completing Bessie's story the way I would have wished her story to be completed.

Yet Bessie's life was hardly over. Sant's death had tossed her world upside down and inside out, but she'd since had time to absorb, if not to accept, the loss. And if she couldn't get the help she needed—*for there is no dependence to be found in anyone*—Bessie had options. She could sell out, trade down to a smaller farm. Or leave altogether. What was keeping her here? Dale could care for Mother and Pa; he was certainly better at it than she was. The deed to the Atascadero land was still intact, much to the consternation of the adjacent rancher who kept sending letters addressed to the dead Sant, offering to buy him out. I've held on this long, Bessie thought—thirty years, come spring—and I'm not about to sell out to some stranger. Now is my chance to see the ocean, to be in a new place. Almonds? Fruit trees? The land was still there, waiting for someone. It might as well be me.

◆

When my great-grandfather died—at 7:30 on a cold December morning a few days before his wife's birthday—he went, as the old-timers like to say, quietly. In his own bed, in the log house he had salvaged from someone else's leavings. Robert Mounts was eighty-seven years old; one of his daughters was already a widow. He had outlived sisters, brothers, nephews, and nieces. He had been married to the same woman for sixty-three years.

The funeral director at Dickerson Funeral Home presented Hattie with an elaborately designed book titled <u>Memories</u>. On one page, a purple-robed Jesus kneels at a rock, light from an unspecified source pouring across his face. On another, a blond angel balances above an open tomb where three women clutch one another, each face paler than

Great-grandfather Robert at Briarwood; a partial list of neighbors attending his funeral in 1943.

the next. Poem after poem attempts comfort: Bryant, Emerson, Whittier, Tennyson. Job 1:21 reminds us of Who gave and Who taketh away. Ornate titles on the top of each page prompt us: Family Record. Our Loved One's Life History. Automobile List. Last Photograph. Flower Remembrances.

The empty pages don't surprise me. Who had the time or heart to fill them in? Certainly not Bessie, though she seems to have tried. Here is her handwriting, the black ink skipping in some spots, smearing in others. Final Resting Place: *Salem Cemetery.* Date of Interment: *December 13, 1943.* The minister's name. A list of the three musicians she chose, along with the six friends and neighbors who comprise the list of casket-bearers. Later, when Bessie has time to catch her breath, maybe she can finish filling out the rest.

A two-paragraph notice appeared in the Lafayette <u>Journal & Courier</u>. On the back of the obituary, which is scissored out carefully, a headline reads "Japs Repulsed by U.S. Forces: Enemy Counterattacks, But is Driven Back With Heavy Loss." When Robert Mounts died, no flags were lowered to half-staff. No public speeches were made.

Still, here they come, arriving at Briarwood—relatives, friends, and neighbors. By auto, buggy, and on foot, balancing covered dishes as they slip and slide up the icy walkway then through the low doorway, crowding into the tiny house, their voices hushed—the Mitchells, McDoles, the Packards and Yundts, the Fickles, Rothenbergers, and Reicherts, the Zinks and Andersons and Funks—and the decades pushing past Bessie's eyes, the droughts and fires and floods and babies, the casseroles and euchre games, dances and dirges, bonfires and laughter. She stands at the door, silently nodding her thanks, for she cannot speak, then politely taking their coats and hats, which she carries to the bedroom and lays across Robert and Hattie's feather bed, or what she can still see of the bed, covered as it is with jackets and vests and heavy capes, wools and plaids and canvas and fur, army caps and hunting hats, black fedoras, felt derbies, and squirrel-tailed caps.

CHAPTER 18

Early photographs of my mother confirm my father's frequent remark: "She was a living doll." Sometimes I correct him, joking that if he's looking to make points, he shouldn't use the past tense. But usually I don't make a federal case about it, partly because the remark doesn't seem to bother my mother, but mostly because his affection for her is so obvious and steadfast. Let's say she's getting up from her chair, where she's been piecing a quilt or arranging photographs in an album or writing a note to one of their fifteen grandchildren. As she moves across the room, my father's gaze will follow her with the admiration of a newlywed, for, if we are to believe his eyes, she is all news to him. Sometimes, out of the blue, he will say to me, "You have an amazing mother, do you know that?" This is a rare gift: for a daughter of any age, let alone a daughter as old as I am, to witness a father's love for her mother. And I mark it here, so I will not forget. If beauty resides in the beholder's eyes, my mother is still beautiful.

Even so, there remains that troublesome past tense: Juanita *was* a living doll.

This is where a different writer, one who lives more sagely from the inside out, would interrupt with wisdom, New Age or old. Wisdom older than the stars. She would speak comfort, telling of earth mothers and Gaea, cosmic wombs, and the mysteries of the Kula flower. Imagine the freedom such wisdom would bring. Imagine being one of those wise, gracefully aging women, the ones you see at poetry readings, on yoga mats at the Y, on the jacket covers of thick books. Look, this one stands defiantly before the camera, barefoot in a field of wheat, her breasts untethered under a cotton tent dress, her gray hair tangling in the wind.

My "living doll" mother, Juanita, in the early 1940s.

This is who I am, her weathered face says. Take me or leave me. I have earned the years. Count them on my ringless hands, in the flesh around my middle.

I have studied such women from afar and have known others who could teach me how to do this natural, terrifying thing called aging. If I wish to learn, I can stand at the edge of my mother's life, or my grandmothers', or the life of Bessie. Or I can return to New York to view Rodin's She Who Was Once the Helmet-Maker's Beautiful Wife in the Metropolitan Museum of Art. Art critics make a big fuss about the sculpture's content—the withered, naked figure, her sagging flesh and shriveled breasts—but it is the work's title that breaks something loose inside me. To be named not by what you are now, in this moment, but by what you once were. As if everything that matters is already gone. The old women pass by on the streets of my town, and I imagine captions floating over their heads: "She Who Was Once the College Professor's Brilliant Daughter." "She Who Was Once the City Ballet's Principal Dancer." "She Who Was Once a Living Doll."

I don't remember when I first suspected that *I* was not a living doll. I do remember a contest that some girls in my sixth-grade class organized. During lunch one day in September, probably about the time the Miss America pageant was due to air, they passed out ballots listing the names of all the girls in our class, and beside each name, four possible boxes that you could check: Beautiful, Pretty, Lovely, and Cute. You were allowed four votes, one girl for each category. By the time the dismissal bell rang, Marilyn Stacklo had been declared Beautiful, Christy Schutz was Pretty, and two girls whose names I cannot recall were Lovely and Cute. There were no check marks beside my name, but Marilyn cheerfully informed me that I had gotten one write-in vote. On the bottom of a ballot, someone had neatly penciled my name, proclaiming me "Sometimes Cute."

The universe offered other clues, and by the time I turned fourteen, I had concluded that though in a pinch I could pass as pretty, I was definitely not a "knockout," a word I'd heard associated with my older sister, and, as the years passed, with my younger sisters as well. My skin was pale at a time when pale wasn't fashionable, especially in southern California; my sisters tanned easily. Plus, they had our mother's dark, expressive eyes. I'd inherited our father's blues, which, according to popular 1960s songs were what every American girl wanted. But who among us wants what we already possess? Desire is measured by what we lack.

On good days, I tell myself I was luckier than my living-doll mother and my knockout sisters. Bessie was, too. Released early on from the expectation of beauty, she could turn her gaze outward, to all that caught her wandering eye, and away from the woman in the mirror, her fading, if imperfect, glory. If aging is difficult for those of us who were only sometimes cute, just imagine how hard it must be for those who knew early on the power of their beauty. My friend Gail, who sensed such power, powerfully, and who has openly mourned its passing over the past few years, has made alternate plans. "I've decided if I can't be beautiful anymore," she says, "I will make beautiful things." Gail makes poems. Other women make other beautiful things: gardens, homes, businesses, paintings, symphonies. My mother made children, then an education for herself, then a licensed preschool. Along the way, the homes she and my father made housed not only their children and grandchildren but also her elderly parents, Great-aunt Bessie, and assorted lost souls for whom the home served as halfway house: a mentally ill niece, a young woman studying at a nearby college, a Chinese immigrant who had no other place to go.

When the house finally emptied, my mother returned to an early passion, hand quilting. Twice a month, she gathers around quilt frames with dozens of other women who make beautiful things to give away. Five of the quilters are in their nineties. One is nearly a century old, and as I watch Gertie bent intently over her work, the intricately carved face and hands seem to me works of art. I do not know if they seem so to Gertie. But if she mourns lost youth, she gives no hint of it. Gertie appears to live her days, as my grandmothers and Aunt Bessie lived, and as my mother continues to live, from the inside out.

Did my grandmothers ever lie in bed, as I do, and wonder where the years had gone, what manner of women they were becoming? Did they touch their soft bellies, their fallen skin, and mourn the changes? Maybe I have been wrong all along about their easy acceptance of all that time did to them. I may be wrong about Gertie and Bessie, as well. And my mother? "Oh, no," she answered recently when I related my brother's proud assessment that "our mother is totally without ego." "That's not true," Mother said. "I am too vain. I always have been." Juanita, vain? My mother, "She Who Was Once the Living Doll"? Is she trying to tell me this isn't easy for her, either, this loss of what has been?

And what of the Helmet-Maker's Wife? Living inside herself, did she feel the shift from *is* to *was*? If so, when did the holding pattern break? To say that the Helmet-Maker's Wife was *once* beautiful suggests a single occurrence. Only once could she be that beautiful thing. In the next moment, the next year, the next decade—depending on how long the *once* lasts—she would become something else entirely. Some other form of beautiful, perhaps. Or thus she might conclude, years later, looking back.

◆

Nearly all the family letters surviving from the 1940s were written by aged women—widows, mostly, or women so long divorced they resembled widows. Although all of these women are now decades dead, as I read the letters they exchanged, the decades rewind and I am in their world, entering the tidy, well-swept rooms their lives have become. With the exception of Bessie, whose traveling feet keep her on the go much of the time, the women generally keep to themselves. Not that they don't sometimes long to be out and about, mixing it up with neighbors or with the growing tribe of grandchildren and greats-, who send postcards now and then or stop by to deliver treats from town, ripe tomatoes from their gardens, or outdated but "perfectly good" dresses from their closets. But the young ones have their lives, and we have ours: such is the consensus of these letter writers. Contrary to common belief—that old people live vicariously through their children and grandchildren, their nephews and nieces—the women in these letters seem quite capable of living their own lives. When they do mention the young ones, the mention is brief: Fannie's girl and her man are living in Hollywood, he is an actor and she has some kind of radio show, isn't that something. Ivan's girl has grown up, so Ella imagines she would never know her now. No one seems to know where Mary and Charlie's girls finally got to after the shootings—is Charlotte still in California? Maitie has heard through the Indiana cousin grapevine that one of Sylvia's sons and his wife are having trouble, and though she's sorry to hear it, it doesn't much surprise her as *things are in an awful mess now days people are so unsettled they don't know what they want or when they want it.*

What do these women want? To live their lives and share them with someone who will listen and understand. *You have my sympthy, I know how it goes,* Robert's surviving sister writes to Hattie a week after his burial. A widow herself, Laura has earned the right to sympathize. As have the Gold Star mothers that Ella describes in the letters she sends Hattie from Tacoma. Never mind the manner in which a son or daughter soldier gave the "supreme sacrifice"—combat, accident, illness, suicide—only another Gold Star mother can sympathize with how the loss "goes." And if the letter writer's sympathy sometimes comes through as complaining, well, that is the fault of the reader (mea culpa) who stands safely outside this circle of women. Women whose aging bodies move like one immense aging body struggling through the world. *I am not any too good but I'm up trying to stagger around,* writes one. *I am just pegging away,* answers another. And if Ella can't keep her heart medicine going, she will *ache & draw all over,* but for now *have enough blood to pump the heart good. Fortune be thanked.*

Fortune is thanked a lot in the women's letters. Luck, too. Things could be worse, and will get that way soon enough, for *time slips by on wings.* Who knows what the next years will hold?

Uncle Bob & Aunt Liz are both in a bad shape he is not able to walk, neither one hardly able to wait on the other.

Margaret & Frank look like shadows. . . . he is very frail and cant live very long, none the children will have him & he is in a home, an awful place Ruth says.

How to live out their last days is a heavy concern for these women, what with recent Social Security shakeups and rapidly depleting unemployment insurance, especially out west. *So many have came in and through . . . some here getting as high as $285. a month for their families & not even here in the state over a year,* Ella reports from Tacoma. Cousin Maitie's California news is almost as bad: *Houses & apts. are so scarce no one can find a place to live but people are coming here by the dozens ever day from the East.* Maitie is afraid she might lose the Long Beach apartment she's been renting for years now. She hopes her new teeth will hold out. She paid fifty-five dollars a few years ago for lower plates and extractions, and she calculates that now a plate like that would cost at least one hundred fifty. And the price of food! Each time Ella goes downtown, everything is raised, a fact that she documents in page after page over a decade of letters: *Potatoes now are 5 cents for old potatoes and new ones 3 for 25 & tax, sliced becomes 75 c per lb., cabbage now 6, 2 bu carrots 17 c, but I bought spinach at one place Sat. for 5 c per lb. onions (dry) yellow 3 for 20C.* Ella's decided she'll have to eat her chickens. She's also taken in a boarder, an elderly logger named Mr. Biehl who can't afford to retire so he just keeps on, sometimes Saturdays and overtime too, and Ella worries herself sick about the dangerous work. *One has to be able to work on booms as well as saw and sometimes they slip in and many drown if they are not strong swimmers and able to fight their way among the logs—& that old sound is deep & cold.*

If Mr. Biehl were to slip in and under, and his body not recovered, at least his family and friends would not have to scurry around to raise money to lay him away. Ella writes that she was at a Gold Star funeral last Tuesday for a woman *8t years old* with *not much to do with, had to work out for a living* because her daughter and her family had taken her Civil War pension to live on. At another Gold Star layaway, members collected money for the flowers and funeral food, with help from the East Tacoma Rebekkahs and the Disabled Veterans Auxiliary. Sometimes it takes all three organizations—women helping women— to put a sister away when the families can't. Or won't. One of Ella's friends has a daughter *not to keep.* And a bad housekeeper, to boot. But at least the girl isn't cruel to her mother. *I see or hear so much of how children treat their old parents that sometimes I wonder why they are permitted to be even near them.*

Not all the women live alone. Ella is caring for an ill daughter (*It's her heart*) as well as cooking and cleaning for Mr. Biehl. And now that the war is ended, two of Hattie's sons are back home at Briarwood, though with Dale working on the railroad and Babe so busy at the filling station he bought with help from Bessie, Hattie seems to be alone most of the time, getting frailer and frailer with each trip to the mailbox. As for Bessie, the California cousins keep sending tempting postcards from "The Land of Sunshine": A field of poppies. The daffodil parade. Orange groves. Turquoise ocean waves curling over the margins.

But Bessie doesn't want to live with cousins. She wants her own place, on her own land in Atascadero. For now, though, she's got more than she can sort out here in Indiana. How did she get herself into such a predicament? Sitting at the kitchen table with her stocking feet stretched toward the stove, she traces it all back in her mind, every step she's made since Sant died. Where did she go wrong?

Trading the big farm for a smaller one? That made perfect sense.

Engaging her nephew to help farm the land? Again, perfect sense: Why bring a stranger into the picture?

Moving in with him and his family?

Here, Bessie hesitated, but only for an instant. Of course. She should have known. What in the world had she been thinking? But she'd found a remedy, she had to give herself credit for that. Her own place, built on the foundation of the burned-out Stockwell house. Perfect sense: Why buy a new plot when you have a perfectly good one waiting?

But she hates the little "chicken house," as she calls it. Hates being cooped up like an old hen. Too much time to think. And when did her mind reverse directions, traveling backward rather than forward? If she doesn't keep a close watch, she'll be wandering into the past like her aunts and cousins, whose letters, more and more, just make Bessie tired. Cousin Maitie, reliving her work on the assembly line at the war plant. Aunt Ella, recounting her job at the hospital where she lifted patients twice her weight, throwing out a vertebra that *still just won't stay put.*

Well, nothing stays put, Bessie's decided, no matter how much you try to nail it down. Least of all, the past. *It was 59 years the 15th of this month that I was married. 36 years-alone,* was Aunt Ella's last sojourn into memory's land. *He is sick, a neighbor of his called me on the phone-*

and said. He wanted to come and see me & how I was. Pretty late I'd say but guess he has had time to learn. Thirty-six years apart from a man who nearly ruined her life, and Ella's still thinking of him!

With her feet still stretched toward the stove, Bessie reaches for the stack of letters and postcards she's been sorting, trying to decide which ones to keep. Hirrell's letters, for sure: *I am an admirer of Lincoln—are you? 'With malice toward none, with charity for all' . . . You spoke of a rose breasted grosbeak, Well I had the same experience when a cedar waxwing came to the bird shelf—they are gorgeous.* Maybe keep one letter from Aunt Ella, one where things aren't dying right and left. *My Christmas cactus has concluded to bloom . . . I had a poincettia give me by the Am. Leg. Aux. and I surely admire the African violet. . . . Come & have squash pie—I cut one I raised that weighed over 35 lbs.*

Much as Bessie would like to see a thirty-five-pound squash—good heavens, she thought, was such a squash possible?—a trip to Tacoma was out of the question right now. Besides, Bessie is quite sure she could not abide Ella's gloom and doom:

> *. . . Sometimes I wonder what life is all about—so many disap-pointments and worry one sees everywhere. I never knew of so much roughness as kids can display—boys and girls both destructive, kids and dogs one can't have anything unless they stand and fight. I some-times wish there were no dogs or kids in the country. Am sure thank-ful I never had grand children to add to my worries. Well that's off my chest maybe I will improve.*

My parents married during a January blizzard so fierce that old-timers in Lafayette, Indiana, still talk about it. "I believe you could skate all the way to Chicago," Arthur announced to those who were able to make it to his daughter's wedding, held downtown at the First Christian Church. Juanita's wedding dress—white satin, with long, tight sleeves—was borrowed from her sister-in-law, who had had it cleaned and pressed in honor of the occasion. In the photograph, the satin train swirling around Juanita's feet is carefully draped, an attempt to hide mud splatters from the not-quite-frozen puddle that my mother had not noticed when she stepped onto the walkway outside the church.

The bridal headdress was heart-shaped, framing the most beautiful face this Indiana town had ever seen or ever would: This is my father's recollection. At the reception, held at Arthur and Sylvia's Circle S farm, Juanita changed into her "go-away outfit" as she calls it, a double-breasted teal wool suit and a black felt hat with fuchsia feathers that matched the fuchsia suede gloves she carried. My father's recollection? Nothing of the suit, the hat, or the gloves. What Paul remembers clearly, now sixty-five years into their marriage: the black high heels, the seamed stockings, and (this knowledge will come later, once Barbara and a friend drive the bride and groom to the Washington Hotel in Indianapolis) the lace garter belt.

Given the mildly delirious state of bride and groom, it's understandable that my parents don't recall everyone who was present at the festivities. Yes, they remember that Paul's parents somehow managed the frozen roads from southern Illinois, along with one of Paul's brothers, who served as best man, and one of his sisters, whose husband was still overseas, as were many of the men on both sides of the family that winter of 1945. On the bride's side, her parents were present, and her sister Barbara. Uncle Ivan and his wife attended, but the other Mounts uncles did not. Juanita cannot remember why. Maybe Babe was still serving in the army. Or maybe he and Uncle Dale stayed home at Briarwood to care for their mother, for whom once again the Fates had not arranged things favorably. Yet even had the weather cooperated that January afternoon, Hattie would have been unable to attend her granddaughter's wedding, as she was now plagued by so many ailments she could *scarcely think above them.*

Neither Paul nor Juanita recalls if Aunt Bessie attended the festivities. They think not, for diminutive as Bessie was, her presence at family events was usually felt and remembered. As were the cakes she contributed to potluck tables, cakes she rose at dawn to bake then place in a tin container with a handle she would grasp tightly with one hand, her other hand welded to an oversized pocketbook stuffed with every conceivable necessity for her journey. For you never know when you might need to stay overnight somewhere—at your sister or brother's, a cousin's, a nephew or niece's. Even without a suitcase, you can manage for a day or two, sleeping on the sofa or in a child's single bed. You can manage. Wash your cotton underwear and stockings in the kitchen sink, hang them to dry overnight beside the woodstove or over the register. Better yet, in a closet or porch, where no one will see them. Once all the lights are extinguished, the last "Goodnight" called out across the darkness and the door to the married couple's room clicked tightly closed, feel your way to bed. Then, starting at the neckline, unbutton your taffeta dress. (Since Sant died, you no longer wear dresses that button in the back—another survival trick you learned early on.) Slide the dress carefully over your head, taking care not to muss the hairdo you hope will last one more day. Slip the straps of the white cotton brassiere down. Lean over at the waist, reach behind your back, unfasten the clasps. Tuck your brassiere beneath the pillow so you can find it first thing in the morning. You can sleep in your slip.

◆

Not long after the wedding, my mother left the gray skies and icy roads of Indiana to join my father. The young, wasp-waisted son of an Illinois

My aviator father, Paul, in the early 1940s.

tenant farmer had already served two years on the Battleship U.S.S. Texas, trained as a glider pilot in Auburn, Alabama, earned his wings as a naval aviator and his commission as a second lieutenant in the U.S. Marine Corps. Now he was training as a fighter pilot in Jacksonville. Juanita had never been farther south than Rising Sun, Indiana. She'd heard how warm it was down in Florida, how you could swim in the ocean nearly all year round. Of course, right now there were the floods to contend with: Would the train make it through? Sixty-five years later, she still remembers how hot and crowded the train car was, filled with sailors and soldiers. When the men opened the windows for fresh air, soot and cinders blew in, settling onto the black crepe dress she had sewn especially for the occasion. Some of the men gave Juanita the admiring looks she'd grown accustomed to since high school. Well, let them look if they wanted to. My mother, a beauty if ever there was one, was already taken.

Juanita had packed just enough to fit in two suitcases, for she and Paul would be in Jacksonville only a few months. Besides, she'd heard that the wife of one of the other pilots—*wife!* the word still felt strange and new to Juanita—had brought a sewing machine all the way from Kansas. So if Juanita needed anything in the way of clothes, she was pretty sure she could stitch something up once she got down there. She'd gotten her 4-H badge in high school, and even back then, she could master any pattern. Heck, she could *create* a pattern if she needed to, but she'd wait to see what the other wives were wearing. She'd brought her black gathered skirt and ruffled white blouse, and had plans for a bathing suit—a two-piece, with a sarong skirt like the one she'd seen in Woman's Illustrated. Maybe she'd even sew something for the others.

Young wives who travel to join military husbands form strong bonds; the more temporary the assignment, the quicker the bonds that form. The alternative? To be marooned in a strange land, away from the smells and sounds of home. Away from the work you have come to know: the office, the plant, the weekly paycheck, lunchtime shopping with the girls, for no one calls them *women* where you come from. Of course you are not alone in this strange land. You have your husband, and everything is still so new: this ring on your finger, this man in your bed. A man who has missed you so much he can't keep his hands off you. But then he is gone again the next morning, and you have the whole day ahead of you. Nights, too, when he is training with the other pilots. So you gather with the girls in the backyard of the rooming house that you and your husband share with three other couples. The widow who owns the house has two Packards in the garage, but no one drives them though everyone wants to. Sometimes you get on the bus and go downtown. You have never been on a bus with black people before, and are surprised that they have to sit in the back. It's not right, it's not fair, but you don't tell anyone because no one seems to notice that it's wrong, not even the blacks. Back at the rooming house, the other girls are drinking coffee and taking pictures with a camera one of the blond girls brought with her. You tell them about the Circle S and they tell you their stories. Turns out, the Kansas wife has left her little girl back home with her mother, and she misses the child something fierce. Juanita listens, trying to take it in. She wonders if it was wrong to leave the little girl. Would *she* ever leave a child behind? Once she has a child, that is. Whenever that might be.

My parents weren't in Jacksonville very long, my mother tells me when I phone one recent morning, anxious to straighten out their story's timeline. "Just long enough for me to get pregnant," she laughs. Hers is a girlish laugh, one that effervesces whenever the subject of pregnancy comes up. My mother's laughter is part habit, part deflection, part accommodation. Accommodation to others, a lighthearted punctuation for *their* stories, *their* myths. Once, when one of my father's sisters asked her how in the world she could let this happen again (Juanita was carrying her fifth child at this point) my mother answered, "I'm just always so happy to see him." Said with a smile, followed by a laugh. Which led to more laughter, chasing itself in a circle around the family table.

From such moments, myths are born.

In truth, the darkest days of my mother's life were inextricably linked to pregnancy and childbirth. Every birth was difficult. One nearly took her life, another her spirit. But it takes a lot of questioning, followed by patient, silent listening, before my mother "lets slip" (this is her phrase, as in "Oops, I didn't mean to let that one slip") the details of the dark days. Her reticence is no selfish act to protect her privacy, but rather an attempt to spare "you kids" as she still calls us, unnecessary pain. I was eight or nine before I learned that a baby named Sylvia Sue had died the year before I was born; I was thirty-three before I understood how much that death cost my mother.

And only recently did I learn that when my parents left Jacksonville in 1945, Juanita was pregnant with what would have been her first child. Her *Might Have Been:* three words I choose carefully, preferring them to *miscarriage,* a term that assigns blame. Mis-carry: to fail to carry, to go astray, to pass into the wrong hands. My mother did nothing wrong. All seemed perfectly right that spring of 1945 as she and her new husband left Jacksonville and traveled north, arriving at his parents' Illinois farmhouse a few days later. Juanita can't recall if she knew yet that she was pregnant. She does remember her confusion. The cramping, the blood, and the confusion. What is happening? Here I am, in my mother-in-law's kitchen, feeling fine and then suddenly, not. What is happening?

Paul's mother knew. Goldie McClanahan, mother of nine living children and two buried ones and probably several *Might Have Beens* over her twenty-five-year course of childbearing, knew right away. She went into action, helping Juanita not to the bathroom, for the farmhouse had no bathroom, but to the closest bedroom, where a basin and pitcher waited on the bureau. The closest bedroom was also

My paternal grandparents, Clarence and Goldie, outside Arcola, Illinois, circa 1935.

the only downstairs bedroom, and since Juanita was in no condition to climb stairs, Goldie and Clarence gave up their bed for their new daughter-in-law. Over the next few days, Goldie watched over Juanita as if she were her own. Goldie had five daughters, not counting the dead Mona Lee, though Goldie had never stopped counting her, and never would.

During the days she rested from the ordeal she still did not fully understand, Juanita missed her own mother and her sister Barbara, who had a husband and a baby of her own. But I am here, Juanita told herself. In Paul's family home. These are my people now. Is this when Juanita started calling Goldie "Mother"? Not "my mother-in-law," not "Goldie," not "Paul's mother." Just "Mother," plain and simple. As simple as "Mom," what Paul called Juanita's mother, from the day of their wedding until the day Sylvia died.

Mother-Mom. As if the two women, combined, formed one whole idea of mother. The way, in my childhood logic, my grandmothers' names formed one bracelet of the world's most glittering elements. I loved to say their names aloud, together: Sylvia, Goldie. Silver and gold. Amazing, I thought. Almost as amazing as the fact that my two grandmothers knew each other! They even wrote letters to each other. Imagine that!

Ah, the loopy logic of young children. The galactic-sized holes in their understanding. Somewhere along the line, I must have understood that my mother was someone's daughter and my father was someone's son. But the fact that they were still someone's daughter or son had somehow escaped me. Paul and Juanita were my *parents.* And my grandparents were my *grandparents.* One set lived in Indiana, one set in Illinois. Grandparents were wonderful, of course—everyone should have two sets of them—but how were they connected? I'd never thought to ask the question. Had I attempted to draw my family tree at this point, it would have looked something like this: one trunk (my parents) with five branches spreading out. One branch for me, four others for my siblings. My youngest sister, the sixth branch, was not yet born, nor did I yet know about the sister who had died before me (*Before me?* What child can fathom such a thought?) nor of any *Might Have Been.*

◆

I used to tease my older sister, calling her "holier than thou" because she'd been baptized twice. "The first time doesn't count," Jenny would counter. "I wasn't born yet, remember?" I can't recall when I first heard the story; I must have been eavesdropping. I was always a nosy kid— hiding in the attic room at the Circle S, where I'd press my ear to the floor vent to catch a breeze of conversation from the uncles gathered around the poolroom downstairs, or pretending to fall asleep on the sofa so that the neighborhood mothers would finish the tales they'd shooed their own children away from hearing. Certainly, neither of my parents volunteered the story of my mother's baptism, not publicly, anyway. My parents were not showy about their faith. They didn't walk the aisle or brag about their journeys of salvation like some grownups in the church. What I know about my parents' spiritual lives, I know because I asked, and asked again, and yet again. So I learned that Paul made a public confession of faith as a young boy in Arcola, Illinois, in the small church his parents belonged to but that his father, exhausted from his tenant farmer labors, rarely attended; a few weeks later, Paul was baptized, fully immersed, as is the Baptist tradition.

My mother does not speak readily about personal issues. Before she answered, she blushed and looked away as if I'd asked her to reveal some bedroom secret. As it turned out, Juanita's conversion took place on a hot August morning as she sat beside my father in the First Baptist Church of Lafayette, Indiana, eight months pregnant with my sister Jennifer. The moment itself, the turn of heart that surprised her that morning, my mother remembers only as the sensation of being lit from within.

A week later, my mother was baptized. I imagine her standing at the edge of the baptistery, preparing to take the five or six steps that will lead her down into the water, where a man in a robe and black rubber hip boots waits. Beneath the white choir robe, she wears a pale yellow slip from her wedding trousseau, onto which is grafted a maternity panel she has stitched herself; it stretches tight around her belly. Her thick black hair, tamed in daylight with combs and nets, is now loose and full, forming a black halo. Earthbound, she is clumsy as all pregnant women are clumsy—her balance thrown forward, her gait a duck's waddle. But once in the water, she is a girl again. Barefoot, buoyant, weightless. The preacher motions her to the center of the water, the scene lit from above to suggest the Holy Spirit in the form of a dove. The robe rises and floats cloudlike around her. The preacher offers his right hand, as if inviting her to dance, and when my mother reaches him, he guides her gracefully to face the congregation, coaxing her hands to form a cross upon her chest. He places his right hand on top of hers, moving his other hand behind her neck for support. Perhaps he whispers some words of assurance—*No need to worry, I have you, you won't fall.* Then he takes her under.

Briarwood Cottage
Dayton, Indiana
August 7, 1947

Mrs. P. G. McClanahan
1510 South Street, Lafayette
Dear Juanita:

Rc'd your Package. Thank you many times. I am trying to make my dress, an my Shearars are so dull they just haggle the goods off an my toes hurt so bad I cannot think above them but I gave them a dose of bread an milk last night an drew out some of the juice so they are some better but it was so hot I had to fan myself to sleep; but first yesterday morning I went out to the mailbox to mail my letter an got back to come in the yard, there my legs Balked, I coaxed an scolded but they wouldnent go, but I did finely get to the house. The clock had stoped too. So I don't know how long I was. Babe has been mowing weeds today an came up to the house looking like he had melted an run all over himself, I have not heard from any of the rest, Tell Jenny Jo to be a good girl and help Mother pick up things. Ha! Ha! Maybe I will get so I can come an see you one of those days come out when you can am always glad to have you an they say the Swimming is fine so by for now with love to you all as ever Grammur.

The last photographs of my great-grandmother were taken at Briarwood on an early summer day in 1947. May, probably, judging by the quality of light. In both photos, late afternoon sun ricochets off the little log house and the surrounding trees, shattering the grass into brilliant shards. Summer was Hattie's favorite time, so maybe that was sufficient reason for the small band of family members to have gathered at the old home place. Or maybe it was Mother's Day. A genealogist intent on merely documenting the who, what, when, and where of family events would no doubt value the second photo over the first. The second photo is more inclusive; other than the photographer, everyone present that day is accounted for.

But I can't look at the second photo without sadness, so I focus on the first photo. In it, Great-grandma Hattie occupies a chair someone has carried from the kitchen out into the yard. She wears a white summer dress, stockings rolled down to mid-calf. She's removed her sunbonnet for the occasion. Standing behind her, my young mother leans sideways into her own mother, their faces sunlit and radiant. Grandma Sylvia wears what looks to be a handmade dress, with rickrack trim running lengthwise down her bosom and a black belt cinched tight; even at fifty-eight, her voluptuous hourglass figure holds its own just fine. Juanita's body is slimmer than her mother's, her aspect more demure. She wears a floral print dress, its loosely tied belt positioned high enough to allow for a delicate swell of belly. Her second child—surprise!—is due in a few months. The first, a daughter in diapers and a soft white shirt, balances precariously on her first pair of baby shoes. The top of

Four generations at Briarwood, 1947. The baby is my sister Jenny, holding Great-grandmother Hattie's hand. Behind them: my pregnant mother, Juanita, and her mother, Sylvia.

Jenny's head is sun-dappled, as if she's wearing a white yarmulke or a lopsided halo. She's turned away from the camera, her Gerber baby face in profile. One small, dimpled hand rests on the folded hands of a great-grandmother she will not remember ever having seen.

Yet in this moment, Hattie *is* seen. Baby Jenny looks directly at her, and Hattie returns the gaze. The beauty—no, the *mercy*—of this photo is in the angle of their faces, the way Hattie looks not into the camera, as in the second photo, but into the face of her great-granddaughter, the two in profile locked into each other as if nothing else exists in this wide, bright world.

Now scanning the second photo, I hurry my eyes along, trying not to look at the seated Hattie. I skim the surfaces of the other faces, panning right to left—Grandma Sylvia, her daughters, Barbara and Juanita; my young father, Paul, holding his baby daughter; Grandpa Arthur beside *his* father, G. E.; and Barbara's little girl, Juanita Anne, whose father is probably the one snapping the picture. A Mounts-Sanders moment. Four generations. Everyone present and accounted for, the document complete.

Except it isn't. Something is missing. Something so hugely gone, we will never get it back. Bessie would have known right away what was missing. One look at the photograph, and she would have known. Her eyes behind their wire-rimmed spectacles would have gone straight to her mother, seated in the middle of her small tribe. Hattie, in a white dress. Her long white hair pulled into a bun on the top of her head. Her toothless mouth closed tightly, for vanity's sake. Her prominent ears with the drooping lobes the Ohio River mammy had pierced for her eighty years before, now bare of ornament. And there, in the center of Hattie's face, where her eyes should be: dark windows. Adumbratio. Umbrella of darkness. The shadow passing over, passing through. Dark windows. Lights blinking. Lights blinking out. *Come and see me. The clock stoped to By for now. As ever. Grammur.*

◆

Mulberry, Indiana, June 10. Mrs. Harriet E. (Ray) Mounts, 85, widow of Robert A. Mounts, died at 7:30 p.m. Wednesday at the family home five miles southwest of here. Born in Switzerland County, she was married in 1878 and her husband died in 1943. Surviving are three sons and two daughters. Dale and Robert W. Mounts, living with their mother. Ivan Mounts, West Lafayette. Mrs. Bessie Cosby, Stockwell, and Mrs. Sylvia Sanders, Battle Ground.

On June evenings in Indiana, light relinquishes its hold slowly. So I imagine Dale and Babe were outside somewhere—in the field mowing, or driving back from town with groceries or some treat for their mother—when Hattie left for "that place from which no traveler returns," as her son-in-law Arthur would say. The 1948 obituary in the Lafayette Journal & Courier cost $2.50, no extra charge for the errors. Hattie's middle initial was "Z" not "E." She married Robert in 1879 not 1878. And her son Robert W. (Babe) did not actually live with his mother. The year before, at age forty-four, he'd finally married and, at his wife's insistence, built a separate house on a plot directly behind Briarwood. Close enough for him to watch out for his mother but far enough from "that woman" to please his new wife.

Unlike her widowed cousins out west who prayed some women's auxiliary would come through with funds when their time came, Hattie needn't have worried about who would lay her away. Her five children gladly shared the cost, Hattie's final tally itemized on a handwritten bill from M. E. Kleinsmith, Funeral Director:

For Funeral Expense of Mother

Casket services	275.00
Vault	80.00
Journal Courier	2.50
Slip	2.49
Cemetery Expense	22.50
TOTAL EXPENSES	$382.49

The funeral gathering at Briarwood was hardly large enough to constitute a crowd. All of Hattie's aging children came, but few young folks were present. Bessie and Babe, of course, were childless, and Dale's only child had left the family circle after her parents' divorce and never resurfaced. Juanita and Paul brought their two children—Jenny, who was almost two, and Jenny's baby brother, Tommy. It was a Thursday evening, and my parents were exhausted. Paul worked nights at the electric plant; days he took a full course of classes at Purdue. Juanita worked at the jewelry counter of the Palais Royal in Lafayette, a job she hated but a necessary one. Her mother kept the children during the day, so Sylvia must have been exhausted too, sitting beside her mother's casket while the young ones filed by.

Ivan and his wife brought their young son, as did another relative. Juanita remembers how serious the two boys looked that night. "Like miniature men," she recalls. Standing by the casket with their hands in the pockets of their best jackets, they seemed to know what to do. They stood still. They furrowed their brows in concentration. Then, in a quiet moment between the minister's address and the benediction, the older one turned to the younger one and announced solemnly, "She was a good woman." The younger one nodded.

Hattie's body had been "prepared," my mother recalls, at the funeral home. No doubt Bessie would have chosen Hattie's dress and arranged her mother's hair as well. Hattie had not cut her hair for decades. Juanita remembers her grandmother letting her "play" with her hair, stand behind Hattie and comb the long white strands that reached halfway down her back. Almost as long as when Hattie was a child. Sixty years past Hattie's funeral, I will find some strands of that white hair, enclosed in a folded slip of paper marked, in Bessie's handwriting, "Mounts."

The pallbearers had planned to carry the casket all the way into the main room, but it wouldn't fit through the frame of the tiny door. So now the body lay in an open casket wedged at an angle in the little alcove Robert had built decades before to house Hattie's flower boxes: *Everything looks lovly this morning after the rain, yellow roses opening.* Listen. Can you hear it? The wasp nest beneath the porch eaves is humming, freshly-caught bass is sizzling in the iron skillet, and Hattie's hand—or is it Bessie's, or is it Sylvia's, or is it mine?—is reaching for the spatula. Oh, yes, it will be a fine dinner, for Brother has caught a big squirrel and Pa got a turtle, awful nice, and there will be Gooseberry pie, more than you can eat. From my desk, I can almost make out the alcove where Robert's empty chair sits, still rocking. He'll just be gone a minute or two, just long enough to check on the little girl running across the yard toward the arbor where, look, the roses are spreading their petals, wide and buttery yellow, as far as we can see.

CHAPTER 20

Sunday night
August 24, 1983

Dear Becky,

    *Have been reminiscing back to 1950—the year you were born—
and to some of the events preceding that event. We had moved to the
country—a little 4 room frame house in White County. Jenny and
Tommy were little. We had a good dog—a Harlequin Great Dane
(purebred) with glass blue eyes. Two hogs, a black cow, some chickens and a garden. In 1949 I was pregnant with my third child, it was
a hard year for me and I resented this fact and was ill for all of the
months preceding the birth.*

It was a hard year for me: an understatement if ever there was one, but
understatement is my mother's way. When hit full force with pain or
disappointment, Juanita absorbs the blow. Later, when questioned, she
demurs, softening the truth to protect her listener, especially if that listener is one of her children. You must dig deeply to enter Juanita's pain
from the inside out. You must read between the lines. Three statements,
strung together with no particular connection to each other: *I was pregnant with my third child. It was a hard year. I resented this fact.* Resented
which fact? That it was a hard year? Keep going, Mother. Tell your story.

    *. . . One day in early March we decided to go to Illinois to visit
Paul's folks, and your Grandma Sylvia went with us—it was like a
holiday and we needed the break. The trip was too much and the
pains came. A tiny premature baby was born, struggling into exis-*

tence. I feel I can say I was in the "valley of the shadow" and wavered there between a desire to die or a will to live.

Dig a little deeper, add up what she isn't telling you in this letter, written on the thirty-third anniversary of your birth. But don't forget: You are the fourth child, not the third. Born in 1950, not 1949. This isn't your story. Just add up the facts. In the fall of 1948, when she learned that she was pregnant with her third child, Juanita was twenty-three years old. She had a two-year-old daughter and a one-year-old son. *There was no bathroom (outside toilet), washed clothes in the basement (wringer washer), carried water from the pump house up steps and down, heated water on the stove.* Her mother watched the children during the day while Juanita worked at a job she hated. Her husband, who received one hundred twenty dollars a month on the G.I. bill, was taking a full load of classes and working eight-hour shifts at the electric plant. Dig deeper. *I was pregnant with my third child.... I resented this fact.*

> *... I've read stories of those who have gone through a tunnel toward a light—I had this experience—but a spirit, a voice constrained me to return. In my weakness I remember Dr. Hollowell and the nurse telling me how well I had fought. I was limp and listless for 3 days. The nurse came with papers to sign and to choose a name—Sylvia Sue was so small she must be taken to Indianapolis to the preemie center. She never made that journey and I never saw her. The day she was buried everyone at the McClanahan farm had to go by horse and wagon to the main road because of a snowstorm. I stared out the hospital window at the grey sky, feeling guilty, sad and lonely. And Paul suffered too. Dad McClanahan provided the gravesite in the family plot.*
>
> *The next year we joined the church in Delphi. The day we joined I wore a black crepe maternity skirt and white crepe blouse, black shoes and a hat. I chose a biblical name for my little girl. The day you were born I did a large washing and canned tomatoes. I felt blessed then and doubly blessed now.*
>
> *Love, Mother*
>
> *P.S. Check enclosed—you're worth a dollar a year at least.*

In August 1950, the month I was born, Great-aunt Bessie was three thousand miles from Indiana. Her mother had been dead two years.

For months after Hattie died, Bessie would startle awake in her little "chicken house," grab for the clothes she'd thrown over the bedpost, and dress hurriedly, bending to lace up her walking shoes for the three-mile hike to Briarwood, before the realization hit her: Mother would not be there. Would not be in the chair beside the raised garden beds, her sunbonnet tied beneath her chin. Bessie was an orphan now—an orphan! Seventy years old, come September, but an orphan all the same. Of course, so were her siblings, but Bessie felt the grief more keenly. Or thus she reasoned. Dale's work on the railroad kept him busy, as did his river and hunting trips. Sylvia and Arthur had the children and grandchildren; Ivan, his wife and children. Even Babe—who could ever have imagined?—had a wife now.

As for Bessie, she had—what, exactly? Her husband was gone, her parents were gone, her big, beautiful farm, gone. She'd held onto a forty-acre plot of soybeans and corn, employing a neighbor to farm it. But the land no longer held any attraction. She would not miss it if it were suddenly gone. And most certainly, it would not miss her. So, what was holding her here?

Nothing.

The word wrenched her mind at first, locked her breath tight in her chest—nothing!—then something broke loose inside, like a great ocean wave, and she breathed again. *Nothing.*

◆

A small album of black and white "Snaps" charts Bessie's westward progress by Greyhound bus, with a brief layover at Cousin Lou's in Albuquerque. Once Bessie arrives in California, she's harder to keep track of, her dance card is so full. Here she is at San Juan Capistrano, perched on a stone bench, her ubiquitous pocketbook clutched tightly in her lap. Beside her is Cousin Goldie and Goldie's extraordinarily handsome husband, who lends an aristocratic air to a creamy felt fedora. Goldie's hat, a two-toned straw number, is broad-brimmed and stylish. Bessie wears a hat, too. It sits unnaturally high on her head, propelled upward no doubt by the force of steel-gray curls that look poised to spring loose at any instant. Had Cousin Maitie, the retired beautician who'd learned her art on the Marcel machines of the 1920s, administered a perma-

Great-aunt Bessie in her "bathing costume" at Morehead City, North Carolina, and with her cousin Goldie and Goldie's husband at San Juan Capistrano, early 1950s.

nent wave? Thankfully, Bessie's features are softened by rounded, wire-rimmed glasses, and her smile shows no hint of her usual dental agony.

A few weeks later, she is posed in profile at the bottom of winding steps leading to Cousin Fannie's home: Lookout Mountain, Hollywood, California. A wall of windows stretches across the frame of the picture, and the roof appears to be composed primarily of sun. Bessie, too. Since her arrival in The Land of Sunshine, her face and arms have browned nicely. She wears a white shirtwaist dress and cushiony sandals, which she probably bought while she was staying with Cousin Maitie in Long Beach, just a few blocks from the ocean. A person could hardly walk the California beach in Indiana lace-ups, for heaven's sake. Your feet need to breathe!

Your hair too, Bessie, so off with the hat, and now isn't that better? Over the past weeks, Bessie's perm has had time to loosen its grip, allowing the gray curls room to spread. Backlit, they form a soft halo around Bessie's face. From a distance, a stranger might read the curls not as gray but as blond. California sunlit blond. Many decades later, when I interview distant California relatives, they will mistakenly identify Bessie as "one of the sisters" rather than a cousin. That's how easily she fit into her new surroundings. "She was a card," they told me. "Cute as a button, and friendly as all get-out. Never a cross word, never a frown." Had the California sun chased the blue devils from Bessie's mind? In the photos, the letters she sent home, and the stories she told to the end of her long life, it would seem so. Even the news that her Atascadero acreage was landlocked, inaccessible for the time being, did not dim Bessie's excitement. (If Bessie had known Spanish, she might have paused over "Atascadero," derived from "atascar," which loosely translates to "stuck" or "hindered.")

Over the next few years, Bessie made several trips back to Indiana to visit her siblings, but whenever she sniffed out an invitation to a part of the world she'd yet to visit, she accepted. She joined our family in time for my first birthday celebration in Cherry Point, North Carolina, where my father was preparing to ship off to Korea to fly the night fighter missions that would haunt him for decades. Bessie had packed the "bathing costume" she'd purchased in California. She wore it every chance she got, along with a white kerchief tied around her head for the beach photos that would later prove her assertion, "I have soaked my corns both in the Atlantic and the Pacific." My mother appears in the beach photos as well, wearing a one-piece bathing suit she sewed herself. In one photo, Juanita poses seductively on a towel spread across the sand, her thick black hair accenting dark, expressive eyes. It's a bathing beauty snapshot, probably taken by my father shortly before he left for Korea. He can't recall if he took the photo with him; maybe Juanita saved it to slip into a letter, one of many love letters that she and my father have wisely never allowed me to see. Paul mailed his letters to Charleston, Illinois, where my mother had taken their three young children to live near the McClanahan relatives during his thirteen-month duty. "I wanted you kids to have a chance to know our other family," Juanita told me recently.

Though rigorous, Paul's stateside training as a night fighter had not prepared him for Korea—the loneliness of flying solo, the darkness for miles around. "Black as far as the eye could see," he remembers, except when the moon reflected onto the snow "an unearthly brightness." Paul tried not to think about what he was carrying, the Corsair loaded with bombs and ammo. Tried not to think of what happened after the world below him lit up, block after block, a circle of fire blasting anything that moved. That *had* moved. A universe away from Arcola, Illinois, 1930. A universe away from the eight-year-old son of a tenant farmer gathered

with the local townspeople, shielding his blue eyes from the sun and staring up, up at the sightseeing plane gliding overhead, begging his mother
to let him please go up—please, Mother, a ride on the barnstormer?

When Paul wasn't flying night raids in Korea, he stayed close to
camp, the "tent city" where, one snowy February day a few days after
my father's thirtieth birthday, the chaplain set up an amateur studio in
his tent and invited the men to make recordings to send to their families for Valentine's Day. I remember listening to the 45 RPM record years
later, once I was old enough to understand whose voice was talking on
the record and why the voice kept saying our names. Nearly sixty years
later, the record survives, marred by hisses and scratches, my father's
voice unnaturally high, like the voice of a cartoon character:

> *Hello there little kids and Mama . . . have to talk into this micro-
> phone . . . I understand Tommy got some cowboy shirts for Christmas.
> They don't have any little cowboys out here, they've got some cows
> though. In fact they even use them to pull wagons. I'll send you some
> pictures of them. . . . Well, I was going to tell you a story about the
> three little Dutchmen but I'll leave Mother to tell you that one, and I'll
> tell you a story about Porky Pig and Bugs Buggy. Name of it is Porky
> Meets the Three Little Pigs.*

Much of the recording is indecipherable, though my father's stuttering
impression of Porky P-P-Pig comes through clearly. It's a loony tale, a
shaggy dog/pig tale in which a mixed-up cast of storybook characters,
each caught up in his own story and blind to anyone else's, finally meet
up in the woods. Because, as it turns out, "we're all in the same book."
But are we? The night world in which my father moved could not have
been farther from the safe, bright world my mother worked to make for
us, homesick though she was for her own people in Indiana. My brother
remembers Dad saying something else on the record, something like
*Tommy, you're the man of the house now, you need to look after your sis-
ters.* But it is clear, as I replay the record one more time, it appears that
Tommy's sisters had jobs to do, too.

> *. . . Little Jenny, I saw a little girl about your size a couple weeks
> ago. She had dark hair and bangs and she didn't have as pretty a
> coat as you have, but she had a coat on. And she had a little sister*

wrapped around her, on her back . . . was taking good care of her. I guess that was the only person this little baby could depend on was her older sister.

Was my father trying to tell us that we needed to look out for one another, that someday we too might have only each other to depend on? Knowing what awaits my father over the next week of his life, I can barely listen to the rest of the recording:

. . . You probably won't get this until after Valentine's Day . . . I love you . . . I guess I've run out of anything to say now. Give all the folks at home my regards. Tell Grandma Sanders hi, too. I miss all of you. All of them . . . and Mama, you be sure to tell the kids about me so they don't forget me. . . .

20 February 52: VMF [Night] 513 Squadron
F4U-5N
Left landing gear collapsed during takeoff

The report, signed by R. S. Hempstead, the captain in charge of the investigation, concluded that the crash of the Corsair night fighter was not due to pilot error. An act of God, then? An act that forced the landing gear to fail, shoving the plane deep into a snowy embankment and hurtling the plane onto its nose. My father was strapped in tight, his body suspended, the radio controls beneath him visible but unreachable. His arms numb, unmoveable, trapped above his head. Snow filling the cockpit. Icy air stinging his lungs. Can't breathe. Sleepy now, dreaming? *Mother beside me . . . a scarf over her hair, wind lifting a few loose strands . . . a man in a leather helmet turning to shout*—quite a view, huh?—*the plane tilting . . . green fields, black dirt, straight rows, tiny barns—look! Wind roaring, wings tilting farther. . . . will it spill me out, Mother's hand pulling me toward her . . .* Wings loaded with ammo, ready to blow. The world would light up, light up inside him. Fingers numb. His breath hard, harder. Pistol against his chest, cold, strapped tight. Must get the pistol. Only way out.

Where did my father's mind go in those moments? Was it the icy snow that defeated him? The fear of the plane catching fire? Or had all the flame-filled nights stacked up inside him?

Moments stretched, to . . . what? Hours? How long until the radio crackled on, a voice through the static calling his name. The pistol still strapped to his chest. His mind free, now, to loosen its grip. To remember who he was: First Lieutenant Paul G. McClanahan. Pilot. Bomber. Soldier. To remember who he was: Paul G. McClanahan. Husband, brother, uncle, son, son-in-law. Father.

◆

After his tour in Korea, my father returned to move the family to our next post, and Sylvia and Arthur began planning a trip to see their three grandchildren in Corpus Christi, Texas. They would drive four hundred fifty miles a day, cook their meals on a camp stove, and sleep in the ancient Oldsmobile that Arthur had modified so that the lean back could flatten at night into a bed for two.

Or, as it turned out, for three. Bessie was visiting the Circle S at the time, and when she heard that a plan was brewing, of course she had to get in on the act. As Arthur would write years later, there was plenty of room *for three small people. We maintained the best of health, and we finished our thirteen hundred mile trip,* a journey that Arthur will remember as *some of the finest days of our lives.* I imagine them, at the end of each driving day, firing up their camp stove for beans and weenies or my grandmother's famous fried potatoes. Soon, Bessie begins to yawn and stretch, making preliminary motions toward bed; she always retired early so as to be up with the birds. Retrieving her travel bag from the back seat, rummaging around for the essentials—washcloth, soap, denture powder. Making her way down the campground walkway to the public restroom, where would begin the nighttime ablutions I would witness years later when we shared a room together.

Sylvia and Arthur followed her lead, preparing for bed. Did they change into pajamas and nightshirts? Exhausted as they were, they probably just slipped off their shoes and climbed into the open back seat, spread with a pallet covered with flannel or soft wool, to cushion their backs. In the scene that plays in my mind's eye, the *three small people* are stretched out in the back of the Oldsmobile: a couple with forty years of marriage to their credit, holding hands under the covers, and pint-sized Bessie, a widow for a decade now, keeping her respectful space on the other side of Sylvia. Bessie, independent as the sun, the big sister who sixty years earlier had slowed her forward-pushing pace on the path to school to accommodate her little sister and brother, now allowing herself to be the tag-along. The extra. The character actress playing her supporting role at the edge of the covers, at the edge of her sister's life.

Grandma Sylvia made another trip to Texas to visit us in the early 1950s, alone this time, on the train. Very late in her life, when I asked my grandmother about memorable trips she had taken, she recalled this one. The way she told it, a young "colored lady" with a baby sat down next to her. The mother was visibly ill and weak, the baby crying loudly, and after several minutes the mother turned to Sylvia and inquired quietly if she would please hold the baby a minute so she could go to the restroom. "Of course I said yes," my grandmother told me. "That baby was so beautiful, so soft. It was a girl, I think. Her hair was soft as lamb's wool. I touched her cheek and rocked her, and she got quiet and started cooing."

I recall the tone of amazement in Sylvia's voice as she recounted the story. As far as she could remember, she told me, she'd been in "close quarters to a colored person" only once before that train ride—more than two decades before, when they lived at the South River farm. I now think of this event as our family's <u>Guess Who's Coming to Dinner</u> episode. It was about 1930, and my mother, who was five or six at the time, remembers few details of the visit, other than her astonishment at being so close to a black person—a minister of some sort, Juanita remembers. "Maybe a circuit preacher." Quite likely, the visiting minister was David Manley, who, after graduating from Indiana Central, continued giving speeches for churches and civic organizations near Indianapolis. If I am mistaken that the visitor to my grandparents' farm was David Manley, I am certain he was someone very much like Manley, someone whose story connected in some way with Arthur's own. Someone with whom Arthur could continue the education he'd begun at Valparaiso two decades before, when he'd copied some of his favorite quotations in his <u>College NoteBook</u>, including this one by the French statesman and philosopher Jules François Simon: "Education is the process by which one mind forms another mind, and one heart another heart." My mother doesn't remember what Sylvia served—maybe her famous beef stew and cherry pie—or much about the conversation around the table, but she remembers that the grownups talked for what seemed like a long time. Hours maybe. How many minds were formed that evening, I wonder. How many hearts? My grandparents are not alive to answer that question. But a black man came to dinner at the Sanders house, and my grandmother served him a good meal, and they talked and ate together until it was time for the man to board the train taking him back to his own home.

Dec. 16, 1952

Bessie Cosby
c/o Baldwin
1169 E. Broadway
Long Beach, California

Dear Aunt Bessie,
    Just a line as you can guess I'm busy & sleepy. The kids are in the bath tub so I have to be on guard. Ha! Poor little Becky was fine until we started from the bus to the car and she turned around & said "where's Behie"—then she cried like her heart would break all the way home like she was scared. She said today though you'd gone on the big bus to California.
    With love,
    Juanita

Until a few years ago, my mother's 1952 letter (into which she enclosed a photograph of Bessie holding a pigtailed toddler) was the only tangible evidence of the early bond between Bessie and her great-niece Rebecca. The most recent evidence, I discovered when I opened an eyeglass case containing old-fashioned, wire-rimmed spectacles. Folded

Great-aunt Bessie holding me outside our family's home in Corpus Christi, Texas, 1952.

carefully beneath the spectacles is a piece of paper on which is written, in Bessie's handwriting, "Becky's hair"; the other side of the folded paper reads "Mounts." Unfold the paper and you will find two different locks of hair. One lock is of coarse, white hair; stretched to its full length, it is nearly a foot long. The white hair is, without a doubt, Hattie's. The other, a short clipping of baby-fine, golden brown hair: mine. My mother has no memory of Bessie cutting my baby hair; she must have done it while no one was looking. Did Bessie have plans for the hair? Would she place it inside a locket, or save it to present to me years later, when, she might imagine, I would have a little girl of my own? Did Bessie save other locks of hair—her own, Dale's, Sylvia's, her dead father's—intending to weave them all together, as her grandmother once did for the Mounts hair picture?

If so, that project will have to wait, as Bessie is on the go again, planted in her accustomed window seat of a Greyhound bus, fanning away smoke from passengers' cigarettes while jotting messages on travel postcards to Sylvia, Ivan, Babe—and to Dale, whom she misses more each day.

Wickenburg, Ariz. Wednesday 6:30
Dear Brother. Stopped here and got coffee. Stopped in Phoenix short
time. Am going to Long Beach by way of L.A. have to change there.
Have eaten very little. Too much smoke, but will get by. Bessie

This message to Dale appears on the back of a postcard showing three colorfully dressed, cartoon drunks scrambling on hands and knees across the floor of a saloon while the bartender, holding a phone to his ear, speaks his bubbled caption: "Yes mam, just a minute . . . I'll see if he's here." Brother Dale was there, all right, at the receiving end of Bessie's postcard, though probably not on a barroom floor. Dale's drinking, a subject rarely discussed among family members, had most likely been accomplished quietly—in the early days, with a few friends or cousins in Wisconsin fishing shacks, and later alone, at Briarwood, the last place Dale would name *home.*

Circle S Ranch
Sunday January 18

Mrs. Bessie Cosby
8816 Lookout Mt. Ave.
Hollywood, California

Dear Sister:

 Got your letter was surely glad to hear from you. Dale has been
sick ever since we came back from Texas or before I guess. Been try-
ing to get along with home remedies but they didn't remedy. He was
getting so weak and had lost a lot of weight. You might be glad you
are not here sliding and skidding around these dark old dreary days.
Well enjoy things for me to and write again.
 Love Sylvia

Bessie responded to Sylvia's news with a breezy get-well card to their brother, posted from Long Beach, where she'd landed after spending a few weeks with her radio personality cousins in Hollywood. In the card, she tells Dale that she's sorry he's having trouble with his stomach, sorry also that she cannot be there at Briarwood to *keep up the fires and feed the hens and the pup.* When she invites Dale to come out to California for a visit, it's clear that Bessie has no idea how sick her brother is.

And the flurry of letters and cards exchanged among the siblings over the next few weeks are a study in misinformation and missed signals.

With his older brother out of commission and Bessie gone yet again, Ivan has grudgingly accepted the role as leader of the Mounts siblings. Letter writing has never been Ivan's forte, but someone has to break the news to Bessie. But dammit to hell, how to phrase it? Better not blow my cover right away. Work up to it slow, smooth things over a little. *Bessie Cosby, 1169 E. Broadway, Long Beach, California. Dear Bessie.* Well that's one helluva beginning, so far so good. Ask her how things are doing in California—*Suppose you had Xmas with roses instead of Xmas trees and tinsel*—then some news about Babe and then when her mind is somewhere else, just slide in something about Dale: *I've been out a couple times this week. Am going to see the Doctor tomorrow and try to have another one or two to look at him.*

Oh, hell, just get on with it, she'll find out soon enough anyway.

> *. . . Now don't get excited because I'm going to tell you what I've suspicioned for some time. The doctor said he was positive of a <u>liver cancer</u>. Dale doesn't know, neither does Sylvia. Art and I thought it better that way. <u>So don't tell Sylvia</u>. We'll let Art do that at the proper time. Dale we won't tell even if and when we know for sure. We think right now it has went too far even for an operation to do any good. This is being a little abrupt but it's the only way I know to let you know the facts as we see them now. As for you coming back here that is for you to decide. Naturally Sylvia will have her hands full and the hospital won't do him much good for he wouldn't be satisfied. Its hard to say what is the best to do. Will close now and hope for the best—*
> *Ivan.*

Friday eve. Feb. 6
Dear Bessie:
> *If you got the letter I wrote the first of the week guess you thought I was pretty excited, well . . . The doctor said tonite when he got all this data, which will be Monday, we would know more. . . . Have the best Doctors there is in the country. Johnson & Gerry. When we find what the decision is will let you know right away. . . .*

VIA AIR MAIL

Monday eve. 9th
Dear Bessie,

Have been to the hospital this evening and talked to the doctor. He say's Dale has a gall stone so is going to operate Thursday morning the 12th. Has had jaundice pretty bad at times. Sat. nite he was awful yellow, but tonite it didn't show much. Shaved him tonite. If you have some business there you just as well do that first if you're thinking of coming home it will be awhile after this operation before he is able to go home. Of course there maybe a possibility of other things wrong to. That the doc wont know till its over with. . . .

Bye, Ivan

The details are murky, and for weeks Bessie agonizes over what to do. How sick *is* Dale? Is Ivan saying she should come home, or stay? To the end of her life, Bessie will debate the whys and wherefores, never finding peace in the matter of Dale. And the family will never understand why Bessie couldn't, or wouldn't, make it back in time to care for her closest brother nor to bury him. Only much later would Sylvia divulge to Bessie the details of Dale's hard end: how he lay on the old red sofa in Sylvia and Arthur's farmhouse, shrunken to eighty pounds, his stomach "on fire," begging Sylvia to kill him.

Those who made it to Dale's funeral remember little about it. If his only daughter was present, family members do not recall. My father, who was training military pilots in Corpus Christi, arranged an instructional flight to Indiana so that he could attend the funeral. My mother, marooned with three young children, mourned from afar, hoping that the get-well cards had reached Uncle Dale in the hospital; she'd chosen funny ones, to cheer him up. I have only three uncles, she thought. No, *had* three uncles. She remembered Uncle Dale's hands, how cool they'd felt on her forehead, all those years ago. She was—what, fourteen? Fifteen? Mom and Dad were up in Detroit visiting her brothers, Barbara was working in town, and Uncle Dale had come to take care of the Circle S chores since Juanita couldn't handle them alone. Couldn't handle them at all, in fact, as she'd come down with the mumps shortly after her parents left. To this day, Juanita remembers the pain and swelling, and of course she looked like a hamster. But mostly she remembers the fever, her head burning up, and Uncle Dale's hands touching her forehead, asking if she needed anything. Moving quietly in and out of the room throughout the day and night, to make sure his niece was okay.

◆

The bus trip from California to Indiana takes three days and two long nights. Time for Bessie to think, to cry, to question herself, to remember, her thoughts unrolling like the chapters of a book. In this chapter, she is twenty and Brother Dale is sixteen. For days they have been hunting mushrooms and greens along Wildcat Creek. But the season is nearly spent now, and they're planning to take the train north to Wisconsin, where spring opens more slowly. Maybe stop overnight at Uncle Clint's in Hammond, but by morning they'll be on their way again. Brother will doze, his head falling against her shoulder, but Bessie will sit straight up as she always does, her shirtwaist buttoned, her traveling bag on her lap, watching out the window as the deep Indiana green dissolves into the pale, early green of Wisconsin. *Menomonie:* She loves the sound of it. An Indian word, she's been told. Years ago, this whole land was Indian land, tribe after tribe, each name more glorious than the next.

Who will be at the train station this time? she wonders, urging the dream on. Uncle Harve, maybe, who will not say a word, will just blush and stare shyly into space. Or old Lafe, with his rough, handmade clothing, his white mustache drooping halfway down his face, smelling of tanning leather and wild roots. Or Aunt Mary if she can find a moment to herself, away from the children. No, most likely it will be Uncle Charlie showing up at the station, walking toward them with that long, loping stride. Once they're seated in the buggy, he'll give the reins over to Dale and they'll ride the rutted road out of town, the whole valley smelling of lilacs and wild onion, patches of asparagus dotting the edges of the road. They'll ride past the cemetery, across the valley and alongside the creek toward the woods. Morels! O the woods are filled with them, and not just around the dead elms, either, but everywhere, in the most unlikely places. Just when you think you've looked everywhere and you're ready to give up, you blink, and there it is: spring's first morel. Long-stemmed, honeycombed, spongy, miraculous. Blink again, and another appears. And another. A whole congregation of morels pointing up at you. They were there all along, waiting to be discovered. You just have to have the right eyes.

CHAPTER 21

January 28, 1955

Mrs. Bessie Cosby
8816 Lookout Mt. Ave.
Hollywood, California

Dear Aunt Bessie,

The only way I can get a letter written is to sandwich it between errands. Right now Becky is ordering lunch—at 9:30 a.m. & Claudia is in her high chair yelling for something—little scavenger. She picks up everything & even eats mud if she can manage it. She has only 4 teeth so far & can she bite.

Glad to get your letter & to hear what you've been doing. Gad-a-bout. Mom says after you go to California you'll end up in Corpus. Well, you'd better come, we may not be here after June or July. We expected orders in January but everybody else's came in but ours.

Write again & let us know what you're doing.

Love, Juanita

This letter, among many that my mother sent to her "Gad-a-bout" aunt during the mid-1950s, was posted from Corpus Christi on my parents' tenth anniversary. If my parents celebrated, the affair would have been squeezed in among never-ending chores, errands, and the care-taking of four young children; the fifth would arrive in June. *The kids have begged all my paper away from me so how do you like the stationary,* Juanita asks Grandma Sylvia, referring to the perforated pages of blank checks from the Corpus Christi National Bank: *Sorry I can't fill in the blanks for you.* On the occasions when my mother could locate writing materials, we sabotaged her attempts to focus on the task at hand: *Here is a picture. Becky made me tear it out crooked.... Tom is having a puppet show this morning. He just stole the doll off the toaster.... Claudia is a big help turning off the light and demanding the pen—Ricky is awake too....* (Ricky, the second son, had arrived by then, born just a week before we left for California.) *The kids have a store in the garage and they just came in wanting breakfast.*

One morning, Juanita decides to repair the lining on the bottom of the living room sofa: *I found the pliers, pencils, scissors, crayons, 2 pens, a dime, pins, dead roaches, etc.,* she writes to her mother. *No wonder the cheesecloth had been sagging.* Sometimes my mother resorts to typing her letters, providing a mechanical barricade between her thoughts and the chaos that surrounds her. When her youngest daughter starts taking her first steps, Juanita ties bells on Claudia's shoes so she can keep track of her while she types. Jingle Bells, as we begin calling my sister, is, according to my mother's letters, a pickle. *Becky got finger paints for Xmas so Claudia painted everything including herself but it's washable.*

If we weren't fingerpainting, we were sewing doll clothes, creating cardboard haunted houses complete with dripping ketchup blood, or clipping euchre cards to the spokes of our bicycles to make them whirr and clatter like motorcycles. Whenever she could, my mother joined our ranks, *pouring plaster molds like mad, also making animals out of newspapers, string, paste and paint. You should see my kangaroo, looks like a prehistoric animal . . . Then too I have been sewing. Have material to make the kids bathing suits, don't know how they will turn out or if they will at this rate.*

Sewing bathing suits? For four—and later, five, then six—children? Yes, bathing suits for all of us and Easter dresses for the girls and jackets for the boys and pajamas and robes and crinolines and dusters and dozens of costumes for school pageants and, in years to come, bridal gowns and veils for her daughters, gowns for the attendants, and three-piece suits for the grooms. But this Christmas, 1955, Juanita gets off easy, just a few Christmas gifts to mail to relatives back in Indiana: *All in all, I made 4 nighties & 6 or 7 houserobes (beside 10 clowns) for the girls, 4 shirts.*

When Juanita isn't sewing, volunteering for Bible School or Cub Scouts or Little League, or being commandeered by her kids into some

money-making project for which she jokes she hopes to receive a commission, she is dragging us out of our sick beds, to the base infirmary.
Mumps, measles, chicken pox, strep throat, flu: We filled our quota of
childhood diseases, and then some. One of my strongest sense memories is of my mother's cool hands, pressed to my face as she checked for
fever. *We keep busy going the rounds of diseases,* Juanita reports.

Still, it's my Marine Corps father who logged the most time in
sick bay, his itineraries often requiring a regimen of shots that made
him sick and feverish. His longest overseas duty was a fifteen-month
stay in Japan. "My daddy's in a pan," my little brother Ricky reported
to neighbors and strangers alike. Who knew what image floated in
Ricky's three-year-old mind? Or in the minds of us older siblings who,
though we could pronounce "Japan," understood little of the circumstances that kept our father from us. We wrote letters and drew pictures, which Mother mailed to him. I once baked a cake in miniature
cake tins I'd received as a Christmas gift. At the time, I was blissfully
unaware that it would be weeks before the cake could reach him. My
mother never told me otherwise. If baking the cake connected me to
the father who had been gone for months, so be it. My father completed the conspiracy by thanking me for the cake, which he pronounced
delicious.

On the occasions when I thought of my father, I missed him fiercely.
It never occurred to me how difficult such separations must have been
for my parents. Not until the breakup of my first marriage would I begin to imagine how hungry they must have been for each other, and to
question whether they remained faithful. Yet try as I might, I could not
then nor can I now imagine either of my parents straying. Too many
ropes bound them, strongest of all their obvious physical affection, coupled with stubborn, midwestern grit; when they made a promise, they
stuck by it. And if I am wrong? If there were moments when the ropes
that bound them began to fray, when their highest intentions slackened
and they found themselves falling toward other lovers? My mother
would have had to drag us along, five—and later six—bags of luggage
she hauled with her everywhere. As for my father? Friends say that I
am naive to believe he remained faithful. "He's a man," one friend says,
as if that settles the question. "He was a soldier, for God's sake," says
another. "It's a different world over there. All soldiers keep secrets from

their wives." I listen, I nod. Still, I cannot imagine it. If my parents kept secrets from each other, I do not want to know what those secrets were.

In the photograph I keep on my writing desk, a young man and woman stand at the edge of the sea. One of her arms encircles his neck; the other, his slender waist. His ears are small and delicately set, and his face is halfway in shadow, the profile of her nose forming a white relief against his jawbone. He is dressed in military khakis. She wears a sailor dress with a short, pleated skirt skimming hips that have not yet accumulated the weight of years and children. Her head is thrown back, the gesture freeing a nest of thick, dark hair. It is impossible not to feel the closeness of their bodies, how perfectly they fit.

The photo is cropped at my father's thighs and just above the hem of my mother's skirt so that their bodies appear to be floating. But I call forth the laws of physics to confirm that they are standing in shallow water, or on the bump of a small sand hill, the closest equivalent to land I can supply, except for a small strip of land in the distance, rising from the reverie of water. You have to squint to see it, but it is there: a ribbon of land miles away, anchored to the earth by buildings I choose to believe are houses and schools and churches. For isn't this what every child, growing or grown, wants? Two parents embracing. Their feet firmly anchored to the earth.

No doubt half the children in today's brutal world "would give their eyeteeth," as Grandma Sylvia used to say—I never knew what the expression meant, but it sounded like a desperate act—in exchange for the childhood I was granted. And *took* for granted, as every child should have the right to do. As she should also have the right to be ungrateful now and then. To pout on occasion and slam doors, to fantasize that she is an only child, or a twin, or that she wears glasses, or doesn't, or lives in an apartment building instead of a two-story, or a two-story instead of a ranch house. And *Please Mom, can't we stay here one more year? One more month? A week, please? Just one more week?*

My parents in Jacksonville, Florida, 1945.

To this day, my worst childhood memories are associated with the perpetual, or so it felt to me, pulling up of stakes. I hated every move the Marine Corps demanded, every loss of neighborhood, church, school, and home. The only thing that made moving bearable was knowing that no matter where we landed, from the moment the movers lifted the first piece of furniture from the truck, my mother would start *making home.* And despite the challenges that life pressed upon her—the constant care of children, the juggling of budgets and schedules, her homesickness for faraway relatives and her longing for the husband who was flying yet another mission in Korea, Japan, or Vietnam—she would continue making home. Each day as I dragged back from school, having made no friends yet, or maybe one, I'd open our door to the thrum-thrum-thrum of the Singer sewing machine or the whoop-splat of fresh sheets being folded or the creamy smell of vanilla and coconut wafting from beneath the kitchen door, and everything else would fall away.

Thus began my infatuation with all things domestic. From my first miniature cake pans to my first whiff of lemon furniture oil to my first whipstitched hem of a calico curtain, I was seduced by the warm, sweet world of home. To this day, I am lured toward domesticity the way some middle-aged women are lured toward Botox, affairs with young men, or overseas travel. "I think you always had that tendency," my mother says, and the way she says it doesn't sound like a compliment, but neither does it sound like a put-down. After all, a tendency isn't something you have much control over. You're either born with it or you acquire it early on, like a stutter or slightly crooked teeth or an attraction to small reptiles or birds. "It's just the way you are," she says. "You were always my helper, my right hand." Yes, I remember those earliest years when I was tied, by choice and often against her wishes, to my mother's apron strings. As I remember the later years: sewing the aprons to which I sewed the ties that bound me more tightly to the world her hands created.

My mother no doubt wondered at my infatuation with domesticity. Like many women of her generation, Juanita had assumed the role of homemaker less by tendency than by fate and circumstance. After a bit of college (a bit being all that Sylvia and Arthur could manage without sacrifice Juanita would not allow) and a brief business career, she married. First, there were just the two of them, love-nested in one-room quarters or upstairs apartments, where my mother made dinner each night on a one-burner hot plate, until it was time to repack their few possessions for the next place, and the next. Soon the first child arrived, then another, and every few years another, and my mother would pack us all up, once again. Not long ago, I asked my mother how in the world she had managed it. She shrugged. "It's what we did then," she answered. "We didn't stop to think how. Or why. It's what we did."

This may be so. Or maybe my mother's constant making and remaking of home was her way of combatting the homesickness that sifts up, like a fine powder, through the mesh of her comical, self-effacing, action-packed letters. Dozens of letters, each with the same salutation: *Dear Mom & Dad. . . . Long time, no write. Christmas over for '55. Terribly disappointed that none of the folks got to come . . . Dear Mom & Dad, We were real homesick but are over it a little now. . . . Dear Mom & Dad, Was surprised to hear from Uncle Ivan, I wish they would pack up and come out but I would never believe it until I see them . . . I've finally given up coming home this summer. It is such a long drive and after the kids were sick I de-*

cided to stick it out here . . . Dear Mom & Dad, Wish I could just go see my people when I want to . . .

Dear Mom & Dad. A greeting so ordinary as to be almost invisible. Why then, does it stop my breath? Don't forget, I remind myself. Juanita was not just your mother, she was someone's daughter. And not just a daughter, but the last child left at home, her parents finally free to squander their full attention on her.

Imagine:

Mornings with your father in the milking barn, balancing beside him on the three-legged stool. First light filtering through the cracks of the rough-hewn siding. The sweet-sour smell of cow and hay, your father whistling. Then, the moment opening to amiable silence, no need to talk.

Afternoons, the school bus wheezing to a stop before the iron gate of the Circle S. Lift the latch, hear the familiar clank. Step inside the cool garage then to the screen door that opens to the kitchen, and already the aroma of baking bread. No, not *baking*. Just *baked* bread, cooling on the cutting board. Drop your satchel, empty your tired self onto the chair beside your mother, just the two of you: Now slathering butter on a slice of warm bread. Now laughing. Now sewing—the 4-H project is due next week and you should rip out that seam, but maybe it will pass. "Yes," Mom nods, looking up from her mending. "It's fine as it is. It doesn't have to be perfect."

To military brats like the McClanahans, home is where the Marine Corps sends you—for a year, two years, four. It's where you sleep at night, where you crash after school, between club meetings, or when you get back late from sleepover camp. Home is the place your mother makes for you. It is portable, changeable; it can cross state lines. Pack your things into a box, they will arrive in a few weeks.

But to those tied to the land and its history, home is one particular spot, traceable on a map. You may change, but it remains.

For my mother, home was and always will be the Circle S farm, never mind that it was sold to a stranger decades ago.

For her mother, Sylvia, who along with Arthur created the Circle S farm and inhabited it for more than fifty years, home was not the Circle S but Briarwood, the little house on Wildcat Creek where she had been raised among Hattie's wild turkeys and Robert's tame squirrels. "Gone

over home," Sylvia would scribble on the back of an envelope (these envelopes survive, more than half a century later) and place on the Circle
S kitchen table in case anyone stopped by and found them gone. For the
homesick Sylvia had once more convinced Arthur to drive the twenty-
five miles to Briarwood.

Yet for Hattie, who along with Robert had created Briarwood and
by all rights should have claimed it as her own, her grandfather Mead's
Ohio River house remained until the end of Hattie's life "the only home
I've ever known."

So it goes, time eating time, memories locked within memories
someone creates for us. Someone works all her life to make a home yet
never truly inhabits it, homesick as she is for some lost place.

◆

And what was home to Bessie, who had created so many beautiful
houses along the way, each floorboard scrubbed, each linen pillowcase
creased, each Mason jar dusted to reveal its fruity, inner gleaming?
Bessie, the family-nicknamed "wanderer" who in later years appeared
to claim as home wherever her tiny self landed for the moment—a
Greyhound bus seat, a sofa shared with a niece, a Murphy bed pulled
from a cousin's wall. Bessie would stay a month or two then be on her
way again, for she no longer had anyone to report to. No husband, and
never any children who might now take care of her. Not that she would
have accepted help had it been offered. Bessie Denton Mounts Cosby
was stubbornly and proudly independent. She'd always worked—as a
young woman in homes, shops, and factories; as a farmer, alongside
her husband; as the widowed owner and manager of forty acres of
farmland and pasture. And though she now hired neighbors to work
the land, she still kept the books and wrote the checks, intervening
when necessary to protect what she'd worked so hard, over fifty years,
to acquire. Bessie kept records of her business correspondence, including the rough drafts she scribbled on whatever writing material she
could find. Shortly before she left Indiana in 1954, once again for California, she drafted a letter on the back of a flyer advertising the "Grand
Opening of the West Side Marathon" service station and a "Free gift of
6 Libbey Crystal Swirl glasses with purchase of 7 or more gallons." Bes-

sie had no need for gasoline; she had no car. And no need for another set of drinking glasses. She had more than she would ever use, packed away in boxes. What she did need was the land, and the income the land created for her.

July 27, 1954

Mr. Wayne Yundt
Stockwell, Ind.

Wayne, I learned only recently that you had continued to use my pasture. I will appreciate your seeing me soon, your bill is quite sizable now and may be easier to pay than later.

I am leaving soon to be away for some time, and naturally do not wish to leave any more unfinished business than I can help.

Hoping you will give this your immediate attention, I am
Cordially yours,
Mrs. B. Cosby

Cordially yours, perhaps. Cordially, as in *I will appreciate, naturally do not wish, hoping you will give*. Still, Bessie's message is clear: I know what you've been up to, Wayne Yundt. And it is time to pay. Now. Because if you do not pay now, it will be harder to pay later. Signed, not *Bessie*. Not the little girl reciting poetry before the schoolmaster's desk, or the young woman who strummed her guitar, sang late into the night, and danced all the neighbors around the barn, showing off the newest steps. Not the Bessie you've known nearly all your life. But *Mrs. B. Cosby*. To whom you must respond with your immediate attention, as she does not wish to leave any more unfinished business than she can help.

Circle S Ranch
January 17, 1955

Dear Bessie and Cousins there in California,

Got your letter today and was very happy to hear from you. I could just see you sitting in a snow drift some-place. Sounds like you are on the go. Well I would like that. We are on the go to but mostly from the house to wood pile and back. I made all the kids rag dolls for Xmas. I made 10 dolls and 7 toaster covers. No aprons though but one cowboy shirt. Arthur wants to know if you can shut your mouth since you got your new teeth? I think he is worried about this—the shutting, I mean. Ha! Ha!

We went out to home place, stopped on our way at the graveyard. I wanted to see the stones as I never knew whether you had seen them before you went away or not. They look nice.

Love Sylvia

It took a while for Sylvia's letter to reach her sister. Like so many others mailed to Bessie during the 1950s, this one had been forwarded several times, one address after another scratched out: *5941 So. Yakima Ave. Tacoma 8, Washington; 5206 Lexington Ave., Hollywood, California; 1169 E. Broadway, Long Beach, California.* Bessie was a moving target.

The stones that Sylvia mentioned were the newest markers in Salem Cemetery, the small wooded lot just a few miles from Briarwood. Headstones that Bessie had ordered to replace the original, cheaper stones that had marked the family graves. Hattie and Robert now shared one substantial stone, a floral etched "Mounts" with two carved boxes beneath, containing the given names the couple had carried all their lives: Robert A. and Harriet Z. The second headstone held only one name, and though this stone too was a divided one, its thin line separated not husband from wife, for there was no wife, but birth date from death date. As if the span of his life was all he had left to claim at the end. That, and his name: R. Dale Mounts.

And isn't this as it should be? Ashes to ashes, name to name. In my several decades of cemetery haunting, I have studied many stones. And though I am saddened by crumbling, decayed, or broken markers, those rubbed nameless by time and the elements, what most disturbs me is the stone that bears not the simple name of the deceased but rather her role as it relates to the survivors: Mother. Beloved Daughter. Son. Loving Wife. Who has the right to claim the loved one? The surviving spouse? The children who pay for the funeral? The parents, now decades dead, who raised the loved one?

Take Hattie: If we had to choose only one identity to carve on her headstone, which would we choose? Mother? Wife? Grandmother? Great-grandmother? Orphan? Daughter? Granddaughter? Great-granddaughter? Sister? Aunt? Gardener? Turkey farmer? Midwife? Friend? The list, if not endless, is daunting. That is what comes from living. If we are lucky, we grow to contain, like Whitman's speaker in "Song of Myself," multitudes. To bury a single person is to bury a family, a village, a continent. A universe of selves.

How little do we know that which we are.

That which we *were*.

◆

CHAPTER 22

Is there a golden time in the life of a family, a community, a tribe? Or is it only by looking backward that we decide when, or if, that time existed? For my father, the four years we spent in Virginia comprised that golden time: before Vietnam and Watts and the Kennedy tragedies, before the world he had known blew apart. He was stationed at Quantico and loved his work instructing new pilots and flying brief stints. He loved our house, too, on Backlick Road in Springfield, a brick two-story with a fireplace, a fenced-in backyard for the pedigreed wire-haired fox terrier we'd nicknamed Topsy. We children were still young then, young enough for buzz cuts and Little League and Bible School and Easter morning photographs. Easter was a big deal for our family; we prepared for weeks. While our Catholic neighbors smudged ashes on their forehead and debated what they would do without for the next forty days, we Baptists rehearsed Easter cantatas and shopped for new patent leather shoes. Our church held no services on Maundy Thursday. We did not fast, ever, or commemorate Good Friday. Apart from occasional pulpit references to hell, which none of us seemed to take personally, darkness was rarely mentioned, even during the holy season. Spring was one celebration after another: Palm Sunday (which I called Donkey Sunday) a bright rejoicing, followed by the brighter rejoicing of Easter, which through the years meant for my brothers new ties and jackets and for my sisters and me new hats, white gloves, and pastel dresses and dusters sewn by our mother.

After opening our Easter baskets, which one year included live ducklings that were not destined to survive the week, we assembled in the front yard for the annual Easter photograph. Though it is pos-

Photo taken by my mother on Easter morning 1961 outside our home in Springfield, Virginia. Back row: Tom, our father, Paul, and Jenny. Front row: Claudia, Rebecca, and Rick.

sible that my father was absent more often than he was present, in the Easter memory I hold onto, the whole family is there. First, gathered in the front yard; then, on our way to church in the gray Borgward station wagon or later the two-tone red and white Chevy wagon and later the Wedgewood blue Olds wagon; then, seated together on a pew close to the front of one Baptist church or another. Since this is my Easter memory and not my siblings', I am seated in the center of the pew, wedged between my parents and clicking my patent leather purse open, shut, open, staring into the space filled with nothing much: a comb, pencil, a quarter for the morning offering. Mother is scented with powder. Her hands are soft white gloves. The preacher's voice plows on, but a thousand words are less to me than the moth fluttering beside my father's sleeve.

Although my parents began their courtship outside the boundaries of the church, by the time we children came along, they were firmly established in what Southern Baptists call a Church Home. (As a child, I assumed all words associated with religion were capitalized.) Within our Church Home dwelled what we sometimes called the Body of Christ but mostly just called the Church Family. The men called each other Brother This and Brother That, and sometimes the women called each other Sister. Just as in a regular family, you fussed and fought with your siblings, you played together and watched out for each other. This wasn't all good. Sometimes you didn't want someone watching out for you, you wanted to do what you wanted to do, period. But mostly you were glad not to be what Sunday School teachers called a Spiritual Orphan. The physical location of our Church Home changed every few years. Yet each time we received our orders from the Marine Corps, each time we packed our belongings and moved to yet another town, another school, the Church Family was there, surrogate parents and siblings to whom I clung more tightly with each successive move.

The best thing about being a Baptist was Sunday afternoon, that holy, five-hour interval between morning and evening services, when our house filled with church kids—the Woolbrights, Tuttles, Pratts, Pedigos, or Eppinettes. Or when one of the childless couples, our surrogate grandparents the Haneys or Fegals, treated all five McClanahan kids (and later six, once our little sister Lana appeared on the scene) to the buffet at Burger Hut or fish-and-chips at the Snack Shop, with its spaceship placemats urging "Take Me To Your Leader."

First, though, there was Sunday morning to survive. If Sunday night services belonged to Jesus, Sunday morning belonged to God, and the difference between the two was the difference between paying a planned visit to a distant uncle, twice removed, and dropping in unexpectedly on a rowdy cousin who liked to tussle on the back porch. Sunday morning was an appointment made by your parents for your own good. The uncle was old and very important; his nerves were bad and his expectations inhumanly high. You dressed in your finest clothes, you whispered, you were careful where you put your hands and feet. When you arrived on Sunday morning, a Body of Strangers was already gathered in his parlor. They were called Visitors. They stood when their names were read from the pulpit during Visitor Recognition, and it was to them you extended the Hand of Christian Fellowship.

Because these strangers weren't part of the Church Family, we regulars had to be on guard. The thin man in the seersucker jacket might be someone's Presbyterian neighbor or Lutheran fiancé, sent to see if we really did all those crazy things he'd heard about. Perhaps he was a lapsed Methodist contemplating joining our Flock. So, each Sunday morning of my childhood, all the things I loved were hidden away—the blood songs, audible amens, baptismal waters, spontaneous testimonies, the Lord's Supper, prayer chains, free-for-all altar calls. Everything, in short, that made being a Baptist *fun*. The deacons closed the cover on the piano and plugged in the organ. Once, they even imported an organist from the university, some stiff-backed musicologist who played songs in minor keys, songs that sounded suspiciously classical. Sunday morning hymns were culled from the thin Praise section at the front of the Broadman Hymnal, with an occasional nature ditty like "This Is My Father's World" thrown in for variety. Nothing about the cross or the bloodied Lamb, nothing about rescuing the drowning thousands waiting for us to throw out a lifeline across the dark waves.

Morning sermons were well behaved, lifeless as professorial lectures; some preachers even used notes. And all of them, including the most frenetic, Tourettic-gestured, handkerchief-wringing preacher, stopped short of inspiration on Sunday mornings. I could see him holding back. A fire would start from his throat, he'd lurch forward and make a stab for the handkerchief in his back pocket, and I'd think, he's going to do it, break into the New Testament, into the smoldering mouth that waits for those who do not now call upon the name of the Lord, but just when he was about to cut loose, some invisible rope reeled him in, and within seconds we were back on the Text of the Sermon as noted on the bulletin. For not only were the ominous Visitors present but also the Women of the Church—young wives in taffeta dresses and seamed stockings, mothers like mine whose eyes had begun to wander to the clock above Brother Woolbright's head. All over the city, timers were ticking in slow ovens, standing rib roasts and turkeys and hams were browning in their own juices.

When the benediction was finally spoken and Brother Woolbright lifted his hand high into the air as if to bless the entire universe, we children were released, climbing over each other on the pew to reach our mother, begging, "Please can Pam come over" (or Roy Wayne or Kevin or Brent or Melanie) and then, "She nodded, I think she said yes!" as we piled into the station wagon. And after we'd stuffed ourselves with mashed potatoes and green bean casserole and banana pudding, off with the patent leather shoes and white socks, and bedroom doors would slam and we'd scramble up onto the bed to test the trampoline springs then jump and jump—"higher, go higher!"—and cover our mouths so our mothers couldn't hear our screams—"higher, higher!"— until the slats loosened and the mattress thumped to the floor and our mothers appeared to threaten us with everlasting separation from our friends, but for now, "Just get down and get ready, church starts in fifteen minutes."

Then we'd be back. Just us, the nuclear Church Family, fifty or sixty of the faithful, whose earthly bodies barely filled the first ten pews. Gone the Sunday morning neckties and double-breasted jackets. Welcome the golf shirts, the unbuttoned Oxfords rolled to the elbow to reveal the dark-haired forearms of the ushers who passed the offering plate, empty except for a lone dollar bill that I suspected had been planted there to prime the pump. Gone the high heels and veiled hats. Our mothers were teenagers, comfy in loafers and plaid skirts. Everyone was fed, the dishes were done, and they could finally lean back in their pews and rest. The organ cover was closed and the pianist's freckled fingers were spread across octaves, thumping out some barrel polka of a hymn and occasionally turning sideways to smile like Jo Ann Castle on The Lawrence Welk Show.

Out came the blood songs with their promises of salvation pouring from the fountain filled with blood drawn from Emmanuel's veins. Buxom sopranos, uncorsetted now, unfolded their magnificent lungs, and second-string altos (like my mother) dutifully trailed beneath. My father was an Irish tenor, pure and simple, and he slid easily into harmony beside my mother, while behind us wavy-haired Waynie Pratt provided the bass percussion, anchoring the rest of us to earth.

"Are you washed?" we would sing.

"Are you washed?" came Waynie's frog-echo.

"In the blood!"

"In the blood!"

Song after spirited song continued, until the deacons stood and walked toward the linen-draped table at the front of the sanctuary. "You mean you observe Communion at night?" my Catholic friend once asked. "It's the Lord's *supper*," I answered. "Not breakfast. We do it the way Jesus did." Beneath the white sheet lay the mysteries of flesh and spirit that had been my first spiritual attraction: "This is my body, broken for you," the preacher intoned. "My blood, shed for you."

"It's a symbol, honey," my mother told me the first time I asked. "Not real blood." Yet even after I'd sneaked into the church kitchen and watched my mother and other Women of the Church pour grape juice from industrial-sized cans into tiny goblets, and crumble saltines into stainless steel trays, I remained Catholic in this one leaning: I believed the miracle of communion. Yes, the grape juice was tart on my tongue, but by the time the preacher had spoken "Drink ye all of it" and I had licked the miniature goblet clean, I felt changed, part of something greater than myself. Following my mother's cue, I placed the goblet in the rubber-lined hole carved into the back of the pew. Around us, heads were bowing, knees creaking as Brother Woolbright began reading from index cards: "Lila Conklin asks us to pray for her mother who is recovering from surgery. Jeff Bobick needs the Lord's guidance as he chooses which college to attend."

Then came the question I'd been waiting for: "Any unspoken requests?" I lifted my head from my church-steeple hands and peeked around the sanctuary. Two rows up, a slender hand rose tentatively into the air. Bridgett Sims's mother. And from the front of the church, a braceleted wrist I recognized as belonging to my Sunday School teacher. What secrets are they carrying? I wondered. What burdens so heavy that they must be lifted up?

For the next ten minutes the Chain of Prayer unwound, snaking its way through the congregation. The Chain of Prayer was totally random and democratic; anyone who felt *so moved* could speak. It seemed miraculous to me that no one ever jumped in too soon, that voices did not collide in mid-air. "It just works out," my mother would say, "like potluck dinners. Sure, fourteen people *could* bring macaroni salad, seventeen *could* bring deviled eggs, but the point is, they don't."

"In Jesus' name we pray, Amen."

"Amen," my father whispered.

And behind us, Waynie Pratt's bass-drum "A-men."

Near the end of the evening, Brother Woolbright disappeared through a side door. The pianist had modulated into a lower key, playing a melody that grew sadder and softer with each measure, like a music box winding down. Overhead lights flickered off one by one, until everything was dark except for one white light above the baptistery. The reflection from the water rippled on the ceiling. I'd been baptized the year before, so I knew that the baptismal tank was only a big bathtub, and the reedy marsh was only a painted backdrop. I'd even seen the preacher's wetsuit and rubber hip boots hanging on a hook beside the stairs, and watching him now, I knew he was only an ordinary man in a white robe standing waist-high in bath water.

The tall woman with the red bouffant and painted eyebrows who was wading toward him was Brad Walters's stepmother, who two weeks earlier had walked the aisle for the first time. She was nearly a foot taller than Brother Woolbright. She crossed her hands over her chest and he placed his right hand on hers, his other hand behind her neck. Her eyes were wide with what looked like fear and I thought for a minute she was going to bolt. Brother Woolbright whispered something to her. She grabbed a few shallow breaths, leaned back, closed her eyes, went under, and sputtered and thrashed to the surface. He placed his hands on her shoulders, turning her to face us. "And lo a voice from heaven saying, 'This is my beloved child, in whom I am well pleased.'"

In a moment Sister Walters will slip in through the side door to join us for the last prayer and benediction. Her red hair will be wet, combed flat against her head. The painted eyebrows will be gone, her face wiped clean of rouge, and Waynie Pratt or my mother or Sister Pedigo or Brother Tuttle will step out of their place in the pew, gesture with their arms, and silently gather her in.

◆

Great-aunt Bessie in Washington, D. C., with my siblings Claudia and Rick, 1959.

House of Representatives, Washington DC.
Admit Mrs. Bessie Cosby for Eighty-sixth Congress

An intricately illustrated visitor's pass, issued to my great-aunt on May 24, 1960, admonishes "no packages, bundles, cameras, suitcases, or briefcases allowed in the galleries." Pocketbooks, however, must have been permitted, as Bessie would never have relinquished her most important accessory to a stranger. In nearly every picture of the tiny Bessie, the omnipresent pocketbook is highly visible, though in my favorite photograph of the Virginia years, taken on a winter day, Bessie's pocketbook is nowhere in sight. Perhaps my mother, who took the photograph, moved the pocketbook out of the frame so as to better focus on her three subjects: Bessie, seated on a stone bench between my younger siblings, Claudia and Ricky. The building behind them is the Smithsonian National Museum of Natural History, our favorite D.C. haunt. Like most kids, we loved the Hope Diamond and the dioramas, but the massive African bush elephant, which had been unveiled in 1959, the year our family moved to Virginia, was our ultimate reward for having endured without complaint the more sedate galleries of the museum.

It's a cold day—you can tell by Bessie's fur coat and the black earmuffs beneath Ricky's cap—but the sun is shining on their faces. All three wear broad, eye-wrinkling smiles—has Aunt Bessie just said something funny? Claudia's coat is tweed; her left hand, in a black wool glove, clutches Bessie's leather camera case. Ricky, who at four is only one year younger than his sister, wears white cotton gloves. One gloved hand rests affectionately on the sleeve of Bessie's fur coat.

I love the white glove touch, love that my often-harried mother dressed her children so formally for an outing to the nation's capital. Did Juanita make Ricky's little coat herself, on the Singer she had brought from California? Probably not, as Ricky's billed cap matches his coat, and though my mother sewed many of our clothes when we were small, to my knowledge she never stitched any hats. If it weren't so cold, if Ricky's hands weren't covered in gloves, he would be stroking the soft fur, as I did whenever I got the chance. Bessie's fur coat was one of the tactile wonders of my childhood. At the time, I never thought to ask what kind of fur it was. I knew only that it was beautiful, plush and brown and luxuriously thick. Had I asked, Great-aunt Bessie would have concocted some story, perhaps about her uncle Lafayette in Wisconsin, how he had made the coat many, many years ago, long before I was born. How he had trapped the minks (or beavers or foxes or squirrels) and stretched their pelts on tent poles just like Indians once did, then stitched them together with a special thread using a needle he'd fashioned from the bone of some long-extinct creature.

Bessie would have watched my face to see if I was buying the tale. Then she would have laughed, and gone on to explain that Yes, Uncle Lafe did indeed make fur coats for his family from animals he had trapped, "but this particular coat I am wearing is not one of them. This coat was store-bought, and though it might look like beaver or fox or mink, it isn't. It is called mouton. Sheepskin. Yes, Becky, sheep have skin. And there is nothing wrong with killing animals," Bessie would have continued. "Certain animals, that is, like sheep. Not pet sheep, of course, like my Debby, no, you wouldn't have known Debby, but your mother did. Most sheep, though, aren't pets. They are bred expressly" ("expressly" being one of Bessie's favorite words) "to provide food and warmth. Which all humans throughout history have required, as you must have noticed—did you not notice?—in the dioramas we saw in the Natural History Museum."

Bessie never missed a chance to educate the McClanahan kids, to explain things that my mother might not know or didn't have time to teach us. Our ancient aunt—for Bessie always seemed ancient to us—could sit for hours studying <u>National Geographic</u> or our <u>American Peoples Encylopedia</u> or even the frayed <u>Webster's Dictionary</u> my mother kept near the family typewriter. Although Bessie had studied many illustrious texts and certainly could have ranked them according to literary merit, she chose instead to sample far and wide. Like the duchess in Browning's famous poem, Bessie's "look went everywhere." Anything made of words was fair game: our biology textbooks, library books, cereal boxes, album covers, even the pamphlets that Jehovah's Witnesses left with her after she'd thanked them politely and closed our front door.

Bessie was always beating us to the door, as if she might be expecting a visitor, though her friends were hundreds—and later thousands—of miles away in Indiana. Once, shortly before we moved from Virginia, I spotted from the kitchen window a cute boy from our church heading up the walkway. Frantic to get to the door before Bessie, I careened around the corner leading to the entry hall, nearly knocking her down. Did I even apologize? I can't remember. What I remember is the angry—or was it pained?—look on her face, and her words, each syllable distinct in its separate, quiet outrage: "Don't. Tread. On. Me." The phrase sounded familiar, had I heard it in history class, something about the Colonial period? But this time, Aunt Bessie did not stop to lecture me, to decode the rattlesnake flag motto every seventh grader worth her salt should have been able to identify. She simply turned from the entryway and walked back down the hall to the room we shared, calmly closing the door.

I wish she had slammed it. Had Bessie slammed the bedroom door, she might have put an end to a moment that I have replayed dozens of times since. How to explain my rude actions? True, we were seventy years apart, but Bessie was my closest aunt, and though I never said the words outright, I loved her. We were two larks in a family of owls, so it made sense for us to share a room. Plus, we were both bookworms. By nine o'clock we were propped up in the double bed we shared, our stack of library books in close range on the nightstand, beside Bessie's denture case and box of Polident. Sometimes we'd read aloud to each other—mysteries and westerns, mostly. We'd take turns, each reading a chapter a night, and at the end of the chapter, right before Bessie removed her eyeglasses and dentures and switched off the light, right before she slipped her embroidered handkerchief into the book to mark our place, we would make predictions about how the story would turn. Because of Aunt Bessie, I never saw books as dead, finished texts. They were living, breathing entities, unexplored territories into which we would venture the next night, and the next. Anything could happen, and we would be present when it did.

December 1963

Well Hello Out There in Pennsylvania. How's the weather?

The broadcaster at the Purdue Station this morning announced that one of the fellows had just come in and he was a bright Xmas red. He said if he just had a green coat he would be all set. It was then 3 degrees above. The temperature was not quite so low yesterday but the wind was so strong, made it seem colder. . . . Eldon sawed some wood some time ago, but it was getting pretty low, he came down and brought some of their coal, three or four buckets, brought a shovel and made a path and carried up to the house what chunks were still in the shed.

Paul and Juanita moved to California. He had to report the 1st of August at El Toro so they are again in Santa Ana. They expected me to go with them but I thought I wasn't ready <u>so</u> here I sit with my feet in the gas oven. I don't know where I'll be for Christmas and don't much care. I still feel struck by the tragedy that has befallen our country. I've no enthusiasm for the holidays. "Merry" hardly seems a fitting word. . . .

I <u>had three brothers</u> and I loved them very much, I lost one and I still miss him. I am deeply concerned in the welfare of the other two. Please write.

If Bessie ever mailed a final draft of this letter to her youngest brother, it would have looked quite different from the scribbled, penciled draft that survives on a sheet of scratch paper filled with multiple cross-outs and revisions. Even when writing to family, Bessie was careful how she phrased things. And in this letter, composed shortly before Christmas 1963, she takes care to mask her neediness, though it's hard to miss the underlined _had three brothers_. Was the past tense construction—_had three brothers, loved them_—a grammatical slip that Bessie later corrected? Or did she employ it purposely, to remind Babe that, though Dale was indeed gone from this earth, Ivan and Babe were in some ways lost to Bessie as well? I see her sitting in the little kitchen at Briarwood, warming her feet in the open oven, stroking the cat in her lap, and grieving. One brother dead for a decade. Two others for whom she is concerned. And now, a beloved president. Unlike her Republican siblings, Bessie had been a Democrat all her life, and Kennedy had been her favorite president since Roosevelt. She still regretted missing Kennedy's inauguration, as she'd been so close, right there in Springfield. Yet even if Paul had been able to take her, they could never have gotten through. Goodness, not even Herbert Hoover could make it: eight inches of snow that morning, the worst traffic jam in D.C. history, and frigid cold to boot.

Still, that cold couldn't have compared to this day. May have to take a warming brick to bed, Bessie thought. Well, that's Indiana weather for you. I could be in California right this minute, making plans for the Rose Bowl. Bessie sidled closer to the stove and studied her list. So many to write to, and me with no spirit for the holidays. She made a check mark beside "Babe" (Check: Done) and turned her attention back to the list: "Major and Mrs. McClanahan." Now where did I put their new address? Heavens, a person needs a secretary to keep track of that family.

CHAPTER  23

◆

August 5, 1964

Hello, Sylvia! Came through fine no one ill, pretty tired. This doesn't give a very good idea of the place in which we spent Wed. night, tis very colorful. The young folks sure enjoyed the pool. Arrived in Santa Ana Sat. PM. Will write in detail later. B. Cosby

Bessie's note to her sister in Indiana is brief, as she had to squeeze the message onto a postcard, one of many that B. Cosby pocketed on her journeys, to use at a later date. This card advertises "Guest House Motel, US Hwy 66, Travelers Delight in the Heart of Oklahoma City." The "young folks" were the six McClanahan children, who, along with Aunt Bessie and Juanita, filled the blue Oldsmobile station wagon for the twenty-three-hundred-mile trip from Indiana. I wasn't yet old enough to drive, but Jenny or Tom took the wheel when my mother needed a rest. Bessie never needed a rest. She'd sit straight up in the passenger seat, pocketbook in lap, her head turning side to side so as not to miss a single billboard, telephone line, or cactus. I'd seen it all so many times I could recite the Route 66 stops without prompting: St. Louis, Oklahoma City, Amarillo, Albuquerque, Gallup, Flagstaff, Kingman, Needles, Barstow. With Dad driving, we sometimes made the trip in three days; without him, it stretched to four.

Usually I got antsy after a day or so, but that summer of 1964 I wanted the trip to last forever. School would start in a few weeks, and I hated the thought of it. Hated returning to the junior high I despised. With all the practice I'd had, I should have gotten used to the uprooting. But our cross-country move the summer before had been the hardest of all.

The move from Springfield, Virginia, where I had sewn my own dresses and sung Peter, Paul, & Mary songs, to southern California where on my first evening, the next-door neighbor, a girl my age but years advanced in knowledge of pancake makeup and garter belts and stockings ("Those anklets will have to go," she said, glancing down at my white socks) took me aside and began explaining everything I needed to know before eighth grade started the following week. Where the Kotex machines were, which girls could be trusted and which girls couldn't, what French kissing entailed. "You mean you've never done it?" she gasped. "That's unbelievable!" So l learned never to say "eagle" or "beaver," because an eagle isn't a bird, as I'd always thought; it's when a boy can see down your blouse. A beaver is a different view altogether. And "69"? Her description sent me flailing into our new house, where I stared at the unpacked suitcases filled with dresses that would never work and white socks and loafers that everyone would laugh at. I'd known in that moment that I would never fit in.

And I hadn't.

Each month the loneliness grew. I woke with a feeling of heaviness and vacancy, as if the best part of me had moved out and left this huge space I had to haul around the rest of the day. The only place where I felt at home—*other* than home—was at the Church Home we'd returned to in Santa Ana. No one at school talked about church, and I never volunteered information. I didn't tell them about Wednesday night prayer meetings, Sunday night services, choir practice, potluck dinners, chili suppers, and revival meetings. Had anyone at my junior high school asked, I would have lied and told them that my parents made me go.

Thankfully, no one could guess the inner sanctum of my most recent shame: I'd started memorizing whole chapters of the King James Bible. The Psalms of David, Ecclesiastes, and the Sermon on the Mount, with its comforting, predictable repetition—*Blessed are the merciful, for they shall obtain mercy. Blessed are the pure in heart, for they shall see God.* Lately, I'd moved on to more difficult passages—sections of Revelation, with its twin promise of judgment and salvation, the Old Testament travails of Job. What fourteen-year-old did this sort of thing? What kind of freak was I, anyway?

Now, wedged in the back seat between Claudia and Ricky, I passed the long Route 66 days rereading <u>The Cross and the Switchblade</u>, a book recommended by our church youth director. I'd seen <u>West Side Story</u> a few years before, but the Dragons made the Jets and Sharks look like Boy Scouts. Dragon gang members were heroin addicts, killers, thieves, and prostitutes; some of the girls were no older than I was. The youth director was hoping the book would convince me to join the "Taking Christ to the World" ministry. Knocking on strangers' doors? Not for me. It felt wrong to trespass into people's private spaces. Live and let live, I thought.

◆

Whenever Bessie joined us on a cross-country trip, the passenger seat was hers, no questions asked. Sometimes one of us older kids got to sit between her and Mother, but the summer of 1964, three-year-old Lana occupied the coveted front seat, where Bessie could keep an eye on her. Or so Bessie claimed. We all knew she just wanted to be close to our baby sister. Who didn't? Though she'd been born long after my parents thought they were finished with children (surprise, again!) none of us could now imagine life without Lana. She was our pet, our mascot. At three, she had only recently given up her bottle, following months of bargaining on my mother's part. The winning bribe was a new Pebbles doll, which existed, like all of Lana's dolls—and Lana herself, when she could get away with it—in a constant state of undress. With Lana, comfort was what mattered, comfort and fun and mischief. Was she spoiled? Of course. Yet, finally, unspoilable. Like her grandmother Sylvia as a child at Briarwood and Juanita as a child at the Circle S farm, Lana was "the light of our home."

Later that summer, our home's light was doubled when little Carla arrived from Oregon with her parents. Carla was a cousin on the McClanahan side, just a few weeks younger than Lana. My father's sister had children from an earlier marriage, but Carla was the only child of Marge's second marriage, to a gentle, bespectacled man named Jim. And Carla would remain their only child for the rest of their lives, her small rocking chair placed by the fireplace as if at any moment she might appear.

Whenever Lana and Carla got together, I'd sing the theme song from <u>The Patty Duke Show</u> ("identical cousins all the way . . ."). The resemblance was eerie: the same dark eyes, the same straight, shiny dark hair fringed with short bangs. Hair so dark it looked black when the

Our baby sister, Lana, 1964.

sun wasn't shining on it. But that September day in 1964 the sun *was* shining on it. I remember watching the girls from the kitchen window, feeling the sadness that had been with me for months now gradually floating out the open window and into the sky above the yard. Get the camera, I thought, but I didn't. The girls were playing on the lawn my father was so proud of. Unlike the prickly Bermuda grass in our neighbors' yards, our lawn was dichondra, a tropical ground cover whose leaves sprouted tiny green flowers. A built-in sprinkler system kept the dichondra perfectly green all year long, cool and spongy to the touch. So of course you had to go barefoot, especially if you were three years old. That day, Carla and Lana were screaming in delight—running, skipping, tagging each other, spinning in circles then falling exhausted to the soft ground. Getting back up, breathless, then stumbling toward each other, reaching out, laughing, the chase on.

◆

Mrs. Sylvia Sanders
Battle Ground, Indiana
Dear Sister:

> *Just a note to tell you Marge's little girl died Tues. at 5 o'clock. Just*
> *about a month ago their family was here, Carla and Lana played*
> *together so happily. Paul & Juanita have gone up to Oregon, taking*
> *separate planes at Los Angeles Airport, Paul at around 3 and J. later at*
> *five. They took Lana to stay at their preacher's house. They thought she*
> *would be happier there. I wouldn't say that for the family has two ram-*
> *bunctious boys and a little girl around Lana's age, terribly spoiled too*
> *and she and Lana also fight. The rest are here. Keeping house. Sort of.*
> *Bessie*

When my parents returned from Oregon, my father's eyes were swollen, his face drawn. A marine known for his silent strength, suddenly he could not stop talking. About how small the casket was, how the congregation sang all four verses of "Jesus Loves Me," just kept singing and singing until he thought he would break in two. He knew his sister and Jim were broken. Jim's own small family—his parents and siblings—were not close, and he had been overwhelmed when Paul and Juanita showed up at the funeral. "I can't believe you came all this way," Jim kept saying. "I can't believe you came."

"Of course we came," my mother answered. "We're family."

As my father told us the story, he kept looking at Lana, who did not fully grasp what had transpired. She'd been told that Carla died, which her Sunday School teacher said meant going to be with Jesus. That much, Lana understood. But *how* did Carla die? Did it start here, that afternoon on the lawn when Carla cut her foot and it wouldn't stop bleeding? Mom and Dad kept saying something about plastic. Something wrong with Carla, about plastic. "Aplastic anemia," is what Paul was trying to explain. A rare sort of blood disease. But Lana heard only "blood," and the word took her back to that day. A month ago, but a month can seem like years to a child of three.

For weeks after Carla died, it was difficult for any of us to look at Lana without thinking of our little cousin. My father's sadness lasted

longer. "To lose a child," he kept saying, letting the sentence hang unfinished. Sometimes his blue eyes would fill, then redden. I never saw him
cry, but I was sure he did, in private. The myth of the cold, hard marine is
just that, a myth. To outsiders, my father might have seemed unmoved
and unmoveable, but his blue eyes have always told a different story.
That fall, the story they told was an old one. It stretched back thirty
years, to a March afternoon in 1934. Another little girl playing, this time
on the playground of a one-room schoolhouse outside the small town
of Arcola, Illinois. It was a Sunday, Visiting Day at the schoolhouse, and
Mona Lee McClanahan had tagged along with her brother Jack. She was
almost five years old. In September she would start school, just like her
big brothers and sisters. She knew her sisters' names, all five of them,
and her brothers' names too—all four, including the one who had died
before she was born. But Mama was going to have another baby soon,
and who knows, it might be another brother, which would make four
brothers again, plus one new name. That would make five. Mona could
already do her numbers, and soon she would learn to read. But today
she just wanted to get on that teeter-totter. Look! A big boy was standing in the middle of it and could help her on and hold it steady until she
could get her legs moving just right!

Mona's big brother Paul didn't go to Visiting Day. Even on Sundays,
the farm chores had to be done, and with his older brother married and
gone, twelve-year-old Paul was the eldest son at home, his father's second hand. It had started to rain by now, and suddenly the McClanahan
porch was filling with people, everyone crying and talking at once, trying to explain to Goldie and Clarence what had happened, how they
had rushed Mona Lee as quickly as they could to Doc Allen's. "The teeter-totter," someone was saying. "A burst appendix." Dead? Mona Lee
dead? But that's impossible, Goldie thought. She was just here, she just
went up to the school a little while ago. Dead?

When Grandpa Clarence's sister heard the news, she packed some
fabric in her suitcase and made the trip to Arcola. Fabric was precious
in 1934, and she had been saving it for a special occasion. Now, she
would sew a dress for her dead niece. Once my great-aunt Laura arrived
at the McClanahan farm, she went to work at Goldie's treadle machine,
pumping to the rhythm of her ragged breath, her tears wetting the fabric. My father remembers little about the funeral. What he remembers

are the steps that led out from the church, his last sight before he went down. Down and out. His sisters all around him, his little brother too, and he the eldest brother at home, who should have been an example (this is how you put one foot before the other, this is how you swallow grief) twelve-year-old Paul broke in two that day. His legs crumpling under him, he fainted dead away.

July 1965

For your Birthday Sister
Dear Sylvia:

> *How time goes!!! Well it is like this: Lana just came in and climbed on my lap eating a chocolate cupcake, then she said she was going to get another one and she would get one for me—she did, then she insisted I read to her and "cubber" up.*
>
> *Have never heard from those people at San Luis Obispo regarding the Atascadero property.*
>
> *Paul is still in VietNam and his father in Illinois is home from hospital, some better but they are keeping oxygen on hand.*
>
> *This is pretty much of a scrawl and no use to date it for I'm not at all sure it will be finished at all soon, but no matter. Have a Fish-nic on your birthday.*
>
> *Bye. B. C.*

This was Bessie at her best, busily absorbed in the lives of the young. Spoiling us with sweets and books and attention, to the point of subverting my mother's disciplinary actions, which, especially when my father was overseas, were mild to say the least. Decades before, Bessie had been extremely strict with her nephews and nieces, insisting that they "comport" themselves properly at all times. But Bessie's disciplinary resolve seemed to have skipped a generation. When it came to her great-nieces and -nephews—especially me as a baby, and now, years later, Lana—Bessie was more co-conspirator than nanny. She took little Lana's part when Lana locked herself in the bathroom as a prank, causing Sylvia to remark later, "Now Bessie, you know that child needed to be chided." On another occasion, Bessie allowed Lana to pull the film out of my mother's camera, exposing a whole roll that—who knows?—might have documented the most significant days of our lives.

Yes, Lana was "a card" and "a cut-up," according to my mother. *A real live wire,* Bessie's cousins would write. And yes, with one of her many preschool accomplices in tow, Lana had been known to autograph our new carpet with lipstick and to redesign the landscape (read: pull up the new shrubs) in our neighbor's yard and to free Claudia's pet rat from its cardboard home, too near the dog's bed to give that story a happy ending. But our youngest sister could charm you right out of your sadness, and that summer of 1965, we needed Lana's charm more than ever. Our father was overseas again. Not in "a pan" this time, not Japan or Guam or Hawaii. The first mass bombings had begun in Vietnam, and for the first time since the Korean Conflict, the B-52s were back in action.

And thirty miles up the freeway from our house, Los Angeles was on fire. Every night, the news was worse—thousands rioting in the streets, hundreds of buildings destroyed, dozens of people injured, many dead. I had read about Martin Luther King's marches and the assassination of Malcolm X, but at the time I didn't understand the Watts riots' connection to Proposition 14. Housing discrimination? Racial segregation? I was clueless; the 1960s were proceeding without me. Marijuana was being sold from Volkswagen vans parked behind the high school gym, and though the dress code stipulated that girls wear dresses that fully cover our knees, as soon as the dismissal bell rang, some girls changed into miniskirts or bellbottoms cut low to reveal their navels. Rumor had it that three girls in our class had gone "all the way," as we called it back then. Hearing the news, I nodded calmly and tried to act cool.

Where to turn? The Church Home, which had always been my refuge from change, was quaking from within. Two girls in our youth group had been sent away to "boarding school." Previously conservative Baptist boys were growing their hair long and claiming conscientious objector status. Even the grownups were losing their spiritual leverage. The deacons, in an attempt to make the church more relevant to the young people they were losing, distributed copies of Good News for Modern Man, a flat, prosy translation of the New Testament accompanied by minimally sketched cartoon drawings. Gone was the stately poetry of King James, which I privately but stubbornly refused to relinquish. Soon, the deacons removed from the vestibule the traditional portrait of a pale, sandaled

Jesus knocking at your heart's door, and replaced it with a painting of a bearded man with savage hair, fiery eyes, and an animal body I associated more with John the Baptist than with his cousin Jesus.

Within months, our youth director bought a guitar, started wearing jeans and floppy hats, and organized weekend mountaintop retreats. Sprawled around bonfires, we sang songs and debated such issues as predestination, birth control, and whether Christians should wear love beads. But the songs, they were *a-changin'*. Gone were the blood hymns of redemption, the missionary anthems, even the praise ballads that proclaimed Jesus our only friend. Now, darkness was our friend, or so said Simon and Garfunkel's "The Sound of Silence." The more we sang, the more I came to doubt, as the speaker of "Kathy's Song" doubted, "all that I once held as true."

◆

Dear Congressman:

For the last few years I have been attempting to make appropriate application for Social Security Benefits. Because of my longevity and the fact that records were not maintained by the State of Indiana, I have been unable to get official documentary proof of my age and marriage date.

I have received no administrative assistance from the Social Security personnel—rather I have been given only the proverbial "Sorry about that" hard time. It is quite apparent that further procrastination may extend to the point at which I no longer can enjoy any benefits offered under the Social Security Benefit Act.

The following information is offered in hopes that you can direct some assistance on my behalf.

Name—Bessie Denton Mounts
Born—28 Sept 1880
Place of Birth—Rising Sun, Switzerland County, Ind.
Father's name—Robert A. Mounts
Mother's name—Harriet Z. Ray
Married—5 July 1904
Husband—Santford M. Cosby

Your humble Constituent,
Bessie Cosby

"Because of my longevity" was an understatement. Bessie was eighty-five years old and, unlike her widowed cousins, had managed thus far without government subsidies. Besides a hefty savings account she'd fed religiously all her life, Bessie still owned Indiana farmland and California acreage she refused to sell, though she'd given up ever building on the landlocked plot. As for Social Security benefits, why start the battle now? Maybe Bessie had finally decided to listen to friends and family: You and Sant worked hard for decades, paying your taxes and contributing to Social Security. You are entitled, Bessie. No shame in taking what rightfully belongs to you.

Or maybe the stony truth had finally dug itself up. Over the past year, Bessie had bumped against it, little stubs of recognition. Despite what Juanita says, those children don't need me any more, Bessie thought. Even Lana—good heavens, kindergarten already, and always on the go. No more "cubbering up" with old Aunt Bessie. Yes, I suppose I must seem old to her. When did that happen? . . . "Further procrastination may extend to the point at which I no longer . . ." If I get sick, if I need care, well, care costs money, and who knows how long mine will last? Best to go back to where I started. Back where I belong.

◆

Dear Mom & Dad and Aunt Bessie,

Monday morning & all off to school & work. We had kids here all day yesterday. Lana broke a mixing bowl of whipped cream all over the floor & it is slippery you know. Too near Christmas I think—the excitement gets to them. It was so cold this morning I had to give Rick his new jacket (Christmas present) but he needed it so bad & he was really tickled so it doesn't matter.

Paul put up the outside lights Saturday—said he needed Dad here. We don't have a tree as yet. He may even be gone—to Vietnam but I hope not. Paul says he hates to send guys over there this Christmas that are bound to be over there for good next year.

I called Barbara Sat. night—needed to hear somebody from home.

Write & Merry Christmas & many blessings.
Juanita

Over the next year, our father would not be the only father missing from our neighborhood and from towns up and down the California coast. Sons, too, would go missing, boys not much older than my brother. I thought of them as boys then and I still think of them that way. Luckily for our family, the 1969 draft lottery was still three years away. Three years until some official's hand would reach into the glass jar rattling with three hundred sixty-six plastic capsules and, on the ninth try, draw my brother's birth date. Until then, Tom was preparing to enter a Texas university not far from the university where Charles Whitman had recently opened fire from a tower and just weeks after Richard Speck had killed eight nurses in Chicago because, in Speck's words, "it just wasn't their night." Every day, another horror appeared in the headlines. If God wasn't dead, as the <u>Time</u> magazine cover had recently claimed that he was, he appeared to be sleeping.

Late one night after everyone had gone to bed, I overheard my parents talking in the next room, my father's voice breaking: "Now I know what it means, 'groanings which cannot be uttered.'" I recognized the Bible verse promising that the Holy Spirit makes intercession for us in ways that are beyond our understanding. Was my father thinking of his father far away in Illinois, growing sicker each month? Was he worried about Jenny's upcoming marriage? Was he remembering Vietnam, or Kennedy, or what he always called "the best years," when we lined up for photos in our new Easter outfits? Lying across from my sleeping sister, I had never felt more alone. Jenny would be leaving home soon. And who knew how long my brother's luck would hold out? If the draft was reinstated, as we were now sure it would be, would Tom leave for Canada as so many were doing? I knew he would never serve. He'd said as much to Dad one night, their voices rising, Tom spewing back, "You were nothing but a hired killer!" And the terrible silence afterwards, a silence that would take years to fill. Years of what Tom would remember as "a severe split" with our father; years until Tom became a father himself, and *to use a cliché-ridden analysis*, he would write, discovered that *I am more like my father than even he is.* But that time was far in the future, a future none of us could imagine that summer of 1966.

I had never heard my father cry. Afterwards, there was a long pause, followed by a labored intake of breath. "I don't know how to pray any more," he said. "It's all just words." Lying in my twin bed, I pulled my knees in tight to my belly, trying to connect myself with myself. This would not be the only time I experienced what I would later learn was a feeling so universal that it even had a name: existential loneliness. But it was the first time. The realization was sudden and fierce, sweeping over me like a cold wind. No one would ever truly know me, the inside me that lived beneath skin and hair and bones and teeth. "From the womb have I known you," began a Bible verse I had memorized long ago. But for the life of me I couldn't remember the rest of it.

Distinguished Flying Cross, Air Medal for Meritorious Achievement in Aerial Flight, Good Conduct Medal, American Defense Service Medal, American Campaign Medal, European–African–Middle East Campaign Medal, Asiatic-Pacific Campaign Medal, Victory Medal World War II, National Defense Service Medal, Korean Service Medal, United Nationals Service Medal, Korean Presidential Unit Citation.

The medals my father received over his twenty-six years of military service could have filled our fireplace mantle, had he chosen to display them. On the day he retired, none of us children attended the ceremony, held on a Thursday, a school day. We didn't see the Commandant of the Marine Corps salute my father and wish him well. Unlike Hattie and Robert in 1918, Goldie and Clarence McClanahan did not receive a letter thanking them for being part of "that Great Army of Encouragement and Enthusiasm which helped to make him," nor did my mother receive official notification that the Marine Corps was "returning him to you a better man." He *was* returned to her. He was returned to all of us, more or less intact. The Atlantic, the Pacific, Korea, Vietnam: Whatever those twenty-six years had meant to Lieutenant Colonel Paul McClanahan were locked away, along with the medals and uniforms, the pistol and rifle, and the gleaming dress sword sheathed in its leather cover and stored out of harm's way in the back of his closet.

June 21, 1967, Wednesday

Mr. and Mrs. A. H. Sanders
Battle Ground, Indiana

Well, we flew to California on a Jet (a red & white TWA) and it is
indeed different than anything ever! We were above "weather" from
St. Louis to Arizona (we were at 35,000 ft.) 65 degrees below zero up
there. I looked down on the desert & could see L.A. OK. Some smog—
not bad. This is even more than you said it is out here. I'll keep you
posted.

    *Love **** Barbara*
    P.S. Lana met us at Airport with bouquets of Sweet Peas.

Once Bessie and her niece Barbara arrived at the Los Angeles International Jet Port, the stewardess removed the pillows she'd placed
under Bessie's feet somewhere over Kansas, when she'd noticed that
the little lady's legs were too short to reach the floor. Before Kansas,
Bessie had been literally floating on air, her white, lace-up dress shoes
dangling. Inside the women's luggage, wrapped carefully in tissue paper,
were the dresses they'd packed for Jenny's wedding. For Bessie, a brown
floral number she would accessorize with white bob earrings, a pearl
choker, and two huge gardenias that one of the church ladies—probably
the pink-faced Mrs. Fegal—would pin to Bessie's dress right before the
ceremony began. Like most of the women at the wedding, my aunt and
great-aunt wore hats. Bessie's was a pillbox with a white bow and a large
white net that from the looks of the home movie seemed to require constant adjustment.

As Bessie hovered thirty-five thousand feet above the scene, my
mother was busily finishing up last-minute details. The attendants'
headdresses were a simple pattern, each coordinated to match the pastel dotted Swiss dresses Juanita had sewn: yellow for Claudia, green for
me, pink and blue for the other two bridesmaids. Six-year-old Lana was
the flower girl, in white like the bride, whose dress and veil my mother
had designed from yards of peau de soie, lace, and satin she'd spread
across the dining room table for weeks. Mother cut, marked, pinned,
basted, adjusted, and readjusted. "I had to keep cutting down the bod-

ice," she remembers. "Jenny was so tiny. Such narrow shoulders, slim waist. Not much bigger than Bessie." In the home movie, that tiny bride stands at the threshold of the sanctuary, preparing to take her last steps as a single woman. Her back is to the camera, her arm grasping the arm of a slim, dark-haired man who would remember little of the moment. "After a while," my father told me recently, "all the weddings kind of blur together for an old man."

How many trips had Bessie made to California—by bus, train, car, and now, jet plane? As she looked down at the Los Angeles canyon, did Bessie sense that this would be her last trip out west? The last time she would walk the long beaches, smell the menthol-scented eucalyptus, see the great oaks, the yellow hibiscus and stalky canna, the jewel-toned bougainvillea trailing down patio walls, the bird of paradise with its pointed, arrogant head. Where had the years gone? The chaos of children filling Juanita's kitchen, sprawled in front of the TV, stuffed into the station wagon for the cross-country trips, the luggage rack packed to the gills with suitcases. Yes, the view from the TWA jet was stunning, but Bessie wouldn't trade anything for the view from that station wagon. From her front row seat beside Juanita, she had seen the Grand Canyon, the great deserts, stretches of green meadows, and mountains higher than she'd ever imagined as a girl lost in the pages of a geography book.

Oct. 31, 1967

Dear Mom & Dad,

Well—"twick or tweat"—Whenever Halloween gets here I think of Uncle Ivan in that Chinese outfit he used to wear and the time we all surprised Aunt Bessie.

Really, though, there is not too much gay activity around here. Do you remember the lovely home I took you up to when you were here? Mr. & Mrs. Fegal, our friends from church. In all the wicked fires it came to Lemon Heights. It all seemed so impending. We searched frantically for them all morning, trying to get through the fire line & I guess we stayed about 10 minutes behind them all the time. I knew Fred Fegal would be up there fighting.

In all the activity she & Fred went back up there & they let them
through to try & carry out some things. They had the Cadillac & the
Cougar parked on the incline, heading out the drive. The car started
to roll & she threw up her hands to try to stop the car I guess and he
tried to throw her out of the way but she was caught—three wheels
ran over her, multiple fractures of the legs, arms, spine but what killed
her was that her chest was crushed. She lived a couple of hours &
massive bleeding. Their home burned to the ground. It was all so fan-
tastic it's unbelievable. At least 50 homes were lost & fire is still going
in some areas.

Love, Juanita.

P.S. I must come up with a Hobo costume for Lana before two
o'clock or my name is mud. I put things away so thoroughly I
can't find the funny faces.

By the time the Paseo Grande Fire was extinguished, it had
burned over fifty thousand acres, its smoke rising ten thousand feet
and carrying ash as far as the Pacific Ocean. Louise Fegal was the
only fatality. In the news account, the <u>Orange County Register</u> misspelled her name. The next day, Mr. Fegal called to say that Louise
had always enjoyed my singing, and would I sing at the funeral?
I didn't think twice about it. I sang solos all the time—at church,
school, in musicals and concerts. My mother seemed hesitant, but
she didn't try to talk me out of it. The next afternoon, we gathered at
the funeral home—a clutch of close friends, some business associates of Mr. Fegal's, clusters of what remained of the Church Family.
The news was still raw, electric; its dark energy traveled through the
crowd. Such a soft lady, such a hard way to die. Mr. Fegal had chosen
a gospel song, a long-ago favorite from their years in Texas. This one
featured Jordan, the legendary river of crossings. I had rehearsed
thoroughly, practicing my phrasing—"winds of sorrow," "billows of
trouble," "ending of day."

The pianist started the introduction. I took my place at the lectern, breathing deeply to fill my diaphragm as my music teachers had
taught. Beside me, in a white casket covered in pink roses, lay Mrs.
Fegal. "When I come to the river," I began, looking out into the faces
emerging like huge white petals—"at closing of day"—between the tall

stalks of gladioli and lilies—"friends have all flown"—then receding with each phrase, faces floating from me as if pulled by an invisible current, a slow-motion film playing backward. My throat thickened and tightened. I looked over at my mother, whose dark eyes were filling—"somebody waiting"—my father's blue eyes too—"I won't have to"—but we do, we all have to cross it, each of us alone, my mother and father, Carla, and Mrs. Fegal, her pink face rising over the hood of the Cadillac then out, far out from me, from all of us.

Briarwood Cottage

Mrs. Sylvia Sanders
Battle Ground, Indiana

Dear Sister,

How time goes! and me with so little to show for that, me who should be making the most of it. The weather being what it has been I have fared very well. Kept busy keeping the fire going and feeding myself and the cats.

Eldon was just in with my groceries. Just got a note off to Barbara. I had a letter from her yesterday, said your leg was much better. I am doing all right so far so don't worry and don't take any chances.

Bye now Bessie

"Taking chances" meant, for Bessie, all those things so-called experts said that women her age should never do—venturing out alone, walking on icy steps. Old bones break easily, and hip fractures are the first step toward the nursing home, so Bessie had heard. So, she'd dutifully dispense advice to her little sister, but as Bessie often wrote, *Ugh! Not for mine!* Good heavens, she'd been going up and down the springhouse steps since she was a teenager. Why should she stop now? Apart from those days when Sant was sick, Bessie had never set foot in a hospital and didn't intend to.

The date on Bessie's letter marked Sylvia and Arthur's wedding anniversary, though this fact seems to have slipped Bessie's mind. If prompted, she could have supplied the details of that icy January day in 1912: the angel food wedding cake she'd baked, Sant stoking the fire, Arthur arriving on the train with a handful of mostly-frozen roses. Lately, it seems the past feels more and more *present,* while the present slips through her hands like a silk scarf. And as for anniversaries, birthdays, graduations, weddings, how can she possibly keep track of them all? Cousins, nieces, nephews, greats, and great-greats. At last count, well, she supposed she'd lost count. Let's see, with Juanita's grandbaby on the way, that makes . . .

> *P. S. Mrs. Bray brought a bag of oranges to me from Florida and one day someone knocked on the door and I called "come in" but they didn't at once so I went to the door and there stood Mrs. Bray holding in both hands a "pumpking pie." She had cooked a big pumpkin and baked several pies so brought one to me while still warm.*

"'Hope for spring!' That's what she'd say," Mrs. Bray recalls when I phone her recently, eager for details of those years when I was missing-in-action from Bessie's life. After Babe and his wife had left for Pennsylvania, the Brays had moved into the house Babe had built just a few hundred yards down the lane from Briarwood. "'Hope for spring!' Come April, Bessie was always out looking for dandelions and who knows what else," Mrs. Bray continues. "Greening, she called it. And mushrooming. We used to laugh at her a little, and now I'm ashamed of that. Now scientists are saying all those things are good for you. Maybe that's why Bessie lasted so long. But back then, we thought she was a little, well, different. Out of a different time." Mrs. Bray pauses. Her voice returns, softer now. "I should have been a better neighbor."

"You *were* a good neighbor." Suddenly it seems important to tell her this. "I just found a letter from Bessie to her sister. My grandmother, Sylvia Sanders?"

"Yes, I remember Sylvia."

"May I read it to you?" I read the part about the oranges, the warm "pumpking" pie, and Eldon bringing in groceries. When I finish, the line is silent. "Mrs. Bray? Are you there?"

"I'd forgotten all that," she says quietly. "The pies. And Eldon Zink. Things are so different now. Mervyn and I don't neighbor with the neighbors anymore. The new ones try to govern in ways we don't agree with. Building big houses. One family even built a big barn, and they *live* in it. Imagine living in a barn, if you don't have to. We did plant a small garden this year, tomatoes, green beans. Just enough to work with hand and a hoe. Mervyn can't use the rotatiller. His hernia. Things are hard but we manage. We're the same old toughies we always were. Just older."

I'm trying to focus on Mrs. Bray's words, but my mind has other plans, images flashing: wild strawberries, yellow roses, a feather bed piled high with quilts, Bessie sitting alone by the gas stove, stroking the calico cat. No letters from her niece Becky, not even a birthday card. Where did I go all those years, how could I have just swept her out of my life?

"Thank you," I say to Mrs. Bray, "for checking in on her." I ask about the log house, how it is holding up; my parents sold it to her and Mervyn a few years ago, a decision reached after many years of difficult choices. "It was time," my mother said the day she called with the news. I'd known this day was coming. Twenty years past Bessie's death, the cabin had outlived itself, and my mother had no choice but to let it go. I suspect she'd hoped she could hold onto Briarwood until one of her children wrested it from vandals, rats, and weedy decay. I could have been the child to do it. Why didn't I? Time, expense, the impracticality of the task?

"We can't keep it up the way we used to," Mrs. Bray answers. "Just the other week while we were gone visiting our daughter, raccoons got in from under the floor somehow, and flung manure and other things around. We still keep the electricity on but we can't lock the door, the ruffians will just break it down, so we just put a wire on the door. The state of the world now," she sighs. "People restless, and school kids have always tried to get into mischief, breaking into the little house."

I tell her we all understand, that kids have been breaking in there for decades now.

"Did you know about the little bridge that runs by the log house?" she asks. "One day a tree fell on it. We heard it, the sound was enormous."

"No, I didn't know."

"Enormous. A huge tree. It just fell by itself."

My nieces and nephews often ask how it was back in the 1960s. They've seen the movies, heard the music. They seem nostalgic for my past. So sometimes when we're driving together, I crank up the Stones, the

Doors, Marvin Gaye, or Jefferson Airplane, the driver's window rolled down so I can steer with one hand, thump my other hand against the side of the car, and sing along, loud. I don't tell them how long it took me to own these songs, or about the young woman in my past, how radically out of step she was with those around her and with the age itself. Part of me wants to disown her, to claim a different history. I think of her in the third person because she seems so far from me now. Some days I catch glimpses. She's alone on her bed, memorizing yet another chapter of the King James Bible or singing hymns to the dark, her eyes closed to receive, what? A blessing, an answer? A touch? Decades later, I search letters, scrapbooks, photographs, desperate for clues, none of which fully answers the loss:

Two months before her high school graduation, Martin Luther King was shot. At a motel, the newscaster on the television reported. In Memphis, Tennessee. Which might as well have been another planet, for all the girl knew about it. Still, the next morning as the school color guard lowered the flag to half-staff, she sensed that something terrible had occurred, a deep, national wound.

The week before the girl's high school graduation, Bobby Kennedy was shot—in a hotel in Los Angeles, just thirty miles from her home. She remembers her mother's pale face, her dark-circled eyes. "What is happening to the world," the mother said, with no hint of question in her voice. It was as if she knew the answer but was afraid to speak it.

The next morning, the girl gathered with other members of the school chorus to rehearse "No Man is an Island" and "Miserere Mei." At the Baccalaureate, some minister delivered a prepared prayer asking for guidance for their troubled nation. The chorus members stepped out from the rows of red-gowned graduates and sang in one voice their miserere mei: *Have mercy upon me, O God, according to thy lovingkindness.* Then they returned to their assigned places and waited for their separate names to be called.

◆

Untethered from the rituals of high school, I'd been set adrift, floating between adolescence and what I thought of as Real Life, a place that both terrified and seduced me. As a toddler, I'd been a mama's baby, one of those milk-contented clingers who must be pulled, bodily, from her breast. Eighteen years later I was still reluctant to leave my mother's side. I lived at home, my only strike at independence the paycheck I earned typing invoices at a printing shop. Evenings, I took classes at the community college, and though I reluctantly accepted my father's offer to pay tuition costs, I insisted on buying my own textbooks. I could afford only used ones, and the more *used* the books, the cheaper they were. At first, I was put off by the underlining, the marginal comments, sophomoric doodlings, and obscenities. Worse still were the cigarette burns and the coffee and food stains.

After a while, though, I began to welcome the marks. I imagined the boy who had splattered pizza sauce across the map of South America. Was he lonely too? Had he eaten the pizza alone, in his tiny dorm room, while memorizing Bolivia's chief exports? What about the girl who had misspelled "orgasm" (using two *s*'s) in the margins of John Donne's "The Canonization"? Had she ever said the word aloud? Was she a virgin like me? The marked-up textbook became my portable roommate, some-one to sit up nights with me, to quiz me with questions I hadn't thought to ask. Not since sharing a room with Great-aunt Bessie had I had a reading partner. Now, years later, I was amazed at the rows of bleary-eyed students slumped around me, their limp hands spread across Nor-ton anthologies. How could someone read a poem by Shelley or Keats and not want to live inside it, not want to add their words to the words on the page? Looking back on my college literature texts, I can trace the journey of those years. In the margins of Wordsworth's sonnets, beside the lines "The world is too much with us; late and soon,/ Getting and spending, we lay waste our powers," I can chart my decision to quit my day job, even if it meant borrowing from the savings account I'd been feeding each payday. "I am done with this," I wrote in blue ink, meaning the commerce of getting and spending, the laying waste of powers I'd yet to discover.

And in the underlined sections of Gerard Manley Hopkins's poems, I can trace the ecstasy of my first literary awakening ("I caught this morn-ing morning's minion") made all the more ecstatic because, since I was unable to understand Hopkins's elliptical syntax with my mind, I was forced to take it in through the rhythms of my body. This was a new mu-sic for me. My heart was no longer metaphorical. It beat rapidly in my chest, my temples, in my pale, veined wrists. Suddenly, within Hopkins's lines, I was breaking in new places—"here/ Buckle! And the fire that breaks from thee then, a billion/ Times told lovelier, more dangerous."

At the time I underlined those lines, I had no knowledge of the fire that waited in the eyes of a young man I'd yet to meet. I saw myself vaguely, like a character in one of the books I fell asleep with each night. In dreams, I drank black coffee at street cafes, lay beneath the branches of the campus oaks, or wandered late at night, as Whitman's speaker wandered, looking up "in perfect silence at the stars." In daylight, I pulled another used book from the shelf and fell into its pages. Could it be that Rilke's injunction "You must change your life" was aimed at me? I wrote in the margin, in bright blue indelible ink, "This Means You!"

Had I chosen to resell these books to the campus bookstore (I didn't, as they'd become part of me) their new owners might one day have read my markings and wondered at the person who had left such a trail. "She needs to get more sun," they might have thought. They might even have responded, as I sometimes do, with an answering note in the margins. It might have gone on and on like that, a serial installment of marginalia, each new reader adding his own twist to Hopkins or Wordsworth—or to me, the phantom whose life pages they were turning.

◆

Looking back on my nineteenth year, I am amazed at how easily I closed the books I'd been living inside. What replaced them were the poems the young man handed me across a restaurant table. "Pretty Brown-Haired Girl" was the title of one, "Monday Rain" another. Some were written in German, and I used my secondhand Cassell's Dictionary to translate them. The poems were not good—I remember thinking this even then—but they were the first love poems anyone ever gave me. I ran my fingers across the words. I folded the papers, put them into my pocket, and later that night, unfolded them on my bedside table. Already the poems were in my head, every ragged line break and rhyme.

At twenty-one he had one of those faces that had probably always looked old. His reddish-blond hair was retreating prematurely, exposing a forehead with furrows already deeply plowed. But his eyes were bright blue, center-of-a-flame blue, simultaneously cool and hot. He wore jeans and rugged woolen jackets. He drove a motorcycle. His mouth tasted of cigarettes. Plus, he could quote Wordsworth, which weakened me even more. He was independently brilliant, a part-time student with an undeclared major, taking classes in subjects like German and astronomy and horticulture, nothing that fit together to form anything close to a formal degree. "Come into the light of things," he teased. "Let nature be your teacher."

Nature taught me so much over the next year that it was all I could do to attend classes, let alone sit up nights scribbling notes in the margins of textbooks. He'd moved into his own apartment, and his marks were all over me—his mouth on my forehead, his tongue on my neck, my belly, the scent of his cigarettes in my hair. All else fell away. I could sense that my parents disapproved of him, and though Aunt Bessie had never met him, I was certain she would have disapproved too. But what nineteen-year-old asks advice from a ninety-year-old? Had I asked, I'm sure that Bessie would have given her opinion; she always did. "Finish college," she would have said. "Travel. See the world." Or, laying her age-spotted hand across mine, "You're too young to give it all up." Had I lifted that hand, stood up and walked away from her as I had so many times before, she might have whispered, "I'm afraid you're going to lose yourself."

May 5, 1970

Mr. and Mrs. Arthur Sanders
Battle Ground, Indiana
Dear Mom & Dad,

> *I know you must think I've forgotten you but not so. It is getting toward the end of the semester and lots of things are piling up in my three classes. Then I'm trying to open a Pre-School and I've done all the legwork so far—all the picky details I hate. Checking with State Dept. of Social Welfare, making application—fire marshall, Bldg & safety, zoning, Soc. Sec., Internal Revenue, Workman's Comp besides getting the equipment, playground, room & teachers ready. Paul has the playground planned & is making some scaled furniture.*

Jenny is very busy with the kid . . . Becky is busy with school and music. We went to a concert she was in last night. Jenny & I cut her boyfriend's hair last week. He had shoulder length blondish hair & has a red beard. Ricky's hair is too long to suit me. There is no dress code at the high schools anymore so anything goes. My policy is—let them alone & they usually come around themselves, but Paul is another vintage & can't quite take it. Claudia wants to be a model and I hope she can. Lana just wants to be a boy I think. Rick is in a talent show this week at school, singing with his guitar. He wanted a suede jacket with fringe all over so I ended up buying a hide and making it myself but I got it done.

We want to go to Texas for Tom's graduation this summer but probably can't. He is student body president and will give a speech. He has received a grant of $2400 from Univ. of South Carolina for Graduate work in his field & we are praying he gets to use it but I'm afraid. He is #9 on draft no. I hope you can decipher this letter.

Love, Juanita.

When life interrupts, you close the book. Or you leave it open, face down on the bed or table, to mark your place. Aunt Bessie taught me never to do this. "You'll break its spine," she'd say, running her hands across the book's cover, and the tenderness in her gesture made me ashamed that I'd ever considered such violence. After that, I took to dog-earing pages to show where I'd left off, but after a while even that seemed too violent. Now, whenever I encounter a dog-eared page, I smooth its wounded edge. Aunt Bessie used embroidered handkerchiefs to mark her place, though she always stopped at the end of a chapter. I fall into books the way I fall into lust—wholly, hungrily. Sometimes the first flush cools or the words grow tired and dull or I grow tired and dull, and I slam the book shut. But usually I keep reading, and lust ripens slowly into love, and I want to stay right there, at the lamplit table or in the soft, worn chair, until the last page is turned.

My mother loved books, too, but she put them aside while she was raising her family. I can't recall, during my childhood, ever seeing my mother sit down except to play Monopoly or Old Maid, or to sew Halloween costumes or Easter dresses. Late at night, when my father was away and she couldn't sleep, perhaps she switched on the light beside their bed and opened a book, maybe her Bible, a beautiful, burgundy-colored King James. I loved to touch the leather cover and the onionskin pages tipped in gold. Unlike me, my mother does not commit marginalia. The only mark in her Bible is a handwritten notation on the flyleaf: "Deuteronomy 29:29. The secret things belong unto the Lord our God; but those things which are revealed belong unto us and to our children forever."

One night after we'd made love, my boyfriend lit a cigarette and leaned back onto the pillows. "I'm in trouble," he said. "There's this girl." Smoke floated around his eyes; he blinked, fanned the air. *"Was* this girl. It's over, but she's been calling." Something hot flashed through my head: *He will marry her and I will lose him.*

"There's this place in Mexico City," he continued. "It's nine hundred dollars for everything, to fly her there and back. I have two hundred."

I had seen the word "abortion" in biology textbooks, but I had never uttered it. In 1969, even at the crest of the free-love movement, abortion was not a legal option in California. I had fourteen hundred dollars in my savings account, all that was left of two years of typing invoices at the print shop. Each Friday I had carried the vinyl savings book to the bank window, where the cashier recorded the thirty dollar deposit, half of my paycheck.

"I'll get the rest," I said.

"I can't ask you to do that."

My next line was from a movie. Something out of the 1940s. I should have been wearing a hat with a feather. We should have been in a French cafe: "You're not asking. I'm offering."

"I'll make it up to you," he said.

The passbook shows no record of the money being replaced. Within a year we were married, and what was left of my savings was pooled into a joint account. Nationwide, the economy was in shambles; even my father had lost his job, as an engineer, at Ford Philco. I still worked part-time at the printing shop, but I'd returned to school, taking night classes toward a literature degree. My husband found work wherever he could—installing patio covers, clerking at a hardware store, drilling holes into bowling balls at the Voit factory. Late one night, while I was studying at the dining room table, he sat straight up on the couch. "I'll bet she was lying all along," he said, as though continuing a conversation he'd started mere seconds before. "Maybe she just wanted a trip to Mexico. She probably spent the whole time on the beach."

I turned back to my book. I hoped the girl *had* spent the weekend on the sand. I hoped she'd gotten a tan. But I knew the girl hadn't lied. I knew because of what had been set into motion since I'd handed over the money nearly two years before. Adumbratio. The shadow of our marriage had made its preliminary approach in the parking lot of that bank, had lengthened and darkened with each month, and has never completely lifted.

The girl had blue eyes and long brown hair, like me. She lived in Garden Grove with her parents. She had a slight lisp. That's all he ever told me. The rest has been written in daylight imaginings and in dreams: She and I sitting beneath a beach umbrella reading books and sipping tall cool drinks, the ocean crashing in the distance. The child crawling the space between our knees is a girl, a Harlequin doll, her face seamed down the center. Not one eyelash, one fingernail, one cell of the child is his. She is the two best halves of the girl and me, sewn with perfectly spaced stitches.

December 16, 1971

Dear Mom and Dad,

How we would love to be home for Christmas but for once I tried to be reasonable & knew we could not really afford to—those old gasoline bills really keep rolling in whether the money does or not. Paul is finishing up his 12 hrs. at Chapman College—he has suffered through those education classes. Becky is still with us, has one more semester to go. Her husband graduates from Basic Training tomorrow—at Ft. Ord. Will go to Chinese language school at Monterey—the trouble is they don't really clear security until 6 months after they start. So if you all are interviewed—Be Nice. Claudia is taking a night course now in modeling. Rick is still strumming, and he really wanted to go this Christmas. I think his aunts spoiled him & his uncles too.

Love, Juanita

◆

"You won't be able to put it down," booksellers claim as they ring up your purchase. But of course you do, you must. The oven timer goes off, your children come in from school, your plane lands, the nurse calls your name, your lover kisses the back of your neck, your heavy eyes close in sleep. By the time you return to the book—*if* you return to the book—you will not be the same person you were ten days, or ten minutes, before. Life is a river, and you can't step into the same book twice.

My college degree brought me no teaching offers in Monterey. During the day, I stood behind the return counter at Sears Catalog Store. Weekends and some evenings, I sang at weddings and funerals to bring in extra money. The Chinese course was difficult and intense; students were expected to attain fluency within a few months. Evenings, head in hands, my husband leaned over a small desk I'd brought from my parents' house, the same desk I'd used since high school. He looked so young, his legs sprawled under the desk legs, his brow etched with worry. I couldn't tell him now, not yet. Just get through the next few weeks, I told myself, until the exams are over. I won't show for another month anyway.

Over the next few weeks, my husband started leaving the house after dinner, saying he needed to study with a buddy. Often he'd stay out past two or three o'clock with no explanation. One Saturday evening, returning from a wedding and looking for clues to his absence, I discovered a woman's jacket dropped behind a chair. It smelled foreign yet familiar—musky perfume mingled with the memory of his cigarettes. They had been here together, in our apartment. When he came home, I would confront him.

My husband had never raised his voice to me. He had never hit me. When his fist finally flew, it landed on the door of the filing cabinet where I kept my old term papers and poetry drafts. The force of the blow was audible: a thud, a crack. Loose papers flew from the top of the cabinet. He cried out then brought the fist to his mouth. Surely the fist was broken, I thought. I rushed toward him, but he held up his other hand as if to block me. Time slowed. White paper fluttered around me like birds. I stared at his hand, and something went out of me, I could feel it, a sucking force, tidal, pulling myself out of myself. Then the moment was over. He turned and walked away, his wounded fist still pressed to his mouth. I knelt on the floor and began to gather the papers together. My eyes were dry, my vision clear. In memory, this is what hurts the most: the clarity of the moment, its sharp focus. Each black word, on each scattered page, distinct and singular.

◆

As it turned out, I didn't have to tell him. Alone one night, doubled over on the bathroom floor, I lost our *Might Have Been*. But the dreams lived on for months, years. In one, I am beside Aunt Bessie on a rubber raft in the deepest part of a murky lake. She's wearing her black walking shoes and the blue dress she'll be buried in—though I don't yet know this. Lying between us is a newborn baby girl. Her skin is transparent. You can see right through her, the way you see the insides of a fertile egg when you hold it to the candling light. The veins and capillaries branch intricately, the bones hardening as I watch. The small red heart is a valentine cut with a child's blunt scissors, ragged and uneven on the sides, pasted onto a background of white doily. In the distance, a pink dock bobs in the center of the lake. My mother, grandmothers, and sisters are dancing on it, waving their hands and gesturing for us to join them. I begin to paddle furiously, but no matter how hard I kick, I can't move the raft. I tug, and Oh, no, now I've tipped the raft over, and Bessie's emptied shoes shoot into the sky, and where is the baby? The water stirs. Now it is clear as cellophane. I can see all the way down. The lake floor is lined with mosaic tiles, and dozens of women lie face-up, each holding the hand of a transparent baby, all of them waving for us to join them.

◆

The next few years are a blur of half-remembered details. My husband and I left Monterey for Fort Meade, Maryland, where I found a job teaching sixth grade. Tom, having escaped Vietnam through a series of bureaucratic blunders, began graduate school in South Carolina. Jenny had a second baby. Claudia stayed in California to be near her boyfriend and pursue a modeling and business career. My parents, along with Rick and Lana, moved back to Indiana where my father had found a teaching job just a few miles from the Circle S. After thirty years of homesickness, Juanita was finally home.

Then it was 1974. Everywhere at once, 1974.

"Strange," Hattie would have said, "how Fate arranges things." In June, Mother was in California visiting her two grandsons. My husband had left for another language course in Monterey while I finished out the school year in Maryland; he'd made it clear he was in no hurry for me to join him. Now, looking back on the scenes that will follow, I want to take the young woman by the hand and lead her through a different door. Get out while you can, I would tell her. If you can't, gather up what remains of yourself and set off on a journey. Alone.

You have no idea, the young woman would answer—if she could still answer. How about this for a plan? You wave goodbye to your self and follow your husband once again. Unpack the boxes, begin making home. When he starts disappearing, you cut off your hair, take the pills the doctors prescribe, beg for more, and lose yourself daily in a gauzy sleep, surrounded by the books that have become your only food. But you have the pills and the books and the bed grown huge by his nightly absence, for he is sleeping elsewhere now with someone else, and he no longer tries to hide it.

If you're lucky, one night your hand will find the phone, and if you are doubly lucky and have a mother like mine, she will arrive early the next day, having driven hundreds of miles in a car large enough to hold several children. Although she is a quiet woman who rarely interferes, in this case she will make an exception. She will locate your husband, demand that he come home, now, and when he does (this is where the details get fuzzy, your self has flown off somewhere) together they will lift you into the back seat of the big car and rush you to the nearest hospital where the attending physician will immediately direct them to the psychiatric wing.

I would remember none of this, which is a blessing. Had I remembered the details, I might have felt compelled to tell the story to anyone who would listen: strangers on buses, prospective employers, longtime family friends, men I met in bars or churches (for months afterwards I would search both places, equally, for comfort). "There's no need to tell," my mother said, and she would repeat this many times, long after I was out of danger. "You don't need more hurt. It's no one's business but yours." This is my mother's way. Though she freely gives to anyone in need—food, comfort, time, affection—part of Juanita, the heart's enclosed, tender core, remains her own. Sitting on the edge of the bed while she packed her suitcase for Indiana, I wanted to be more like her. More like my grandmothers and Aunt Bessie. Less needy, more singleminded in forward resolve. Though I had rehearsed his leaving for months, when he finally left, for good this time (isn't it strange how we use "good" to mean "final"?) I was devastated, terrified to imagine my future. "What should I do," I begged my mother. "What would you do?"

Juanita has never been one to give advice. Experience, in her view, is not transferable. It is not an inheritance you pass on to your children, no matter how much you wish you could.

If her words held no answer, I decided, I would read her life: She had left her parents and home to follow her husband from one military base to the next; waited out his long absences; buried one child and raised six others; watched as friends and family members suffered divorces, financial ruin, alcoholism, depression, life-threatening illnesses and accidents; nursed loved ones through difficult years. And survived, intact. "Take me with you," I begged, meaning back home, to the home she and my father had made.

My mother remembers this as one of the painful moments of her life. "I wanted more than anything to say yes," she recalls. "But I knew if I did, you'd never find your way. It was time you found your own way." Juanita cupped my face in her hands and said No. No, I could not follow her, I could not come back home. Then, while she packed her suitcase, she packed mine too. And so that I would not be alone if worse once again came to worst, she made a one-way plane reservation to my brother's town in South Carolina. Half a world away, or so it seemed to me.

Everywhere at once, 1974.

Friday, Oct. 11, Lafayette Journal & Courier
Log Cabin Reflects History

While modern vehicles rumble by on nearby Interstate 65 and jet planes knife through the sky above, a wispy, 94-year-old Tippecanoe County woman occupies a small corner of the 19th Century in a log cabin. She is Mrs. Bessie Cosby, and she lives in a five-room log cabin that is more than 150 years old. She said her father, Rob-

Log Cabin Reflects History

Log Cabin Home

It probably is safe to say Mrs. Bessie Cosby, Rt. 6, Lafayette, is the only 94-year-old woman living in a log cabin in the Lafayette area. She apologizes for her unkempt lawn, saying "I just don't have anything to mow it with." She said she used to have lots of flowers...

By JACK ALKIRE
Regional Editor

While modern vehicles rumble by on nearby Interstate 65 and jet planes knife through the sky above, a wispy, 94-year-old Tippecanoe County woman occupies a small corner of the 19th Century in a log cabin.

She is Mrs. Bessie Cosby and she lives in a five-room log cabin that is more than 150 years old. The old house, nestled in a small, wooded triangle between County Road 900-E and the South Fork of Wildcat Creek, has electricity and a telephone, but no other modern conveniences.

The years have been kind to the cabin's occupant. Her mind is razor-sharp, she hears perfectly, and she does most of her reading without using the spectacles that rest in a case on her kitchen table.

"I do read a lot. I suppose I should be doing something else," she said.

How is life in a log cabin today? "I don't mind it, but it does need more conveniences," she says.

One of the conveniences missing is running water. Her drinking water comes from a hand pump in a well located down a flight of concrete steps in the rear of a small outbuilding behind the cabin. Mrs. Cosby fell while fetching water last May, and since then a neighbor drops by at least once a day to tote a bucket of water into the house.

Talking about the fall angers her. "It was caused by the crazy heels on the shoes I was wearing," she said. She was given the shoes by a relative. "These young people are always getting something new, and they give me lots of things they don't want anymore. I burned those shoes after the fall and I have been...

She does have a source of water in her kitchen that would stimulate memories of Americans reared on farms and in small towns in the 1920s and 1930s. It is a cistern pump that provides water for dish washing and other domestic chores. Cisterns, for those unfamiliar with the term, are shallow-dug wells that provide water that generally is not safe to drink.

"I may live in a log cabin," she declared, but I've been around. I've soaked my corns in both the Atlantic and Pacific oceans."

Several years back she flew to California with a sister and a niece to visit relatives.

Time no longer means much to Bessie, and she has trouble fixing dates. She thinks she has lived in the cabin three years, coming there from a home in Stockwell, where she lived for many years.

She and her husband, Sanford Cosby, operated a 300-acre farm near Stockwell for many years. Her husband "died a long time ago," she said.

The log house in which she lives has been in her family since about 1890. She said her father, Robert Mounts, dismantled the cabin on a farm in Clinton County, moved it to its present location and re-assembled it. She and her family lived in it several years when she was a girl.

Although Bessie and her husband never had children, she does not lack relatives. She was the eldest of five children, and she is blessed with nieces and nephews, grand nieces and nephews, great grand nieces and nephews. Shelves and walls of her home are covered with photographs of youngsters who are five-generation relatives.

Three of her brothers and sisters are still living. They are Ivan O.

BESSIE COSBY

canoe County and they stop by often to bring groceries and do small chores. They are nephews Leland and Merrill Sanders.

Although it isn't evident from the outside, the cabin contains two small bedrooms in a second-story loft area. The downstairs has a combination kitchen-dining-living room, a more formal living room and a downstairs bedroom.

The house is heated by an oil heating stove in the kitchen area. A majestic, black and chrome wood heating stove occupies a prime spot in the living room.

The cabin's owner has a large vocabulary and speaks in soft, cultured tones. In the last century she would have been known as "a well spoken woman." She will stop in the middle of a story and apologize: "I hope I'm not boring you?" She is...

Article from Lafayette Journal & Courier featuring Great-aunt Bessie at Briarwood, October 1974.

ert Mounts, dismantled the cabin on a farm in Clinton County, moved it to its present location and reassembled it. The old house, nestled in a small, wooded triangle between County Road 900-E and the South Fork of Wildcat Creek, has electricity and a telephone, but no other modern conveniences.

"I may live in a log cabin," she declares. "But I've been around. I've soaked my corns in both the Atlantic and Pacific."

The years have been kind to the cabin's occupant. Her mind is razor-sharp, she hears perfectly, and she does most of her reading without using the spectacles that rest in a case on her kitchen table.

"I do read a lot. I suppose I should be doing something else," she says. She apologizes for the unkempt lawn, saying she doesn't have anything to mow it with.

The cabin's owner has a large vocabulary and speaks in soft, cultured tones. In the last century she would have been known as "a well spoken woman." She will stop in the middle of a story and apologize: "I hope I'm not boring you." She is not boring.

With her background of log cabin living, has Mrs. Cosby considered running for president?

"I hardly think that's for me," she chuckles.

Time no longer means much to Bessie, and she has trouble fixing dates. She thinks she has lived in the cabin for three years, coming there from a home in Stockwell, where she lived for many years. She and her husband Santford Cosby, operated a 300-acre farm near Stockwell for many years. Her husband "died a long time ago," she says. Although Bessie and her husband never had children, she does not lack relatives. She was the eldest of five children, and she is blessed with nieces and nephews, grandnieces and -nephews, and great-grandnieces and -nephews. Shelves and walls of her home are covered with photographs of youngsters who are five-generation relatives.

The house is heated by an oil stove in the kitchen area. A Majestic black and chrome stove occupies a prime spot in the living room. Her drinking water comes from a hand pump in a well located down a flight of concrete steps in the rear of a small outbuilding behind the cabin. Mrs. Cosby fell while fetching water last May, and since then a neighbor drops by at least once a day to tote a bucket of water into the house.

Talking about the fall angers her. "It was caused by the crazy heels on the shoes I was wearing," she said. She was given the shoes by a relative. "These young people are always getting something new, and they give me lots of things they don't want anymore. I burned those shoes after the fall and I have been wearing my own ever since."

Had 1974 been a census year, census takers would have found Bessie Denton Mounts Cosby wearing her own shoes in her own home, and Juanita and Paul's tribe of children split into three equal parts: two in Indiana, two in California, two in South Carolina. Spread coast to coast, but none alone. And thank God for that, Juanita thought. She typed a

single letter—*Dear Becky and Claudia*—and mailed us each a copy, apologizing for the duplication. *Becky, guess Tom and Robbin gathered up a
few things for you to set up housekeeping with. Claudia, I know you must
feel very low often—and everyone inquiring as to Stephen's progress. It must
seem like an interminable time since all this has taken place. I don't know
what to say to help you bear up.* Though pain pulses through each line
my mother writes, Juanita is Hattie's granddaughter, so tell the news!
Lana and her friends have been riding the ponies at the farm, Grandpa
is stacking wood for winter *high as the house . . . I made Grandma Sylvia
a new slack suit—she said she would never wear them but she really tries to
keep up with the times. She's already planning how she is going to make the
next one.* Mostly, though, my mother wants to hear from us. To be sure, as
Hattie would have phrased it, that we are *still among the living.*

Barely.

Three months earlier, while I was in South Carolina stuffing my
brain with cotton—that's how it felt when I took the pills—Claudia
and her boyfriend were vacationing in Mexico, riding the back roads
in Stephen's sports car, when an approaching pickup truck driven by a
drunk driver crossed the center line, sideswiping the car and sending it
out of control. All told, five vehicles were wrecked that day. By the time
Stephen was finally transferred to a hospital in California, a nightmare
journey in itself, he was in a deep coma. Claudia had suffered minor
injuries, if fear, uncertainty, and guilt—the guilt of the survivor—can be
considered minor. Stephen underwent three brain surgeries, but there
was little hope for a full recovery. *Everything just seems to get harder for
me each day,* my sister wrote to me. *. . . It breaks my heart to see Stephen
this way . . . Please let me know how you're getting along. I try not to worry
about you, but it's hard to keep from it.*

I saved the letters Claudia sent me during the darkest days, her days
and mine. For months she kept vigil at hospitals and rehab centers,
staying with Jenny and with the Tuttles, one of the closest branches still
remaining in our Church Family. Every morning, Mrs. Tuttle fixed Claudia a poached egg and toast, and sat quietly at the table until Claudia
had eaten. "It's all that kept me going sometimes," my sister remembers.

Thousands of miles from Claudia, what kept me going? Although
the pills no longer had the power to put me to sleep, they lifted me to a
place of soundlessness and ether. A place of blessed forgetfulness where

it was impossible to recall—for full moments at a time!—the shape of my husband's hands, his furrowed forehead, the flame-cool blue of his eyes. I thought of T. S. Eliot's hollow men, their heads filled with straw. The image of scarecrows was comforting, too, as were thoughts of helium balloons, slow-floating dirigibles, and anything submerged in water. I was an aquarium, enclosed within myself. Amniotic silence surrounded me hour after hour, then suddenly—What's that noise, I'd think, startled, amazed to discover it was my own breath in my lungs, my heart thumping, the blood thrumming in my own ears.

When this happened, when I was brought back to myself, I'd think No, please not that. I had forgotten for a while that I was alive, that there were fingers at the ends of my arms, fingers that could burn on the gas stove, the iron, the teakettle's steam. The world was too much with me. Why bother? I fell back into bed, finding comfort in Eliot ("This is the way the world ends . . . ") and then in Job. The New Testament was too full of promise and light, but Old Testament sufferings were redemptive. I was long past questioning why a loving God would destroy Job's house and cattle, afflict him with boils all over his body, and kill his children. The worst is yet to come, I thought—and almost said, aloud, to Job. *Happiness* is what you should fear. If God answers, out of the whirlwind and the chaos of destruction, beware of what will be given: healing, forgiveness, six thousand camels, a thousand she asses, seven sons and three daughters, each fairer than the next, your life overflowing, another high place from which to fall.

I didn't want to live but I couldn't imagine dying. How to gather the energy? I didn't own a gun and could see no way to get one. I had no courage for knives. Pills seemed an easy way out; I tried, but my stomach refused to accept them. Over the next weeks, I started taking long drives on country roads, staring at the yellow line and thinking how easy it would be to pull the wheel to the left, into the oncoming truck, which was heavy enough, I was sure, to bear the impact without hurting its driver. I didn't want to hurt anyone, not even myself. I did not want to die. I wanted not to live. There's a difference.

Better yet, pull the wheel to the right, into that stand of pine trees.

What terrified me was not the thought of the mangled metal, the row of wounded trunks, or even of the sheet pulled over me—a gesture that seemed a kindness, something a loved one would do. What terrified me that early autumn day was the sudden greenness of the pines, the way their beauty insinuated itself into my vision—peripherally at first, vaguely, and without my consent. I blinked to stop what felt like tears, which I hadn't tasted for so long I'd forgotten that they were made of salt, that they were something my body was producing on its own, long after I thought I had shut down. Okay, I said to the steering wheel, the padded dashboard, the pines. If I can think of five reasons not to die, I won't.

When I got back to my room, I pulled from the pages of Eliot a blank prescription refill form I'd been using as a bookmark. I found a pencil in the nightstand, one without an eraser, I recall. I remember thinking that I couldn't go back on what I'd written, couldn't retrace my steps if I made a mistake. Slowly, deliberately, I wrote the numbers (1. 2. 3. 4. 5.) with a firm period after each one, as if preparing to take a spelling test. I thought for a minute then wrote beside number one, "My parents," immediately wishing I'd have split them into "Mother" and "Dad" so I could have filled two lines. Then suddenly the blanks were filling—my siblings, but there were five of them, so another number and then another and another—Grandma Sylvia and Grandpa Arthur and Grandma Goldie and Aunt Bessie and Aunt Barbara and my nephews and the Pedigos and Woolbrights and Tuttles, tears falling on the page now so black with names I couldn't bear it any more—the stab of hope, the possibility.

As the months passed, the world slowly continued to make itself known, appearing in small merciful gestures, as if not wishing to startle: voices, a pair of hands, golden leaf shadow, a suggestion of sky. Then one morning, for no reason that I can recall, the world lifted her veil and showed her whole self. She looked strangely familiar. Yes, I thought, it's coming back. Put on shoes, brush teeth, smile into the mirror, pour orange juice into a glass. *This is the way the world begins. This is the way the world begins. This is the way.*

◆

How many ways can a world begin? Begin, again? Sylvia, pulling herself from the bed in the rented upstairs room. Choosing a name for her dead child: William Hayes. Charlie's daughter selecting two caskets, arranging for separate funerals for her father and brother, then packing up to leave the Valley. Hattie, every January for seventy years, vowing to get straight and *start the New Year square.* Arthur, a year past the deaths of his wife and sister (Sylvia and Vena would die in 1981, within weeks of each other) returning to Circle S to check on things, and *it is hard to believe,* he wrote, *but those two ancient hens are laying eggs again. They chuckle and sing, and seem just as happy as if they were starting life all over again.*

Recently, I asked Claudia about the autumn of 1974, how she finally made the hard decision. I've always struggled, I told her, with the question of how much to give those we love and how much to keep for ourselves. Where do we leave off, and others begin? *At some point,* my sister wrote back, *Mom and Dad came out and assured me that I had done all that I could do and that I should consider continuing my education. I was scared to leave him and scared of losing my own life. I was depressed and confused. Shortly thereafter, as I was wheeling Stephen around the hospital grounds, he pointed me in a direction that I had not visited before. We ended up in the women's wing. He directed me to a particular bed and then waved as he had always done when he was ready for me to leave him.*

Claudia took Stephen's gesture as a sign: she could remain with him, in a bed in the women's wing, perhaps? Or she could move on. He was, she believed, releasing her. *On a plane,* she wrote, *we are told that in an emergency, put the mask on yourself first so that you can save your child. Ultimately, I believe that my needs are their needs and theirs are also my own. We are one. I talk in circles . . . but perhaps the circles are what I am trying to say. It is the circle that answers the question.*

Sometimes at night I watch my husband sleep, his arms stretched gracefully across the pillow. I love Donald's arms. Thirty-five years ago, they were what I first noticed about him, the tendons of his forearms and the way the dark brown hairs lay so obediently down then swirled with a delicate flourish at the wristbones. Barely a year out of a disastrous marriage, I was still punch-drunk from the blows, loose-kneed and terrified of getting back in the ring. Not that I didn't take advantage of opportunities that came my way. Everywhere I looked, the men were there. Men I met in bars, at the school where I taught, in my classes at the university, even in the church choir I'd joined to fill my evenings with the songs I'd lost years before. The more men I dated, the less possibility I would need only one. Meet, date, bed, goodbye. *Men* could never hurt me, I'd decided. Only a *man* could do that.

Strange how Fate arranges things. It was an early spring evening, 1975, the air heavy with the narcotic sweetness of Carolina jasmine. I had a date to see <u>Shampoo</u>, a Warren Beatty flick set in 1968 on the eve of the presidential election. I'd read the reviews. Just what the doctor ordered, I thought. Dramatic irony. We know something the characters don't yet know: Nixon, Humphrey. And because it is 1975, we know where the story will end up six years past the election. Where we will all end up, a nation of shell-shocked citizens staring out from our sofas into television screens while an ordinary looking man with soft skin and loose jowls looks directly into the camera to face his public with his public shame, but who cares anymore at this point: . . . "quarter of a century in public life" . . . "strived for" . . . "sometimes failed. . . ." Then and now, back and forward, was and is, was and is.

Nearly a year past Nixon's resignation, on that jasmine-scented evening, I was tying the straps on my halter top when the phone rang, my date calling, asking if it was okay if his friend joined us for the movie, along with a woman I didn't know, a blind date he'd fixed Donald up with. "He just got divorced," my date said, "and he's in town for the weekend to see his little boy."

"Sure," I answered. "The more the merrier." What difference did it make anyway? My date was just another guy. Another guy, another movie, another satirical spin on life as we once knew it.

When I answered the door, my date was standing there. "She couldn't come," he said, "so it's just the three of us. Hope you don't mind." He motioned to the driveway, where a late-model American car was idling. The driver's window was down, and an arm was extended, adjusting the rearview mirror. Shirtsleeves rolled to the elbows. When my date opened the passenger door, I slid onto the seat between the two men, my eyes facing directly forward. Introductions, names, heads nodding politely, glad to meet you, a scent, heady, is it the jasmine, no not sweet, sweetly musky, breathe it in. His arms on the steering wheel, bare forearms finely muscled, dark brown hairs, delicate wristbones, prominent veins pulsing on his hands. Hands positioned at ten and two o'clock. A careful driver, trustworthy. A man here for the weekend, a father visiting his son, close your eyes, breathe him in, no not now, not this, this is not my life, it's too soon, not now.

I have never believed in love at first sight. The notion is preposterous. But I did not fall for a notion, I fell for a man. No, not fell *for.* Fell into. Into the expanse of Donald's arms, all his past and future lives. When you are as empty as I was that year, you can't feel the emptiness until it begins to fill—against your will, you feel it filling. Days pass, weeks. The man himself will be enough, that's what you think at first, but once the emptiness begins to fill you need it all, you want it all, his history and his promise: his dead grandparents, the ex-wife, the young son who rides on his shoulders, the combat boots and Army-issue fatigues stacked neatly in the back of his closet, all the photographs he has taken with his black camera, and those yet waiting to be developed.

I have loved you Dear since before you were born, Sylvia wrote to Arthur one hundred years ago. When I met Donald, I hadn't yet read my grandmother's letters to her future husband, but as the weeks passed I must have sensed that Sylvia, of all people, would understand what was happening to me. Why else would I pick up the phone one moon-bright night and dial the Circle S, delirious with joy. And why else would she be the one I most wanted to call that November afternoon a year later, after Donald and I had walked out of the South Carolina courthouse with the signed papers in our hands.

When my grandmother answered the phone, her high-pitched voice scratching out "Hello," I heard her obvious delight at the news. She had hoped for this, she could tell Donald was the one for me, she couldn't be happier, what had taken me so long?

Looking across the room at Donald, the phone pressed to my ear, my past and future filling up, spilling over, I could not stop talking, telling her about our plans, my new job at the university, Donald's little boy, how I was fixing up the guest room with a new bedspread and toys and Donald's old train set, and I can't wait for you to meet his son, Grandma, for him to meet you. Now, looking back at the calendar (*everywhere at once, 1976*) I can't believe I did not think to ask Sylvia how *she* was doing. Or how Bessie was doing, twenty-five miles from the Circle S, alone at Briarwood. They'd buried their little brother two weeks before. Had I even sent a card? I can't remember.

Lafayette Journal & Courier October 27, 1976
Ivan O. Mounts, a retired Army first sergeant, died at 4:20 p.m.
Wednesday in Home Hospital. Born in Tippecanoe County, he was a lifelong resident of the area. He retired from the Army in 1946 after 24 years of service. He was in World War I and World War II. . . .
Surviving with the widow are one son, one daughter, one brother, and two sisters . . .

I had three brothers and *I loved them very much,* Bessie had written to Babe thirteen years before. *I lost one and I still miss him.* I replace Ivan's obituary in its envelope, wondering if she'd drafted a similar letter after returning home from Ivan's burial. Returning to the log house where her little brother had been born seventy-five years before. Bessie had been twenty-one when Ivan was born, old enough to be his mother: mother of the five-year-old Ivan walking hand-in-hand with Sant on the "liars, thieves, sons-a-bitches" day; mother of the sixteen-year-old "Skinny" who ran away to enlist, *going after them old Germans allright;* mother of the man who shaved his dying brother Dale, and the next day wrote Bessie with the news, *This is being a little abrupt but it's the only way I know . . .*

I had three brothers and I loved them very much.

Surviving with his widow are . . . two sisters.

◆

> *Briarwood Cottage*
> *A Friday morning in October,*
> *cloudy, chilly*

Dear Sylvia:

Thanks for sending check, will repay you some of these days for stamps and envelopes. Larder rather low along some lines, particularly (bet that isn't spelled right) cat food. Got 20 pints of tomatoes canned, made a little chili sauce yesterday, 8 small jars and got some green tomatoes to fix somehow. Tinkered around in the cellar some yesterday. Big kitty caught a mouse but let it get away, goes out gets sand burrs in that big plumy tail. Such a tail was never intended for roughing it. Groc. have arrived.

Bye now. Bessie.

P.S. Eldon says if nothing happens he will clean out stovepipe in the morning. Too wet for soy beaning.

Dear Sister:

Here it is the middle of the week. I am constantly amazed and wondering where the time has gone. I washed yesterday and ironed a piece or two. I must try to can some more apples today, don't see how I can get away this week. If Eldon can get help to fix the roof I should be here I think.

Thanks for the card. I like it, it fits. I enjoyed my birthday very much. The day was perfect. But O, there is so much to do! Monday it was so overwhelming I just told myself "I am going to run away" and so I got ready as quickly as I could, gathered up my birthday cards and went up to Rosa's.

Bye now. B.C.

Grandma Sylvia (left) and her sister, Bessie, at the Circle S Farm, 1978, less than a year before Bessie's death.

O there is so much to do. I am going to run away. The two opposing forces that had always defined Bessie. Stay or go? *Remove the mold of ages past* or push forward *across the young orchard, down the hill, across the spring?* O there is so much to do, for *I am leaving soon to be away for some time, and naturally do not wish to leave any more unfinished business than I can help:*

> Hereby signed & Acknowledged Bessie D. Cosby, September 16, 1977: Escrow Receipt, Affidavit, Trust Deed for Lot 21, Block 28 of Atascadero Colony, Mail to Bank of America, Atascadero, California.

> February 1, 1978. I, Bill Frantz, hereby agree to cash rent the 14 acres more or less property of Bessie Cosby. Bessie Cosby does hereby agree to pay the expense of any limestone required by proper testing of the soil.

> Witness my hand this 2nd day of March, 1978. Power of Attorney appointed my niece Juanita A. McClanahan.

This 2nd day of March, 1978. I set my hand and seal to this Last
Will and Testament.

What finally convinced Bessie to say yes to my parents' urging?
To pack up the log house, store what was left of her belongings at the
Circle S, and move in with Paul and Juanita? The fall down the springhouse steps had injured her shoulder, but she'd managed for years
since then, wearing her own shoes, thank you very much. Her little
brother's death a year before had shaken her badly, but Ivan was not
the first brother whose death she had mourned, and might not be her
last: Who knows if Babe would survive her? Anything can happen and,
as Bessie had come to believe, usually does. So, at what moment did
she finally decide it was time—to relinquish her pride, her independence, her life as she had always known it? The handing over of her
Lafayette National Bank checkbook to my mother on September 27,
1977, one day before Bessie's ninety-seventh birthday, seems to be that
moment. Check #482 was entered in Bessie's hand, check #483 in Juanita's. Eldon Zink was paid for his handyman services, Wayne Yundt for
"combing of corn."

Bessie purchased her last pair of shoes for $21.83 from Smith's Shoes
on July 8, 1978, just in time for Lana's wedding and Sylvia's eighty-ninth
birthday party, the last birthday Sylvia would celebrate at the Circle S;
my grandparents would move in with my parents just a few weeks after
Bessie's death. But for the time being, Bessie was the only relative sharing the McClanahan home with Paul and Juanita. My parents had made
room for her things in the dresser and closet, but Bessie kept her small
tan-colored suitcase packed at all times, placed on a chair near her bed,
"as if she were ready to leave at any moment," my mother recalls. "She
kept all her important things in there—papers, underwear, a complete
outfit, her teeth in a container, her toiletries. And always, a pair of shoes.

"She liked to rummage in the suitcase. We would hear her in the
middle of the night. Paul would poke me and say 'I think Aunt Bessie's
up,' and we'd lie there in the dark, hoping she would calm down and
go back to sleep. Sometimes we would hear her putting on her shoes:
clunk, clunk. The old black shoes. Then I would get out of bed and go
downstairs to check on her. I would say something like 'Can I help you,
Aunt Bessie?'

"As soon as someone appeared, she got quiet, my mother continues. "She would just be turned a different way, looking out the window, maybe, like she was expecting someone. She didn't fight me. She was docile then. You could soothe her. I don't know, maybe she just wanted the attention. I would adjust her nightgown, or just touch her, and she would say 'thank you' then get back into bed. She never attempted to leave in the daytime. It was always the nighttime, always. Maybe she'd forgotten where she was, or she thought she didn't know where she was. She knew she wasn't home, though, and she needed to go somewhere."

◆

I can't remember when I last sat in a church pew, but here I am in the First Christian Church of Lafayette, Indiana, where my parents married more than sixty-five years ago. My father sits at my left side, my mother at my right, her thick hair tarnished with gray, her face lined and still beautiful. All week she's been pointing out old haunts: the small white farmhouse where they lived when I was born, the church where she was baptized when she was pregnant with Jenny, family burial plots, Briarwood, the Circle S with all its changes since the auction and final sale. This is unlike my mother, this urgency to open the past, and it concerns me. Today is Palm Sunday, the beginning of Passion Week. We find our place in the hymnal and fall into our accustomed parts: my father's lyric tenor, my mother's alto, my faltering soprano. Just this morning, after breakfast, I'd lifted the cover on their piano and begun to play some old hymn, a remnant from childhood. In a moment they appeared— my mother from the kitchen, her hands damp with dishwater, and my father from the basement stairs, his plastic heart valve clicking audibly from the exertion—and we sang some words about the kingdom of heaven, what it is made of.

Now, from her place four pews ahead, a young woman in an orange blazer turns to stare at us. Her face opens widely, like a child's, revealing a toothy grin. She waves. A few minutes earlier, as the service opened, she had greeted each member of the congregation with a furious, nonstop wave and thick, guttural laughter, and I'd studied her surreptitiously—hair cut in a severe, no-nonsense style that ensures easy maintenance; large, floppy earlobes studded with pearls. Had she dressed herself? Maybe the elderly woman sitting beside her, who has the look of a paid keeper, had assisted. Another young woman, wearing a bright yellow dress with ruffled sleeves, sits on the other side of the elderly woman, her shoulders slumped, head lolling. The woman in orange motions to her, smiling and snorting, stabbing the church bulletin with her finger and saying, over and over, "Mike. Mike's getting baptized. It's Mike." Is he one of their own, I wonder? Maybe they all live together in a group home, and the older woman is their housemother.

The candelabrum beside the altar is a crude wooden cross, the kind a child might hammer together to mark a pet's grave. Five purple candles are wedged into the wood, and elsewhere, throughout the sanctuary, purple reigns: in the minister's shawl, the choir robes, the ribbons decorating the arrangements of palms on either side of the pulpit. Purple is the color of royalty, of kingdoms won and lost. The color of the robe placed over Christ's shoulders on his way to Golgotha, the Place of the Skull. The color of passion—suffering, but also worldly desire, what we cannot resist. At her wedding reception, my mother wore fuchsia suede gloves and a felt hat with fuchsia feathers. A living doll.

The pipe organ surges as the aisle fills with small children waving palm branches and proceeding toward the altar. When I was the age of these children, I called this day "Donkey Sunday"; the significance of the palms was lost on me. Maybe it was a hot day, and they were fanning Jesus to keep him cool. All that long hair and everything. The picture in our Sunday School book showed a grown man straddling a little donkey, his long legs dangling. I liked seeing grownups looking foolish, like at the circus where red-nosed clowns circled on tricycles. The fact that Jesus was making his last triumphant entry into Jerusalem never occurred to me. *Last* means nothing to young children: last triumph, last week on earth, last moments with those you love. Sitting on the pew with my family, I would draw pictures on the church bulletin or fidget with my patent leather purse. Sometimes my mother would moisten a handkerchief with her tongue and reach to rub a smudge from my cheek, and I would push her hand away.

When the organist segues into "Come Dove Divine," the young woman in orange begins to bounce excitedly, waving the church bulletin in her hand. Then she turns once again to stare, unabashedly. Her eyes sweep side to side, taking in the three of us, as if attempting to frame us within one lens. She must sense that we go together. I wear my father's blue eyes, his chiseled nose and clenched jaw, but my hands are my mother's and my rounded hips and thighs are too, visible even beneath this long, loose skirt I selected as camouflage. I smile politely, blood rising in my cheeks. I feel stripped, naked, as if she can see right past the trappings—my carefully selected clothes, the mascaraed eyelashes, the forced smile—to the child inside. It's the same unnerving stare that babies give you, dead on, unblinking, their round eyes all pupil, in crayon shades of brown or green or blue so clear that you can almost see yourself reflected in them, blinking back.

The organ swells as wooden doors below the altar open to reveal the baptistery, which more closely resembles a Jacuzzi than the River Jordan. The minister has waded to the center of the baptistery and is now extending his arm. From behind the screen a figure emerges. It's a child—no, a man with a mustache, but he's so small, is he walking on his knees? It's a cartoon image, and it takes a moment for sense to settle. The head of the man-child comes to just above the minister's waist. His body is nearly as wide as it is tall, plump arms standing away from the torso, a neck thick as a stump. The face that opens to the congregation glows pink and innocent, bisected by a thick black mustache. "Mike! Mike!" the woman in orange calls out.

The minister, unruffled by the outburst, begins to speak slowly, calmly. "Except you become as a little child, you shall not enter the kingdom." He crosses Mike's hands over his chest in a gesture reminiscent of sleep or death. Mike's body relaxes into the minister's arms. I bite my lip, trying to stop the tears, but it's useless, they're falling harder now. My mother reaches into her purse, and pulls out a handkerchief, and for a moment I'm eight again and she's coming at me, the ritual spit bath, but no, she's handing the handkerchief to me. I take it, swiping at the smudges of mascara, the red clown nose.

Now the deacon is reading from the gospel, reminding us that in the last days of Passion Week, Jesus left the noise of public life, choosing to be with the few that he loved intimately, his flock, his small kingdom. He called them his "children" and gathered them around him. Together they talked, walked, ate, slept. He washed their feet and allowed them to wash his. He knew what was coming—the solitary garden, the betrayal, the hunger. But for now there was adequate light, and "having loved his own which were in the world, he loved them unto the end."

City of Lafayette, Indiana
Department of Health

NAME: Bessie D. Cosby

DIED: April 4, 1979 at 7:15 AM at Home Hospital

IMMEDIATE CAUSE OF DEATH: Broncho-pneumonia

SEX: Female

COLOR OR RACE: White

MARRIED, NEVER MARRIED, WIDOWED, DIVORCED: Widowed

AGE (in years): 98

PLACE OF BURIAL or REMOVAL: Salem Cemetery, Near
Stockwell, Indiana

I am the hybrid daughter of a farmer and a pilot. My mother's eyes are the rich brown of earth; my father's, the blue of skies and distances. The summer I was ten, he drove the family to the Lafayette airfield, chartered a two-seater, and took each of us up, one at a time, for our first flight. I remember how clean everything looked, how perfectly planned and ordered. The clouds—whole herds of them!—whiter and fluffier than the dusty sheep whose black faces followed me across the fields of my grandparents' farm. From that day on, my favorite perch was the haymow window where I could watch the world spin on without me. Below in the fading light, my sisters and brothers were living their real, necessary lives—patting together mud pies, combing burdock from the horses' manes, building the Kon-Tiki raft for tomorrow's float down the creek. I liked the view, the tops of heads. From a distance even the cow-pies were beautiful, dusted with moonlight.

One autumn day, as I've been told, a salesman knocked at the farm-house door. Arthur had just huffed in from the pasture where he'd been repairing a fence that the lively bull had once again kicked in; manure was drying on his boots. Sylvia was at the sink examining a basket of eggs, still warm and caked with feathers. The salesman, dressed in a navy blue suit, held out a large photograph. It was an aerial view of what appeared to be a perfect toy farm: Gabled house and twin barns looped by a continuous white fence. Fields dotted with tiny horses and cows that stayed obediently where they were planted. An outhouse tastefully camouflaged in golden foliage, the scene so awash in autumn that the colors appeared to have been painted on.

"It's beautiful," my grandfather agreed. "Where is it?" Then, as if he'd suddenly been granted new eyes, he blinked, collapsing into the nearest chair. "I never knew it looked like that. Sylvia," he said, turning to my grandmother, "we've got us a beautiful farm."

My grandfather bought the photograph, and now, decades later, it hangs in my parents' den. I have a photograph of the photograph: twice removed. My copy is slightly blurred around the edges, like a movie frame about to dissolve into flashback. No, it is not the squawking reality of the henhouse, the chigger-ridden grasses, or the slice of rhubarb pie warm from the oven. But I forgive my grandfather for loving the photograph, in that instant, more than he loved the real farm. At times, we all require a proper distance from what is ours, to be reminded of its beauty.

Hattie and Robert have been dead more than sixty years, Uncle Dale nearly as long. Of the five Mounts siblings, Robert "Babe" Wayne lasted the longest, though his wife informed none of the Indiana tribe of his passing. Barbara learned of his death months afterwards, when she and her husband knocked on the door of her uncle's home in Pennsylvania and Babe's wife delivered the news, asking in passing if they'd like to see his grave. Of my four grandparents, Clarence died first, leaving Grandma Goldie a widow for over a decade. Sylvia would never be a widow; Arthur would outlive her by nine years. He would die at ninety-eight, the same age as his sister-in-law when she died. Bessie had taken ill on April 2, 1979. My father drove her to Lafayette Home Hospital, where she was admitted for the first hospital stay of her life. Her final bill for two inpatient days—a one-hundred-sixty-dollar deductible—was covered by Medicare. Bessie had finally received Social Security benefits a few years before, along with a hefty check for retroactive payments.

During Bessie's brief hospitalization, Juanita and Paul came to visit, as did other family members, alternating shifts, keeping watch at her

Aerial view of my grandparents' Circle S farm, Tippecanoe County, Indiana, circa 1968.

bedside. Had Bessie been able, she would have laced up her shoes, made her way down to the check-out desk, and signed herself out—*right here, Mrs. Cosby*—on the dotted line. Instead, she seems to have waited for the door to close and Juanita to step out for a minute to go to the canteen for a cup of coffee. It was early morning, just a little past seven, Bessie's favorite time of day. The attending nurse heard something from Mrs. Cosby's room, the little lady calling out names and more names, a whole string of names. By the time the nurse made it to the door, Mrs. Cosby had expired.

Bessie Denton Mounts Cosby was buried beside her husband, parents, and brother in the cemetery in the middle of the woods where she used to go mushrooming and greening on April mornings. Luckily, on this April morning it was not raining, for, as she'd written in her diary, *O it is so bad to put anyone away in the rain.* A few weeks later, my father received the bill from Hippensteel Funeral Home. Each item was listed—concrete vault, serving vault, casket spray, dress, cemetery charges, minister's services, certified copies of death certificate, newspaper notices, state sales tax. The total cost for Bessie D. Cosby was $2,879.28. After the fifty-five-dollar dress charge was deducted (my mother supplied the blue dress she had sewn for Bessie to wear to Lana's wedding) and the thirty-dollar charge for the two singers added, and the discount for early payment was figured in (my father, like Bessie, always paid his bills on time) Bessie cost her estate $2,811.87. Not counting the forty-dollar charge from Thompson Monuments for cutting the date, 1979, into the stone she had ordered decades before: "Bessie D. Cosby." Bessie had always known who she was. She just wasn't sure how long she would last.

As the months went by, Bessie's possessions were distributed to family members. One niece got Bessie's guitar. Juanita received most of her books. Lana inherited Bessie's library table, converted now to a dining table around which tribes of noisy, exuberant children and neighbors gather to feast, laugh, and play music. And as for the great-niece who is writing these words? She inherited Bessie's small, tan-colored suitcase. Inside is Mother Mounts's timeworn Bible, two of Hattie's handmade sunbonnets, a gold pocket watch passed down from Aunt Phebe, Dale's 1896 composition book, Bessie's 1897 diary, and Bessie's walking shoes, placed neatly, side by side, as if readied for a journey.

If you reach into the side pocket, you will find a leather eyeglass case. Snap open its hinge and look inside: Great-grandpa Robert's wire-rimmed spectacles. A calling card with a feathery bird holding a banner in its beak—"Bessie D. Mounts, Faithfully Yours." And a faded piece of paper, folded carefully. Unfold the paper and you will see two distinctively different strands of hair—the long, white, fragile threads of an old woman and a short lock of baby-fine, golden brown hair, delicately intertwined to form a nest that should not be disturbed.

◆

As I write these words, my nieces and nephews number fifteen; my greats-, thirteen. My namesake, Rebecca, was born a year ago, and I am happy to report that Rebecca is aging quite well. She came into this world already nine months old and if the universe permits, she will continue to age. If she keeps growing old, like her Great-great-great-aunt Bessie did, perhaps one day a century from now, some sculptor will cast her likeness in bronze as Rodin did the likeness of "She Who Was Once the Helmet-Maker's Beautiful Wife."

According to Ingmar Bergman, he who was once a beautiful woman's lover and director, Liv Ullman's face is remarkable because it is "a face which can lend itself to an immense number of roles." How many roles did Bessie play throughout her long life? Baby daughter, big sister, factory worker, niece, wife, suffragette, farmer, nurse, widow, landowner, manager, cousin, aunt, great-aunt, nanny, and finally, the lone survivor of Briarwood. How much of the stubborn, independent Bessie was sacrificed along the way, only she knew. It was not Bessie's nature to confess, especially in writing, having *no desire to start a conflagration.*

When a reporter asked Ullman why she had decided to leave her aging face alone, she answered that she is curious to see what time will do to her. What a fine gift to bestow on her beholders, and an even finer gift to Ullman's child and grandchildren: to let time have its way with her, to clear a space for her daughter then her granddaughter, so that the natural order can continue. In her last decades, Grandma Goldie would shake her head side to side until her jowls wobbled, then laugh and say, "Silly old grandmother with the chicken neck." She let us grandchildren—and later the great-grandchildren—touch the silky folds that hung beneath her once-taut jaw. And when I sat on Grandma Sylvia's generous lap, I leaned into her round belly and stroked the loose, soft underside of her upper arms. She never pulled away or asked me to stop. Even scrawny Aunt Bessie allowed me access, anticipating what I wanted when I reached for her hand. Without complaint, she would turn her hand palmside down, offering it to me so I could do what I always did: pinch the thin, spotted skin, then count the seconds before it settled back into shape.

On and off over the years, I have thought back to that evening in 1965, wondering at the source of Bessie's tears: "It hurt to see you look so old." Watching me onstage, did she see herself, the ancient self that others had been seeing all along but which she had never fully recognized, living, as she did, from the inside out? Did Bessie, for the first time, glimpse a future in which "She Who Once Was . . . " would be no more?

If my great-niece Rebecca continues growing *old,* and one day some sculptor casts her image. . . . Wait, let me try that again, with the emphasis on *growing* rather than *old.* To remind myself of flowers, plants, grasses, and trees, and all living things, for *growing* is a living word with forward motion, even if one is growing old. As opposed to *staying,* which has no motion, which is a dying word. Though I will not live to see Rebecca's progress into old age, I pray she lasts a long, long time. As Bessie lasted, as Goldie and Sylvia lasted. As the array of old women in my city are lasting. Just yesterday, on my afternoon walk, I came upon a woman—ninety if a day—at the edge of the park. She had positioned her cane between two benches as if it were a barre, and she was performing, excruciatingly slowly but with classic precision, each of the five ballet positions, gesturing gracefully with one thin arm, the other grasping the cane for balance.

Aunt Bessie's caption might have read, "She Who Was Once the Young Woman Holding a Guitar Close to Her Face and Leaning Visibly Into the Music." And what will my caption read, once I gain the courage to move boldly forward? I would choose "She Who Loved All That Was Given to Her Without Looking Back." If I squint into the mirror, I can almost imagine that time, can throw myself into the prime of my future, when that time comes. As it must come, as it will. There I am on the stage of a niece or nephew's house, their children tumbling on the floor around me. If a great-niece reaches to touch my neck, she will be rewarded with a handful of extraordinary folds. And if she wants to pinch my hand, I will offer it to her. "Here," I will say, patting my lap. And we will sit, "The Child I Once Was" and "The Old Woman She Will Become," our moments together so swift and sweet we will barely feel them pass.

AUTHOR'S NOTE

Most of my sources for *The Tribal Knot* were primary sources, gleaned from a large cache of family letters, documents, photographs, and personal effects spanning more than a century. Secondary sources are noted within the text itself, as are interviews and informal conversations. In some segments, I reconstruct scenes or move directly into characters' thoughts, imagining their internal landscapes based on what I learned about their lives through the documents, interviews, oral or written histories, or from what I experienced firsthand.

The book is not intended to be a complete or exhaustive family history, but rather a multi-generational memoir of several interwoven strands of the extended tribe.

In my research, I discovered variant spellings for some family members' surnames and given names, in addition to nicknames used by close associates. To aid the reader, I have standardized the spellings of names, and, in most cases, assigned each character one main moniker, which is used throughout the book. Following is a guide to variant spellings, with primary monikers underlined:

<u>Babe</u>, Robert Wayne Mounts
<u>Charlie</u>, Charles, Charley
<u>Clint</u>, Dewitt Clinton Mead, Jr.
<u>Father and Mother Mounts</u>, William and Mary Mounts
<u>Hattie</u>, Harriet, Harriett
<u>Harve</u>, Harvey
<u>Lafe</u>, Lafayette, Leif
<u>Lucippa</u>, Lusippa, Lusippi

Mounts, Mounce, Mountz

Phebe, Phoebe

Throughout this book, I use actual names of historical personages, family members, friends, neighbors, and acquaintances, with the exception of the following names, which I supplied in Chapter 22 to aid the reader in imagining the church scene: Lila Conklin, Jeff Bobick, Bridget Sims, and Brad Walters.

When referring to African Americans, I apply the terms that appear in the letters, interviews, and oral histories.

An account of the Mounts family "hair picture" appears in *Let Us Come and Settle—Town of Lucas Wisconsin,* a self-published book by Joanne "Dode" Thorud.

In chapter 2, Kyger's inscription is a slightly inexact paraphrase of Byron's lines; the line breaks are Kyger's own.

At the end of chapter 4, Bessie characterizes her great-aunt Phebe Mead as a single woman until Phebe's marriage at age 43 (to John Wesley Houze, Phebe's first cousin.) This is consistent with the information that Bessie gave me regarding Phebe's marriage to Houze. However, in my research I discovered a second marriage license, issued to Phebe Mead and Thomas E. Smith on February 19, 1867, when Phebe would have been only 15. Therefore, it appears that Phebe was married twice.

Some genealogical records appear to conflate biographical details for Dewitt Clinton Mead and Dewitt Clinton Mead, Jr. I am confident that the marriage and divorce details included in chapter 5 relate to Dewitt Clinton Mead and not to his son.

In chapter 14, the song that Barbara remembers hearing Aunt Bessie sing is probably a version of "Stay in Your Own Backyard" by Lym Udall and Karl Kennet, published in 1899.

REBECCA McCLANAHAN
is the author of nine books, including *The Riddle Song and Other Rememberings* (winner of a Glasgow Prize in nonfiction), *Deep Light: New and Selected Poems*, and *Word Painting: A Guide to Writing More Descriptively*. Recipient of the J. Howard and Barbara M. J. Wood Prize from *Poetry*, a Pushcart Prize, a Governor's Award for Excellence in Education, and literature fellowships from New York Foundation for the Arts and North Carolina Arts Council, McClanahan teaches in the MFA programs of Queens University (Charlotte) and Rainier Writing Workshop. She lives in Charlotte, North Carolina, with her husband, video producer Donald Devet.

CPSIA information can be obtained at www.ICGtesting.com
Printed in the USA
LVOW01s0230260315

432087LV00028B/623/P